FOREWARD

Maybe you have been [...] by the promise of 'a comical accoun[...] [...]ter 4. Why? Well let me explain.

Several years into t[...] I began to write reports of our var[...] e *great Minibus Adventure*' (see cha[...] received by the charity's supporters I decided to write another report after we delivered a car to the Hope & Future Foundation; *'Road Trip'* (chapter 4). This particular trip was with my brother Adrian and our good friend Tony Morgan. Tony always lit up any activity with his endless wit and sarcasm bringing laughter and joy to any situation, so naturally this particular report was flavoured with the comedic events inspired by him.
The reaction to this style of writing was very positive and so I was inspired to write all future reports with a humorous bent

Sadly, we have lost Tony since that report was written but hopefully, what he inspired will live on.

So, the first few chapters give some background to how it all began and an outline of the events which occurred prior to the reports.

It is my hope that the first few chapters will clearly show that God has been my strength and guide throughout this sometimes difficult journey and that in amongst all the jokes and tomfoolery He will be revealed and get the glory for all that has been achieved.

So on second thoughts, don't go straight to chapter 4; start at the appropriately titled chapter one *'In The Beginning'*

Andrew

CHAPTER ONE
In The Beginning ….

As I sat in Church that particular Sunday morning I began to get my first sense that God was starting something.

My interest in overseas mission had been born through a friend at Sticklepath Community Church; Joyce Philips had been visiting China with CCSM and her reports of life in the mission field both enthralled and excited me. The miracles she reported were amazing and I knew that I wanted to be a part of God's work overseas. I attended many CCSM meetings and continued to listen to Joyce's stories but never really felt called to China.

So when Brian Glover came to preach at our Church and used his work in Bulgaria as the basis for his message my heart was ready to hear from God. What happened from this point wouldn't become completely clear for many months. God set off two very separate reactions which carried on completely oblivious to each other but which were intrinsically linked.

Ann Underwood was also in Church that morning and when she heard Brian talk about the orphanage in Barzitsa, Bulgaria she paid special attention as on that very day her husband, Des, was in Bulgaria looking for an investment property. Moved by what she had heard that morning Ann phoned Des to ask if he was anywhere near Barzitsa and was delighted to hear that despite the size of Bulgaria, Des was only 20km away. She urged him to go there to visit the children Brian had talked about.

Des made arrangements with an interpreter and driver to go to the orphanage in Barzitsa but this wasn't as straight forward as it might have been as no one had heard of an orphanage in Barzitsa. We later learned that many of the orphanages in Bulgaria were historically hidden away in very rural locations so that even the locals didn't know of their existence. When they eventually found the orphanage the driver was reduced to tears as he had no idea that such plight existed on his doorstep. So it was there, in the orphanage in Barzitsa, that God spoke to Des having already spoken to Ann in Sticklepath in rural Devon and between them they pledged that whatever property they eventually bought in Bulgaria would be used for the benefit of the children. However, they had no idea at this point as to how this would happen.

My own personal response to what I heard that Sunday morning was to join one of the trips organised by Saltmine to Barzitsa orphanage. While I was there I learned a little of the future which lay ahead of the children who lived there and it was pretty disturbing. At age 18 they are forced to leave the orphanages and fend for themselves out on the streets. They leave with no home, no job, no family, no money and no hope. Inevitably they are lured into the criminal gangs where they will spend their lives engaged in prostitution or pick pocketing. Over the years we have seen just how organised these gangs are and they start grooming the children several years before they leave the orphanages.

In the same way that God had spoken to Des in that very place I can clearly remember God speaking to me. I stood in the yard of the orphanage looking out across the fields of the rural landscape. It was stunning, golden sunflowers as far as the eye could see set against a brilliant blue sky; it really was God's creation in all it's splendour. God challenged me, "What are you going to do about these children?" I had no idea what but I knew I had to do something.

A little while after returning home I was invited to speak at Church and tell people about my trip to Bulgaria. At that time I still had no idea what God was calling me to do and so I didn't mention anything about God's calling. Instead I asked the Church if they would be willing to help the orphanage buy a new cooker. Now this might sound a little strange but it was an extremely important foundation which God was putting in place although once again I had no idea at the time. The director of the orphanage, Mrs Zlateva, had shown me the cooker which had a huge hole in the door of the oven and only two of the six hotplates were working. It didn't escape my attention that there was only one cook, a lady in her seventies cooking for seventy children. On the menu for this day was cabbage stew; I saw the cabbages which only affirmed my desire to do something for these children. Whilst I was in the dark as to God's long term plan, raising money for a new cooker was something I could definitely do and I encouraged the Church to get involved. *

Following the service Des approached me and held out a cheque. "I was sat in my office yesterday", he said "and was prompted by God to write out a cheque for £200 but to leave the payee blank. Now I know why, who do I make it payable to?" I was stunned, what an amazing start towards the £900 target and a confirmation from God that I was on the right track. However, something far more amazing was about to happen. Des asked me, "What's really on your heart?" "What do you mean?" I replied. He pressed home his question "What has God laid on your heart?" I explained about the fate awaiting the children when they reach eighteen and how I wanted to do something to help them. "What do you need to make this happen?" Des pressed again. I was floundering, I didn't really have a plan just some 'half baked' idea about a safe house so I said, "a house". Nothing could have prepared for what God did next. Des said, "I have one, you can have it."

Des explained how Ann had told him to go to the orphanage and about their commitment to use their Bulgarian house for the benefit of the children. He explained how they had been unable to do anything about their commitment due to the pressures of work and this provided the perfect opportunity to meet that commitment.

As I began to see all the threads which God had so carefully laid and was now pulling together I was amazed at how intricately, how wonderfully, how majestically God was working in our lives. And so it was that right there, in Sticklepath Community Church, a tiny village in rural Devon, God revealed the first part of His plan. An incredible adventure had just been launched.

The significance of the cooker wasn't revealed until much later. Mrs Zlateva had pitched the cooker appeal to many different people all of whom had promised to help but delivered nothing. The simple fact that the people of Mid Devon enabled me to deliver the cooker meant that I now had the full trust of Mrs Zlateva who was able to open doors for me that would have made the subsequent work impossible. God was truly in every detail of forward planning.

CHAPTER TWO
The wilderness years

The next few years were a mix of highs and lows as I tried to steer what at times felt like a rudderless ship through some stormy waters. Of course, God was in control but I was at the foot of a very steep learning curve which felt like a learning cliff at times, one which I spent more time falling off than I did climbing up. It is only with the benefit of hindsight that I can truly appreciate how God was training me and more importantly, putting in place all the building blocks I would need later.

Looking back over this period I believe the greatest gifts God gave me were patience and determination. Despite several 'wobbles' God never allowed me to lose sight of the vision He had given me and each time I fell off that cliff He sent another miracle to reassure me He was in control and I should persevere.

I met with several groups and organisations trying to form a partnership with someone with the experience necessary to help me set up the halfway house but all to no avail (although later I enjoyed a profitable season with the Trussell Trust). I was totally ill equipped for the task ahead as I had none of the skills required to do this alone. I'm not a fan of Christian clichés but there is one which is wholly appropriate in this circumstance. *'God does not call the equipped, He equips the called.'* This is so true for me and over the years I have come to realise that God called me because of my lack of skills in order that He gets the glory.

I made many trips to Bulgaria in order to get the house ready for occupation but the work was slow and there were many setbacks; the voices of the enemy started to creep into the work. At the lowest point I was accused of wasting people's money and reprimanded severely for "not helping one single child." The accusation haunted me for a while as I couldn't name one child who had benefitted from all that I had done so far. However, each time the enemy came visiting God gave me the strength to resist and carry on. God reminded me of Joseph who was given a vision as a young man but it was at least 22 years later that the vision was fulfilled. I must admit I didn't much like the idea of waiting 22 years but I was grateful for the faith God had given me to trust in Him.

It's difficult to pinpoint an event which I could describe as the turning point, the point at which God started to direct me out of the wilderness. Each time I think it was this event or that one I recall a previous linked event which had to happen first. Once again the intricacy of the way all of my experiences work together can only demonstrate the hand of a mighty God at work. Each experience dependant on the last, each taking me another step closer to finding the path God had prepared for me.

But if I had to pick one moment to represent the turning point I think it would be the day I got a call from Ian Freeland. I knew Ian through Okehampton Baptist Church so he was aware of my work in Bulgaria. He was Assistant Principal at Launceston College and a plan to take a group of students to an orphanage in Africa had broken down so he was looking for an alternative. This was a completely new direction for me but I relished the proposition and agreed to try and set something up.

I met with Pastor Plamen in Provadia as he had previously told me that his wife often visited the orphanage there so I thought he might be able to introduce me to the director. Plamen had been helping me with the work on the house as he is a builder by trade. It was an arrangement that suited us both well as he needed the work and I needed a reliable, trustworthy builder.

Plamen made arrangements for us to meet the Director and we called in at the orphanage at the appropriate time but she wasn't there and no one could tell us where she was or even if she would be back that day. This was a problem because it was my last day in Bulgaria and I didn't want to have to go back to Ian and tell him I had failed to make arrangements for his students to make the trip. We had a few other jobs to do before we left so we set off in the car through Provadia. Suddenly Plamen yelled at me, "Stop, stop!!" I had no idea what all the sudden panic was about but I hit the brakes as commanded and Plamen jumped out of the car and ran down the road. He had seen the Director of the orphanage and literally chased her down the street. He brought her back to the car and introduced her and we made arrangements for the student visit over the bonnet of the car in the middle of the street. Once again God put us in the right place at the right time. The odds of us just happening to pass the Director in the street like that are so immense it could only have been God at work.

Whilst the student trip was a great success it wasn't the trip itself which defined the direction the work would take but it got me on the right path and set everything up. This trip led me to organise another one when I took a small family group to join with the children in celebrating Christmas and New Year. It was the end of this trip that brought some clarity to the 'new' direction. I was chatting with the director about organising another trip for the following summer when she said, "if we are still here." It turned out that the orphanage was under threat of closure due to the dreadful condition of the building. The Director had been manipulating the meagre budget trying to save up sufficient to make the necessary repairs but it was a hopeless task and she was woefully short; she pleaded for my help. Could I finance new windows? There were thirty windows, most of which were huge, I estimated a minimum cost of £50,000 plus labour. To date most of the fundraising I had done was tiny in comparison and the balance in the account at the time was £3,000. My head said, "no" but my mouth said, "give me a month and I'll let you know" What I thought I was going to do in that month I didn't know.

In a dramatic pause I will leave that thought hanging for a moment while I tell you of some other pieces of this complicated jigsaw which God was drawing together. For our first trip to Provadia orphanage I arranged for Milena to be our translator but at the last minute she had to pull out and so the Pastor of the Church in Varna 'appointed' a reluctant replacement, Didi. The first words out of Didi's mouth when I met her were, "I didn't want to come, I don't want to work with the children." But God had other plans for her. During the week God broke her heart and she fell in love with the children and there began a whole new ministry which resulted in Didi setting up the Hope & Future Foundation through which she now devotes much of her time to ministering to the children, catering for both physical and spiritual needs.

We also met Tatiana and her two daughters Alex & Dobs. Tatiana was one of the staff and her daughters often came to the orphanage with her to play with the children. I thank God regularly for Alex who is now a key part of all the work we do in Bulgaria and I simply couldn't do the work without her. She translates for us, organises accommodation, transport, meals and everything we could possibly need or want. On top of that she joins in everything we do whether its games with the children or helping the builders. Nothing is too much trouble for her.

So you can see why Provadia orphanage represents such a pivotal point in this story. Many pieces of the jigsaw were brought together here. But what about the windows?

Back in the UK I contacted a friend, Roger Thorne, as he worked for Okehampton Glass our local window company and asked for his guidance. Roger grasped the nettle and together with his boss (and owner of the company), Andy Ewen, started ringing around his suppliers looking for help and to say they came up trumps is the understatement of the century. They got all the frames donated for free and the glass donated for the nominal sum of £600. Now as amazing as that is it wasn't exactly the solution I had imagined as now I had to figure out a way of getting 30 huge windows to Bulgaria. The freight costs of such an enormous load were horrendous but once again God stepped in we found a company in Bristol who would take them to the orphanage for just £2400 all we had to do was get the windows to Bristol. We were blessed by a local haulier who agreed to do this for free.

I was blown away that God provided all this for £3000 – the exact sum of money in the bank account. Wow, God had given me the faith to step out and trust Him and then given me the windows and labour. In the face of this it is impossible to deny God at work. As I said earlier I have none of the skills to achieve this so it can only be of God. He called me and He equipped me.

At last I had stepped on to the path which God had prepared for me. The first part of my training was over and the work was just about to begin.

The enemy threw everything at me to stop the windows being installed in Provadia. The trip coincided with the infamous Icelandic Ash Cloud which brought aviation to a standstill and our flight was cancelled. Twenty four hours later we were stood in the check-in queue for our re-arranged flight when I received a call from the Mayor of Provadia in which he told me, "Don't come, we don't want you here." We went anyway and I left the builders twiddling their thumbs on site while I went to do battle with the Mayor. With MTV blaring in the background and his attention firmly fixed elsewhere I presented our case to him but he wasn't budging. Eventually, maybe just to get rid of me, he relented when I said to him that we would do all the work and he could take all the credit. After reminding him of his earlier promise to repair the roof if we renewed all the widows he agreed to let us start work. Despite the loss of nearly two days the team worked tirelessly and fitted all the windows.

From this point I began organising regular trips for college students to visit the children and for building teams to repair and renovate crumbling orphanage buildings which is how I have spent the last few years fulfilling God's will for my life.

There have been other trips too, the next one was to provide a minibus for the Hope & Future Foundation and this is when I started to write reports of my travels. 'The Great Minibus Adventure' was my first report and was well received so I carried on writing after each trip but with an element of humour to entertain the reader thus driving home the message of the work in an easy to read style. Therefore the remainder of this book is made up of those reports, I hope you enjoy them.

CHAPTER THREE
The Great Minibus Adventure
December 2010

Most of you will be familiar with the troubles we experienced in getting the bus ready to go. Insurance, winter tyres, International Driving Permit etc but at 4am on Dec 14 Rhys (my son), Rose and I set off for Varna, Bulgaria.

The bus was packed full of donations for the children in the orphanage we couldn't have squeezed another thing in – or so we thought.

In Salisbury we stopped to pick up Bob Taylor (or Santa Claus as he became known to the children with his big red coat and white beard) who, with his wife Chrissie had been busy collecting donations from the local school in Codford. With a lot of pushing, pulling and squeezing we managed to find room for another sizeable donation.

Day one was fairly straight forward. We made Dover in good time and the crossing to Calais was very smooth. We passed through France, Belgium, Holland and into Germany without any trouble. We spent a comfortable night in an Hotel and set off to cross the rest of Germany.

Regrettably, Germany turned out to be one long queue of traffic courtesy of endless miles of roadworks. Eventually we got to Austria but seriously delayed and now starting to experience the first of the bad snow. The temperature dropped significantly and we started to experience difficulties keeping the windscreen clear as even the antifreeze in the screen wash was freezing so we decided to pull in and find accommodation for the night. Here we discovered that the nearest hotel was approximately 40km away (25miles). The snow was adding to the problem of the falling temperature but we had no option other than to push on and find lodgings for the night. After roughly 15km we faced a fork in the road. One way was our planned route, the other was the road on which we were told the Hotel lay. Should we go out of our way to try and find the Hotel we were told of or stay on our route and hope we come across a hotel soon? The terrible conditions helped us to decide to make for the Hotel even thought it meant going the 'wrong' way. We were very pleased when the hotel came into view and even more pleased when they confirmed they had rooms for us.

As we set off on day three we returned to the fork in the road to get back onto our route. We made a conscious decision to look out for the first hotel so that we could see if we made the right decision the night before. I can't help thinking our decision must have been divinely inspired as it took four hours of travelling before we came across anywhere to stay.

The journey through Austria was truly amazing. The scenery as we traversed the Austrian mountains in the snow was spectacular. And so we progressed through Slovenia and on into Croatia. With Serbia approaching and the day coming to a close we knew we had another decision to make. We had heard many stories about Serbia which meant we had no desire to stop there. We were now almost 24 hours behind schedule and under a little pressure to get to Varna by Friday afternoon (the next day) to complete the registration paperwork before all the offices closed down for the weekend. So do we stop in Croatia and miss our deadline or push on through the night in the knowledge that we had to make it through Serbia. We decided to push on.

Day three should have ended with us tucked up in bed in Varna having safely delivered the minibus but actually ended with us in a fuel station in Serbia filling up with diesel. Little did we know what consequences awaited us as a result of this apparently harmless fuel stop and so we pushed on to the Serbia/Bulgaria border. Just as we had the Bulgarian border in our sights the dual carriageway disappeared and were taken onto a single track mountain road. A combination of the poor road, bad weather and relentless drag up and up and up the mountain meant progress was very slow and a journey we expected to take an hour took nearly four.
We weren't sure what to expect at the Serbian border, we had heard all sorts of stories of delays and difficulties. It was a little confusing how to proceed through the border as there were several 'booths'. We pulled up at the first one and were waved through and thought that was it so joyfully drove on into Bulgaria – well not quite!! The guard in the second booth was very unimpressed as we sailed by. Fortunately, Rhys had seen him try to flag us down and we were able to reverse and await our fate. However, despite our confusion the guards were satisfied with everything and allowed us to go on without any fuss.

So that was it, we were in Bulgaria with a huge sigh of relief only 500km to go. Unfortunately, we had not anticipated that in 50 metres there would be yet another border control to allow access into Bulgaria (I guess experienced travellers are thinking "obviously" – and on reflection so do I now!). After such easy passage through Serbia we were deeply disappointed to find the Bulgarian border the worst of all – particularly as we were delivering aid to the country.

I think the freezing weather probably worked to our advantage as the guards weren't too keen to be standing around in -10°C temperatures. They asked us for paperwork which simply doesn't exist, they made it up as a prelude to saying we could 'buy' the necessary papers; for cash of course. But to our surprise and relief they put up only minimal resistance to our protestations. So whilst the Bulgarian border crossing was the most difficult of all, we passed through and reflected that things could have been much, much worse.

By now it was the early hours of day four and so we took the decision to push on and drive through the night. We thought that having climbed so high through Serbia we must have been on the very top of Europe but not so. More climbing ensued through Bulgaria. Naturally, as we got higher so the temperature dropped even further and we were about to find out the true cost of our fuel purchase in Serbia.

As we climbed the mountain the minibus started to lose power until the engine cut out all together and we were coasting. Just ahead there was a tunnel and so we hoped to be able to coast far enough to get into the shelter of the tunnel. Then something very strange happened despite the fact that we were still going uphill and the engine had cut out the minibus just kept on rolling. The bus rolled up the hill and in to the tunnel where the road started to go downhill and just over the crest of the hill there appeared a very welcome sight – a fuel station (albeit closed). We were able to pull in and park relieved that we had at least reached a point of relative safety. There were several other cars in the station who had all stopped to rest, engines were running and heaters were blowing; we were just a little jealous as our engine refused to start and so our heater was inoperative.

One of the occupants of the 'warm' cars decided to try and help us but despite a lot of effort we couldn't get the frozen engine to kick into life. So we contacted the AA but despite the 'European Cover' logo on our card, still wanted to charge us £350 simply to get us towed to a garage where we could pay extra for any repairs necessary – they don't tell you that in their advertising!!

Luckily, we were in Bulgaria and have many friends there so were able to make a distress call and arrange for help. By now it was 2am and very, very cold so we prepared as best as possible for the long wait for rescue. We had blankets and warm clothes, we even had a gas cooker which we lit for heat.

Fortunately we didn't have to wait too long and a rescue truck arrived, the problem was quickly diagnosed as a frozen fuel filter caused by bad fuel which contained water and thus the full extent of the consequences of being sold dodgy fuel in Serbia were revealed on that freezing Bulgarian mountain in the wee small hours. The rescue truck carried us to a repair garage with an open fuel station. The fuel station had a rest area with a hot drinks machine; never had a rubbish half cup of over expensive coffee been more welcome. It could just have easily been nectar from Heaven.

Duly refreshed and warmed we were delighted when the mechanic arrived and replaced our frozen filter and we heard the sweet music of a purring engine once again. The whole episode cost just 88 Euros. We were very glad not to have parted with £350 for a tow with the AA + unknown repair fees!!!

The rest of the journey was fairly uneventful and so we arrived in Varna about 18 hours late, tired but happy.

The snow and freezing conditions had taken their toll in Varna as in the rest of Europe and we were told that the Orphanages we wanted to visit were cut off and we couldn't get there. We were also told that the children had been confined to their bedrooms for three days because of the fear of them falling and sustaining an injury for which no ambulance could get in and no vehicle could get out of the villages where the homes are located. We were desperate to see the children and to give them some relief from the boredom of their unwanted confinement but the conditions were too poor. We were given some hope for Sunday, if conditions improved we would be allowed to collect some of the children and take them to Church. They had been rehearsing for months to sing in the service and everyone wanted to see the fruit of their work.

Meanwhile we occupied our time with other activities which on the face of it were wonderful (we saw a magnificent sunset over the Black Sea on a snow covered beach while drinking hot chocolate in a beachside restaurant) but the pleasure was hollow as all we wanted to do was get to the children.

Finally, on Saturday afternoon, we were given the go ahead to collect the children for church the following day. We were so happy we didn't even flinch at the 5:30am start! Normally the trip would take 3 hours (there and back) but we had to make allowances for the bad weather. We were 'encouraged' to make it back to Varna for 10 o'clock in time for the start of the service – everyone wanted the children to be at Church so badly. And so we made it to the outskirts of Barzitsa by about 7:30am but the road into the village (approx 5 miles) was barely passable; we gingerly drove on and eventually made it to the Orphanage. We had such joy meeting and greeting the children. Only a few were allowed to come and greet us. A group of 8 children had put themselves forward to form a singing/dance group and it was this group who were coming to Church. They had woken early and were eating breakfast waiting for us to arrive. A few of the boys helped us to unload all your donations and their eyes were as wide as saucers as they saw the bounty before them. Their reward for helping us was first pick of a few items – they all chose trainers and were overwhelmed by the gift.

Eventually, we got the kids into the bus and left for Church. With such a precious cargo we limped through the village on ice and snow careful to protect the children. We had such fun on the journey, the bus was filled with laughter, singing and all sorts of other happy noises. Everyone was filled to overflowing with joy.
We made the Church for bang on 10 o'clock. Cones had been put out to ensure we could pull up right outside the church and deliver the children like royalty.
I cannot begin to describe the atmosphere in the Church when the children sang. Maggie & George sang solos and were pure joy. They were so very nervous but the congregation simply cheered and called out their names to encourage them and then the tears flowed as they sang like angels.
During the service the official handover of the minibus was affected and the Pastor blessed the bus.

After Church we took the children to a restaurant which was a bit of an eye opener. At first they seemed reluctant to choose their meal until it was revealed that this was their first visit to a restaurant and they had never seen a menu before (they are aged 15-17). However, once the food arrived all that was forgotten and they had the time of their lives.

We returned to the Orphanage and were treated to a display of traditional Bulgarian dancing from the children. We also spent some great time with the rest of the children who joined us in their hall. Our time there was over so quickly and it was time to move on. A few more tears and we were on our way.

Krivnya Orphanage was our destination. A few of the children we know and love had been moved to this specialist home for children with learning difficulties. We had never been there before and didn't know what to expect. We were delighted to find a wonderful, warm, loving home. The children slowly came to see these strange visitors and before we knew it we were like long lost friends and we enjoyed a short time playing and laughing with the children. We definitely hope to return to Krivnya again sometime.

Well, that's a brief overview of the highlights of our trip. I hope you have enjoyed sharing our journey.

The trip home was and adventure too but I won't bore you with the details except to say it took 24 hours due to travelling conditions in the UK. The plane was diverted to Stansted (which was a lot better than Amsterdam where we nearly ended up). It took two and a half hours to get off the plane and another two hours waiting for our baggage. A coach took us back to Gatwick and then three trains (Gatwick to Basingstoke, Basingstoke to Clapham, Clapham to Salisbury) took us through the night to Salisbury where Chrissie was waiting to take us to Codford to collect my car and drive home to Okehampton.

It truly was a wonderful adventure and any difficulties with travel just disappear in the memories of the day spent with the children. Maggie and George singing in Church is a memory which I will cherish forever.

Thanks to everyone who made the trip possible. So many people contributed time and finance to ensure we could donate the minibus. And special thanks to everyone who prayed. I am conscious that readers of this newsletter will vary in their faith but I know that we were constantly in God's protection and the prayers of His people were answered. The miracles we witnessed are all the proof I need. Have you ever heard of a minibus, which has cut out and has no working engine, gather speed going uphill in order to get you to the safety of a garage?

Thanks to everyone. I can assure you that the minibus and all its contents will make a very real difference to the children who were so grateful to receive them. And it's all down to you for making the effort to help.

Andrew

CHAPTER FOUR
Road Trip
April 2011

"Never again!!!" With those words still ringing in my ears after preparing the minibus trip last December I found myself doing it all over again. What kind of madness provokes such a foolish return to the cause of so much stress?

1 Corinthians 2:14
The person without the Spirit does not accept the things that come from the Spirit of God but considers them foolishness, and cannot understand them because they are discerned only through the Spirit.
1 Corinthians 1:25
For the foolishness of God is wiser than human wisdom, and the weakness of God is stronger than human strength.

So often on this walk with the House Of Rachel (HOR) I have embarked on projects which have looked foolish in the eyes of man but thanks to the faith God has given me and His bountiful grace He has used HOR to achieve great things.

And so, despite all the trauma of preparing the minibus trip, here I was doing it all over again. I have heard ladies say that the trauma of childbirth is forgotten once the baby has arrived. Maybe there is a shadow of that sentiment here too as the trauma of the trip preparation was forgotten once the minibus had been delivered.

Our latest trip got off to a great start when my brother Adrian and a good friend Tony Morgan from Cardiff agreed to come on the trip and share the driving.

Everything was falling nicely into place when, with just a few days to go, the car we were taking had to be withdrawn. Almost before I had time to panic another car became available and God opened a new door for us. New arrangements were hastily put into place and the time soon came.
So why were we going again? We had received a fabulous donation of brand new trainers (42 pairs), duvets, duvet covers, sheets, towels etc which needed to go to the orphanage in Barzitsa. To send them by a

carrier company would have cost in the region of £500. So the decision was taken to use the money to finance a trip instead so that we could do some other essential work while in Bulgaria. The car was donated to HOR and we were able to donate it to the Hope & Future Foundation along with sufficient money to tax and insure the car for a year.

The trip started on 27 April when I drove to Cardiff to pick up Adrian & Tony. At 1am on 28 April we left Cardiff bound for Varna on the Eastern edge of Bulgaria 2000 miles away. We established a strict rota of 2 hours driving/navigating/resting and quickly found ourselves in Dover well ahead of schedule. We were able to board an earlier ferry and got to Calais in France about 2 hours earlier than expected – which was just as well. It soon became apparent that someone's navigational skills left a little to be desired – that someone was me! My very first navigational duty was to get us out of Calais and on to the road to Belgium – I failed. After a few miles of driving I had to confess that I was unsure that we were on the right road, after a few more miles my concerns were confirmed and we had to find a junction to turn around and go back to Calais to find the right road. If I had known what was coming later I wouldn't have tried to so hard to make excuses. Fortunately, I was travelling with two kind hearted, loving, forgiving people who hardly mentioned my failure – NOT! I didn't hear the end of it and there was worse to come.

We made good progress for the rest of the day (I wasn't navigating) and made the Austrian border on schedule and booked in to a pleasant motel for the night.
It's amazing how time distorts memories, if only I had remembered the Youth Camps Adrian, Tony & I (and others) used to run when I lived in Cardiff I would have booked a room in a different hotel. When I was awoken to the sound of thunder I had a crushing recollection of those long, sleepless camp nights. It wasn't thunder it was Tony snoring. Ah well, it added to the good humoured banter in the car the following day(s).

And so, after breakfast we set off again, through Austria, Slovenia, Croatia & Serbia. There may have been another navigational issue today, I can't quite remember. Unfortunately, there's no way the others will let me forget the fact that, once again, I sent Adrian down the wrong road. My brilliant map reading skills to get us back on track were very quickly forgotten as my reputation for navigating was in tatters.

Added to the minor navigational misdemeanour was the problem of time zones. Our schedule missed the time zone change on the Bulgarian border resulting in us arriving in Bulgaria approx 2 hours late. However, we passed through customs with minimum fuss which was a relief.
We had an arrangement with a Church in Sofia to sleep there for the night but we were expected at 11pm. However, the pastor of the church, Ludmil, was very patient and gracious and said not to worry when we phoned to explain.

Now if I had the sole responsibility of trying to navigate through Sofia I might have had to carry an even bigger burden but fortunately I couldn't be trusted and so Adrian took control of the map. I was very relieved that between the three of us we struggled to find our destination. Eventually, after a series of phone calls to Ludmil he agreed to come and collect us from the monument where we parked to look for help. It was a little surreal when a car stopped in the middle of the road and a man we had never seen before beckoned for us to follow him – and we did. We questioned our sanity but we were very tired and perhaps just a little deranged with fatigue and managed to persuade ourselves that this unknown man was Ludmil and he would lead us to our beds. The fact that I am writing this report will be a clue to the fact that we were right and arrived safely at the Church. After some very complicated instructions about the highly technical burglar alarm which none of us understood it was time, at last, to get some sleep. God was smiling on us that night as there was a wall separating one of the three beds in the room and so Thundering Tony could be isolated and Adrian and I could get a good night's sleep.

If we thought getting into Sofia was hard, it was nothing compared to finding our way out again. Clearly, Sofia's budget for road signs limited it to two signs, both of which were written in Cyrillic and both of which were wrong. At least, that's the conclusion we came to in order to explain why it took us an hour to travel the three miles to the edge of the city. It took so long to travel those three miles we had to stop for fuel on the edge of the city and it was here that I found it necessary to check Tony's papers. He claims to have been a mechanic but this was brought into question at this fuel station. Oh yes, he made up some story about a two phase release cap but he couldn't hide the fact that taking the cap off a hot radiator was not the most sensible thing he could have done. The volcanic eruption which followed was testament to that. For that few minutes as Adrian and I fell about laughing, we all forgot about my navigational incompetencies, for just a few precious minutes Tony was the clown, not me.

We soon recovered that situation and got on our way again. The Bulgarian roads were completely different to the motorways & dual carriageways of the rest of Europe; and the drivers!!!………. well the less said the better. Some of you will be familiar with the Beatles' song Day In The Life and the lyric "four thousand holes in Blackburn Lancashire". Have you ever wondered where those holes have gone? Well I can tell you, they are on the roads of Bulgaria – the majority of them concentrated into a few square miles in Varna (our destination town). We arrived in Varna in good time and were proudly patting ourselves on the back for a great journey and commenting on how good the car had been. My ability to find my way around the city had almost caused the others to reconsider their assessment of my navigational abilities. 1,999 miles covered, only 1 mile to go – Adrian, Tony, Andrew and a Citroen ZX had made it. BANG! We had hit a pot hole which would have easily passed itself off as the Grand Canyon and guess who was driving? Guess who couldn't even navigate his way around a pot hole? And so it was that less than 1 mile from our destination on the furthest edge of Europe I wrecked the front, drivers' side tyre. Never mind the tyre, my driving reputation was destroyed much to the amusement of the others.

We limped to the Church, parked the car and went to find Mitco who had the key to our room. I wish someone had told us Mitco was a chameleon as we couldn't find him anywhere even though we were assured he was there. As we sat around contemplating our next move a few girls came out of one of the rooms and I seized the opportunity; in my very best Bulgarian I asked "Kudeto se Mitco?" (Where is Mitco) to which the girl replied, "Sorry I don't speak English". Adrian & Tony found this hilarious as I had looked so proud speaking my best Bulgarian only to be shot down in flames by that response. So, no Mitco, no keys, no room. We went for a walk to explore the surroundings and by the time we got back we were able to get into our room and rest.

The following morning we attended Church. It's a Pentecostal church in the heart of the city and I'm guessing there were about 300 people there. We were led by a great worship band in a time of music and song then we were able to listen to the message in English via a little earpiece. The quality of sound made it a little difficult to follow every word but never the less we felt part of the service

Before we could go to Barzitsa Orphanage later that day we needed to get a new tyre for the car. We were bemused when Didi took us to Carefour Supermarket but apparently in Bulgaria you buy tyres from the supermarket and then take them to a garage to be fitted and so that's what we did. We also took the opportunity to buy a few footballs to take to the orphanage. And so we were ready to go to the Orphanage with the donations for the children. As usual we were greeted with great enthusiasm by the children and within a short space of time a game of football was underway. Adrian and I joined in while Tony, Didi & Claudia (from Varna Church) entertained the children indoors.

I learnt two important lessons – 1. don't play football in glasses (a bloody nose confirmed this) and 2. don't try to keep up with fit teenagers. These boys had boundless energy and a lot of talent but were very humble and we had a brilliant time. However, our time was over all too quickly and we had to go.

Our next stop was the orphanage in Krivnya (for children with special needs). There are approx 25 children here with varying degrees of special needs some of whom I knew from Barzitsa but had been transferred. Another exhausting time of playing all sorts of weird and wonderful games and the room was filled with laughter and joy. It really was a wonderful time. However, there is only so much tickling, poking, prodding and slapping games anyone can take and so we took the games outside. Here Adrian and I discovered just how much the earlier game of football had taken out of us and we creaked and groaned around the playground trying to keep up with children aged only 11. But we all had a brilliant time and made a few new friends in the process.

I was later quite pleased to learn that Adrian, who is younger than me, was suffering more than I was. He pretended to be ill but he wasn't fooling me.

By now we had become regulars at the 'Happy' restaurant and so naturally made our way there for an end of day meal. Clearly the staff there had never encountered anyone like our very own Adrian 'two puddings' Morgan before but after a little confusion managed to provide multiple desserts for him. If ever you find yourself in Bulgaria make sure you have at least one meal in a 'Happy' restaurant, fantastic food at a great price, but think twice before you order two puddings!

Another day passed and another began. This time we needed to get the car registered and meet the Mayor of Provadia. We headed for the 'DVLA' (equivalent) in Varna but it was closed for lunch so we decided to go to Provadia.

In Provadia we discovered that bureaucracy and red tape is not unique to the UK. Before we could register the car we needed a contract drawn up by a solicitor to cover the transfer of ownership. The solicitor told us that before we could get a contract drawn up we needed to get the car valued. The valuation was a farce, with the car parked at least half a mile away a man sat at a desk asked us how much it was worth, we suggested 400 lev, he wrote it on a form and that was it. We paid the man 12 lev for the privilege. It was hardly worth putting my wallet away because we then had to go to the Bank to pay the tax for importing the car – another 12 lev. Guess what, the bank charged a fee for collecting the tax (that really made me feel at home). Now we were ready to go and get the contract from the solicitor which they happily provided for 70 lev. The total cost was less than £50 so not too bad but we still had to register the car. This would eventually be done by Didi after we returned to the UK.

And so to the meeting with the Mayor. The purpose of the meeting was to discuss the next phase of the building work at the Provadia Orphanage. But I was completely blown away by what I heard. First of all I was delighted to learn that he had kept his promise to renew the roof and carry out remedial work to crumbling foundations. But I wasn't prepared for what came next.

Due to our dogged determination in persuading the Mayor not to close the Orphanage but allow us to repair it and the consequential installation of new windows and his roof and foundation repairs we had aroused the interest of Central Government. Now a grant has been made available to complete all the works. But that wasn't all, not only were they prepared to pay to repair the building but build an extension for two additional facilities. Once complete the unit will consist of a 'family' style orphanage with apartments for 12 children, a transition home for 8 children aged 18-25 and a rehab unit for orphaned children with physical difficulties. The rehab unit will be open by July 2011 with the rest to follow.

The perfect scenario in this line of Charity is for us to be able to hand over a project for the Bulgarians to run themselves so this news was brilliant. And so it seems our involvement here may well have come to a natural conclusion.
Back to Varna for a celebratory 'Happy' meal and two puddings.

I had a great chat with Didi about future projects and have sown the seeds for further work. One of those projects would make great use of our building team who had been expecting to go and finish the Orphanage renovation but are now 'redundant'. Did has set up The Hope & Future Foundation and bought some land with a view to providing a facility for children to have summer camps. The children are at their most vulnerable during the school holidays. Some are sent to abusive families, some just roam the streets, all are prey to criminal gangs looking to recruit pickpockets & prostitutes or to those involved in sex trafficking. So by taking the children to summer camp they are protected from this threat and get a great holiday thrown in too.
To achieve this Didi has asked if HOR would be interested in a project to build log cabins and playground facilities on the land. There is a lot more to talk about here but it's something worth exploring in more detail. It is probable that Didi will come to the UK in June when she will bring some plans for me to show our builders/supporters and discuss everything in more detail.
Independently of this Adrian was touched by the hopelessly inadequate facilities at Krivnya and raised the possibility of some outdoor play equipment for them. Some more food for thought and maybe a future project.

On our last day we went to see the land Didi has purchased for The Hope & Future Foundation and she explained her thoughts for how she would like to use it. We walked around the area and chatted through a few ideas but nothing concrete as yet.

Our time in Bulgaria was coming to an end and it was time to return home. Didi finally took possession of the car and dropped us off at the Airport. Unfortunately, the flight was delayed by 1hr15m due to bad weather but we eventually took off at 9:30pm.
We arrived in Luton and made for the car hire site where we discovered that I was not able to drive as I didn't have my counterpart licence so the

responsibility fell to Adrian & Tony. We hadn't got too far when we came across a road closure which would have been ok but there were no diversion signs and so we had no idea where to go. This gave me the ideal opportunity to redeem myself for my earlier navigational failings and I was able to direct us onto the A303 and in the direction of Okehampton. If Adrian & Tony were impressed with this brilliant piece of navigating they didn't show it but it was very late so I will forgive them.

We arrived in Okehampton at 4:00am and my journey was over. However, Adrian and Tony still needed to get back to Cardiff so after a quick cuppa they were on their way again while I went to bed to try and get a few hours sleep before starting work at 9:00am.

As you may have gathered the trip was a great success. A great team of drivers who had a good laugh (usually at each other's expense) was a key factor in the success.

However, I am acutely aware of God's presence and guiding hand throughout the entire trip. I am also aware that so many people were praying for us – thanks to each and every one of you. But most of all, thanks to our God who sustained us and blessed us and is the author of all the good things which HOR is able to do. To Him be all the praise and Glory.

In His service

Andrew

CHAPTER FIVE
FUNDRAISER
The Coast To Coast Cycle Ride
November 2011

At 7:00am on Saturday 12 Nov the intrepid team of Roger 'the navigator' Thorne, Tony 'two bikes' Hemingway, John 'saddle bag' Stepto and Andrew 'wish I had a road bike' Morgan left Okehampton bound for Illfracombe (thanks to our drivers, we appreciated the lift).

At 8:45 we set off on our bikes for the first leg of the challenge. The sun was shining and a cool, calm day followed affording us ideal cycling conditions.
The first few miles was a steady climb out of Illfracombe followed by a gently undulating route around the estuary of Barnstaple, Instow & Bideford.

I say gently undulating but even the slightest bump seemed to cause John's antique saddle bag to fall off. We were beginning to suspect it was a ruse to take regular breaks but John insisted it was a problem with the saddle and to prove it we stopped off in Braunton to buy a new saddle complete with appropriate fixings for the saddle bag. At least John claimed it was a saddle, to the rest of us it looked like a instrument of abject torture and we winced as he dared to sit on it.
We couldn't help but notice the proprietor of the local antique shop taking an interest in John's saddle bag but the lack of a Carbon Dating machine meant he couldn't date it accurately. The last we saw of him he was making a hurried phone call to the 'Time Team' producers.

At 12:15 we had our scheduled lunch stop where we discovered Roger can eat even faster than he can cycle - if it had been a sponsored eat-a-thon we could have made a small fortune. We were very grateful to Roger's Mum & Dad for meeting us at the Puffing Billy and providing us with an endless supply of food.

During the afternoon we discovered some of Devon's steepest hills - why are they always up! But with lungs and legs pumping for all they were worth we made good progress - until Hatherleigh where the first puncture occurred. Not a problem, we had spare inner tubes and a pump - oh! If only we had checked the pump worked before we left. However, a quick phone call and a short wait saw the cavalry arrive and we were on our way again.

Shortly after 4:00pm we arrived at Okehampton Baptist Church to a wonderful reception plus some very welcome tea & cakes.

Sunday was a little overcast but still cool and dry as we set off at 9:00. Tony had changed his bike and was really feeling the benefit of slimmer, faster tyres (The rest of us felt the benefit of no longer having to listen to his whimpering cries of "Ow this hurts so much". As he is by far the youngest and fittest of our team he got the appropriate amount of sympathy – none!).
We reached Tavistock at 10:45 in time to see the start of the Remembrance service/parade. Tony had brought a Poppy/Cross to leave at the War Memorial. He wrote a message on it, signed our names and left it in the Church yard as we couldn't get near the War Memorial. A poignant moment for us all but particularly for Tony who is ex-army and has seen active service.

Leaving Tavistock brought quite a shock as the climb was relentless, the road was wet and slippery and made for a very tough ride.
Fortunately (?) John got a puncture and we were all relieved to take a break at the top of the hill to fix it. This time we had a working pump and the repair was made rather too quickly for those of us still wondering if we had left our lungs somewhere on the hill.
Around the halfway point the challenge changed from us riding the bikes to the other way round as we heaved the bikes onto our backs to climb the ridiculously steep forest path through mud and rocks.

I was particularly disappointed as when I was told about this part of the route I secretly thought, "I'll be OK cos I have a Mountain Bike." This should have been my moment, the one point of the leg where having a Mountain Bike was an advantage. "How Tony will regret switching to a road bike", I sniggered to myself. But oh, how wrong could I be. It was absurd that such an obstacle should be on an official bike route. Roger told me about a £4m investment in a new section which offered me hope but this was shattered when his sentence finished with, "but it isn't open yet". Thanks Roger, I think I would prefer not to know that!

Not only was the track VERY steep it was completely impossible to ride on due to copious amounts of mud separated by rocks and boulders.
Do you know how heavy a Mountain Bike is? I do.

And so it was that instead of leaping up the hill like a gazelle looking back at my poor colleagues struggling on their inferior road bikes I ended up with my bike on my back like a Sherpa climbing Mount Everest looking ahead at those carrying feather light road bikes with just a hint of envy.
We thought we would be relieved to get back onto our bikes at the top but the wind which greeted us was quite incredible. It was so strong we even had to peddle to go downhill; the uphill stretches were extremely difficult. There was very little conversation on this stretch, but I seem to remember something about a business plan to set up a wind farm.
This was the situation for approx 5 miles but once we got into the shelter of the trees we had a long descent into Plymouth that we all enjoyed.

And so we arrived in Plymouth in the early afternoon tired but satisfied. Just before the finish line we enjoyed the irony of a sign on National Cycle Network Route 27 which read, "Cyclists Dismount". However we were allowed to get back on our bikes just in time for the cobbled area of road. It is here I had my very brief moment of joy watching my colleagues bounce painfully over the cobbles on their flimsy road bikes while my robust and wonderful Mountain Bike took it in its stride and in some comfort. What a shame it was only about 30 metres long.

The final few hundred metres to the Ho was soon completed and our challenge had come to an end. All in all it was hard work but very enjoyable thanks to great company and (mostly) good weather.
Now the hard work begins - collecting the sponsor money !

Thanks to everyone who helped make this possible and to those who have sponsored us.

Andrew

CHAPTER SIX
4355 miles
(Fawlty Towers is alive and well)
December 2011 – Jan 2012

Four of us gathered to make the epic journey to Bulgaria. My mum, who had been staying with me over Christmas together with my brother Adrian and his son, Cai who had travelled from Cardiff during boxing day evening.

Our schedule had us down to leave at 01:00 27 December but we were all ready at 22:00 on the 26th. The plan was to get a few hours sleep to prepare us for the journey but it was then that I announced my 'good idea'. "Why don't we leave now and catch the earlier ferry so that we get a head start on the trek across Europe." A quick check on the internet confirmed a ferry at 05:35 so we decided to leave.

The journey to Dover was fairly uneventful and we arrived feeling a little smug and ready to congratulate me on my 'good idea'.

The first sign that things were wrong came when we realised that we were in Dover even too early for the 05:35 ferry so decided to pull in to the 24 hour services specifically designed for people, like us, waiting for their ferry. However, despite the huge, red 24 on the side of the building which enticed us in, it was shut. There was no indication as to which 24 hours they were open – maybe one a day for 24 days, we will never know. Never mind we can always get a cuppa at the port.

And so we drove the few remaining miles to the ferry port ready for a break and some refreshment. But a man in a fluorescent jacket had other ideas when he waved us into a barn where a lady from HM Customs walked over to the car with a very bored expression on her face. Not surprisingly there were very few vehicles around at 04:00 and clearly she was looking for something to do to alleviate the tedium of a long cold night on Dover Ferry port. Mercifully, she limited her search of our vehicle to one bag which was put through an x-ray machine then, apparently satisfied that all was well with the remaining contents of our car we were allowed to proceed.

Feeling pleased that we had allowed enough time to absorb this unscheduled delay we went to book in. It was here that we received the bad news. Between checking on the internet at 22:00 and arriving at the port around 04:00 the early ferry had been cancelled and so we were booked onto the original 07:45 ferry as per our schedule.

I don't know if you have ever been to Dover Ferry Port but it's not the greatest place to while away three hours. There's a toilet, a café and a shop. On the positive side, there was no queue for the toilet but we quickly made for the café. Adrian and I approached the counter ready to order but something was wrong. Do you remember the Mr Men books? Well, I'm as sure as can be that the lady behind the counter was Mr Grumpy's even more grumpy wife. She was polishing the counter right in front of us while simultaneously ignoring us. How long is it polite to wait before saying something? Long enough for me to wonder just how much cleaning the counter required when there wasn't any sign of any other customers. Long enough for me to wonder if I had become invisible. Long enough for me to wonder if I hadn't actually had the 'good idea' but had in fact gone to bed and was in the middle of a very peculiar dream. After a few minutes of pondering and the odd pinch to make sure I was actually awake I ventured to ask, "excuse me, are you serving?" At least those were the words which came out of my mouth but I can only assume that perhaps she had trouble with my accent because her reaction suggested I said something more along the lines of "Oi, you, get your lazy butt over here now, put some deodorant on, clean your teeth, brush your hair and give me some coffee immediately." After a little while and a lot of grumpiness she gesticulated to another counter to her left which, according to my phrase book of grumpish, meant my cup of tea was over there. And so I collected it and waited for Adrian to endure the same routine for his coffee. We re-joined mum and Cai and explained why we had been so long. It was then that mum pointed out the sign above the counter 'SERVED WITH LOVE'. This Irony kept us amused for the next few hours and before we knew it we were on the Ferry and crossing the channel bound for Calais. Basil Fawlty would have been proud of her but the true Fawlty Towers experience still awaited us.

The rest of the journey was uneventful. France, Belgium & The Netherlands passed relatively quickly before the long haul through Germany. That really is a marathon slog but our incentive to keep going was the Hotel we had booked on the German/Austrian border.

I have owned the car we were travelling in for about 18 months but never knew that there were two beds in the back. Mum and Cai managed to sleep for the majority of the day; actually I think Cai slept for the entire journey. I have made a mental note that should I ever suffer from insomnia I will simply climb into the back of my car where sleep is apparently guaranteed, nay unavoidable.

The hotel was very nice and provided our next instalment of amusement (you'll clutch at anything remotely interesting after six hours of motorway through Germany).
The receptionist struggled a little with our booking but this was not a problem and eventually she invited us to go to the cashier to pay. The cashier looked remarkably like the receptionist but we thought little of it until the girl who came to show us to our room also bore an uncanny resemblance to the receptionist and cashier. Mum and I decided to have a bite to eat in the café while Adrian and Cai went to the counter to buy a sandwich and drink. Strangely, the waitress and shop assistant once again appeared to be the same girl. As it turned out it was the same girl doing all the jobs. She was running around being 'all things to all men' and to be fair, doing a remarkably good job. We felt a little sorry for her as in addition to being all the staff on her own there was a fault with all the hotel room doors which meant that every time anyone wanted to return to their room she had to run up the stairs to let them in.
With the simple addition of a fake moustache and a few hats I feel sure another episode of Fawlty Towers could have been inspired by this situation. However, even this was not the true Fawlty Towers experience; read on............

04:30 alarms greeted us the following morning and we made our way down to breakfast (which was very nice) and we were on our way once again. As dawn tried to break through the dark we were a little disappointed to find a heavy mist had descended and our hope of seeing the Austrian mountains in all their glory faded into the grey which surrounded them. But God was smiling on us and halfway across the mountains the sun broke through and lit up His glorious creation revealing the stunning views which we craved. I have driven this route three times now and this is definitely a highlight of the trip.

Slovenia, Croatia and Serbia followed but fog meant that we did not get the full experience all these countries had to offer. We entertained ourselves by bird spotting instead. Now either there are hundreds of Buzzards sitting on every 10th fence post on the Croatian roadside or one very energetic Buzzard was shadowing our every move. I suspect that they/it were/was watching us too as clearly they could not hunt in the fog and so indulged in a bit of human spotting.

In Serbia the dual carriageway ended and so we started the climb into the mountains; it's a long and slow climb through villages and tunnels cut into the mountains but eventually we started the long and winding descent towards the Bulgarian border.
We made the border in good time and we passed through passport control and customs without incident. Sofia (Bulgaria's capital) was only 30 miles away and this is where our next hotel was booked. Incidentally, when we left Okehampton we had nothing booked and had no idea if we had somewhere to stay as our original plan had been thwarted a few hours before we started our journey. However, during the journey, thanks to the wonders of texting, we managed to secure a booking at the Kabu hotel somewhere in Sofia.

Followers of our previous trips will know that I am not famed for my navigational skills so thankfully (for my passengers) I was driving as we arrived in Sofia so the navigational responsibility fell to the others. We agreed that we needed the Sofia ring road and should head for the Airport, this would take us in the general direction of the Hotel. However, we didn't appreciate just how big the ring road was; it seemed to go on forever. Our mobile phones came to our aid again but this time it wasn't texts but maps which helped us. It amazes me that I can simply press a button on my phone and a map of my surroundings appears with a flashing dot showing my exact, current position thereon – in Bulgaria!
By inputting our destination a line appears on the map showing us exactly where to go. Cai also had this facility on his phone and so both he and Adrian were giving directions and getting us closer and closer to our destination.
But one thing the phones couldn't tell us was the whereabouts of the roving Police checkpoints and we were pulled over. I wound down the

window and in my best Bulgarian greeted the officer with a cheery, "Dobur Vecher". Now I don't like to show off but clearly my excellent command of Bulgarian and precise pronunciation fooled the officer into thinking I was a local but it's true that pride comes before a fall as when he spoke back to me in Bulgarian I didn't have the first idea what he was on about and had to resort to the other two words of Bulgarian I know, "Ne razbiram" which translates as "no understand".

I have travelled around Bulgaria quite a lot over the years and have always been warned about these spot checks which are often used as an excuse to extract money from unwary travellers. I guess the roofbox, right hand side steering wheel, GB sticker etc were acting like a big sign which said, "travelling ATM – withdraw cash here". But I was prepared with a file containing all the documents they might ask for and was quickly and efficiently able to meet all their requests – oops, more pride but on this occasion there was no fall and the officer sent us on our way.

Eventually, we arrived in the heart of Sofia and our maps were telling us we were in the vicinity of our Hotel but one shortcoming of the maps was that they didn't show if a street was one way or if right/left turns were not possible. So we pulled over on the side of the road to study the map in more detail. After some discussion I was instructed to drive again but to look for somewhere to turn around as the hotel was behind us. After a few seconds the shout went up, "hang on, this is the right way, the map was upside down" this was closely followed by, "there it is". In all our efforts to read the map we had failed to look out of the car window and see the huge building with HOTEL KABU written in massive letters rising high into the skyline.

We checked in and got to our rooms by 00:30 which for all sensible people is bedtime and so mum and I made our way to our beds. However, some of you will know that teenagers are not normal people and their body clocks are completely different to the rest of the human race. Teenage body clocks are very much driven by their stomachs and so it was that Adrian found himself taking 13 year old Cai to the 24 hour McDonalds just down the road. It wasn't just the lateness of the hour which made this trip undesirable but there was snow and ice on the ground and the temperature was -5 degrees. But Adrian has learned that you do not ever come between a teenage boy and his food, the consequences are unimaginable.

However, a bit of a theme was developing on this trip and once again we found a 24 hour facility closed. Somehow Adrian managed to feed Cai and eventually got to bed.

The following morning was a much more civil affair and we got up with the sun and made our way to the restaurant for breakfast. I smugly opted for the cereal and orange juice healthy breakfast while my fellow travellers went for the cholesterol and calories option. Pride, fall …….. Guess what's coming now! I was served cornflakes on a napkin with a huge pyrex bowl of luke warm UHT milk. My family didn't try to hard to stifle their laughter as I looked on enviously at omelette and sausages whilst picking dry cornflakes from my napkin – the milk, unfortunately, was, judging by the smell, not fit for this human's consumption. But our family bonds are strong and they all pitched in by offering me the tomato they couldn't eat because they were too full.

At last we had reached a point in the trip where we could fulfil one of the reasons for going. We met up with Patrick & Letty (and baby Nina) at their apartment and dropped off some of the donations we had been given. We gave them bags of clothes and boxes of toys & games for the Children of the RETA project. This project looks after children whose lives have been ravaged either directly or indirectly by the demons of drugs & alcohol. The children will usually end up in a RETA home with absolutely nothing and so the donations you gave us will be put to very good use.
We spent a lovely but brief time with Patrick and Letty drinking tea and eating cake before we had to get on our way again.
It was very heart warming when Patrick texted us later (after looking through the bags & boxes) to say it was much more than he ever dared to expect.

Crossing Bulgaria was great as the sun came out and stayed with us throughout our journey. Our highlight was a visit to the Happy Restaurant for lunch. A visit to Bulgaria is incomplete without at least one meal at a Happy Restaurant, although we didn't know it at the time it would be our only Happy visit on this trip but it was, as always, a very enjoyable one. We made Provadia by 18:30 met briefly with Alex, our translator and friend and settled in to our Hotel.

The following morning, before going to the Orphanage, we went to Kichevo to meet Didi and make our second drop of donations. Didi runs the Hope & Future Foundation which our charity supports and they have rented a small property to provide an 'offsite' facility for the children from nearby Orphanages. Preparations were underway for the first 'event' to be held there – a winter camp for the older children from Barzitsa Orphanage (due to start on the day we left Bulgaria).

The main donations here were 15 magnificent, hand crafted quilts donated by the ladies from Okehampton (it's worth noting here that not only did they donate the quilts but a considerable cash gift to facilitate their transportation which, in part, made our trip possible). The quilts were very well received and on a later visit I saw them all on the beds and they filled the rooms with colour and cheer. Since returning to the UK I have received an email saying how much the quilts were appreciated and how warm they kept the children. I know that on at least one night the temperature dropped to a bone chilling -11 degrees.

I love the fact that ladies here in Okehampton helped to keep these lovely children warm at the other end of Europe in Eastern Bulgaria. Proof if ever it were needed that we really can make a difference in the lives of vulnerable children no matter how far away we are.

At last we were on our way to the Orphanage. We had loads of craft and sports equipment to ensure that we could provide four days of fun for the children. More donations meant we had really good quality equipment to delight the children.

Within a few minutes of our arrival a football match had broken out and so Adrian, Cai & I started our marathon football session. I clearly remember at 16:55 precisely, with the light fading I said, "we have to go at 5 o'clock" but buckled under the pressure to stay 'just a little longer' and so it was we played football until it was simply too dark to carry on.

Meanwhile, mum and Alex set up the craft in the big hall where they made all sorts of delightful jewellery with the 'indoor' children. They might have thought that they had the best deal being indoors while the boys played outside but they hadn't factored in the stereo. The hall was also home to the children's stereo and I think that even if it had been The Albert Hall the music would still have been too loud for the surroundings. Now I don't mind loud music so long as it is good music but this was truly awful American drum & bass. If you're reading this thinking I must be getting old and grumpy I would like to point out that even Alex who is just 18 agreed (that the music was awful, not that I'm old and grumpy!!). Alex found communication extremely difficult amidst the deafening boom, boom, boom so I've no idea how mum coped when she can't even speak the lingo. Judging by what I saw of what the Children made they clearly managed OK and the children all looked very happy indeed.

We finished the day off with a meal in a local restaurant where tradition (i.e. our charity tradition) dictates that one of our party has to go and ask for the bill in Bulgarian. The staff there know us well and are familiar with our tradition so play their part in pretending to understand our laughable attempts to converse in the local dialect.
Unusually, it took quite a lot of effort to persuade someone to be bold enough to undertake the task. Eventually mum put the others to shame and after a lot of rehearsal took the long walk to the till and said, "monja lee smetcata molya?" No doubt she was suitably proud when the bill arrived if not relieved that she had not been tricked into saying, "Will you please cover me with feathers and chase me around the building"

Day two at the Orphanage was New Years Eve. At this point I must reveal that there is something I haven't mentioned – but that's the point, I hadn't mentioned it. When I was planning the trip I had it in my heart to treat the children to a Firework Display on New Year's Eve but after sharing this with a few people at home I realised that it would be impossible to get permission to set off fireworks in an Orphanage and so I didn't mention it again although the idea never really left me.
Imagine my joy and surprise when I received a phone call via Alex with a request from the Director of the Orphanage to provide Children's Champagne and ……. Yes…… fireworks for the Children. I hadn't breathed a word of my desire to anyone in Bulgaria or even to many people in the UK but clearly God had heard my silent prayer and blessed me by granting my silent wish.
And so New Years Eve started with us visiting the supermarket for Children's Champagne and Fireworks. Cai had been given a cash donation which he brought with him and it was exactly the right amount to buy what we needed.
Off we went to the Orphanage for another session of art, craft, sport and sundry other activities. One of the great joys of working with the children is their overwhelming desire to give us things. Often the craft items they make are given to us as gifts, this is very humbling indeed.
It was very cold outside today and so we decided to have some indoor sport, out came the table tennis equipment and before we knew it there was a Bulgaria v England world cup final in progress. Now at this juncture I need to point out that ALL of us are Welsh but experience has shown me

that trying to explain this to the Children of Barzitsa is a painful, drawn out, exasperating experience and despite the obvious insult it is much easier to agree to be 'England' for the purpose of a table tennis match. (There has been a little improvement in this area and the very mention of Ryan Giggs or Gareth Bale brings a dawning of realisation to at least some of the Children i.e. the boys who follow international football.)

There's something about sport which brings out the competitive spirit in most men. The fact that we were playing little Orphan children got lost in the 'must win' red mist which engulfed Adrian and I as we battled for our honour. Actually, the older boys are very talented and gave us a very close game but you will be delighted to learn that we did not let you down and came away victorious. We were suitably humble in our victory and restricted our celebrations to just the three laps of honour and gentle shouts of YEESSSSSS, Champions, Champions!! There were various re-matches in both singles and doubles, even one staff member got involved. I don't remember if Adrian or I lost any games (funny that!) but I do remember that we all had a great time even though by the end of it our fingers were so numb with the cold we could hardly punch the air in (humble) victory any longer.

Around 5 o'clock we packed up and told the children we would return around 10 to join them in seeing in the New Year at midnight. So we made our way back to Provadia and it was time to wind our weary way to the restaurant for some well earned sustenance. But, shock horror, we couldn't get in as it was fully booked and so we went to the local shop (think Spar) for supplies. I never realised before but sandwiches seem to be a very British thing as we couldn't get them anywhere on our journey through Europe. If you are the sort of person who isn't prepared to experiment a little with 'foreign' food you could easily starve in Provadia. The shop has a deli counter with a small section devoted to hot food so with some pointing and gesticulating we purchased some unidentified meat like things and took them back to our room. I've no idea what we eat but we were filled and it stayed down so all was well.
While all this was going on the innocuous snowflakes which had started fluttering down during the afternoon began to take on a more threatening nature. There were a few centimetres of settled snow on both the pavements and roads and it looked like it was getting worse. Now we faced the agonising decision of whether to cancel our New Years Eve party with the children or risk life and limb on the treacherous Bulgarian

roads. We took advice from Alex's dad who said that the roads would freeze later and that it would be too dangerous to travel. As we needed his daughter to be with us I could understand his concern and so, with enormous reluctance and sadness we took the decision to cancel. I guess we will never know if I made the right decision but I can take some comfort from the fact that we are still alive and well to tell the tale so if the decision wasn't right it definitely wasn't wrong. The ice on the ground the following morning helped to soften the blow of having to make that decision and suggested it might have been the right decision.

On New Year's Day I travelled with Alex back to Kichevo while the others stayed behind to 'sort out all the craft equipment which had become very disorganised'. Three people to tidy one box? I wouldn't say I was suspicious but their beds were still warm when I returned.
The purpose of my return to Kichevo was to do a site visit of the land set aside for the proposed summer school.
In brief, we have agreed to help create facilities for a summer school to be used in conjunction with the building The Hope & Future Foundation are renting (i.e. the venue for the winter camp mentioned earlier in this report). The building will provide the sleeping facilities while the land, a short walk away, will provide the site for daytime activities. In order to get the site ready a certain amount of work is required and I was going to get a clearer idea of what would be required of us.
It was a very cold day and there was about 20cm of snow on the ground but the sky was blue and the sun shining so a lovely day for a site visit. We are asked to do the following:
Lay blocks for a car park area (which will also be where the minibus we previously donated will be kept)
Lay a footpath
Level a playing field
Build a caretakers home and storehouse (to include cess pit)
The site will also have a playground which is being donated from Germany.
There will also be a camping area but this does not need much work
I am hoping to put together a team of builders/labourers to go and do this work in May/June. A number of people have already expressed an interest and are lined up to go. The target is to have it completed in time for the first summer camp in July. It is hoped that the camp will be active throughout the summer drawing several different groups of children from various Orphanages in the region.

I have also been asked if we can arrange groups to go and run the activities at the Summer Camps (similar to that which we do at Barzitsa Orphanage with Okehampton College).

New Years Day afternoon we returned to the Orphanage but with snow and ice everywhere we were limited as to what outdoor activities we could run. Meanwhile, Alex and mum had plotted to run the craft activities in a different room away from the stereo but didn't realise the other room actually doubled as a fridge in its spare time. There was a wood burner in the room but it must have taken a full hour to get it going despite all our best efforts.

A few of us dared to venture outside with a baseball bat and ball which despite the bitter cold turned out to be a success as a small handful of younger boys never seemed to get bored with smashing the ball all over the place and watching me, Adrian and Cai struggle in the ice and snow to retrieve the ball with all the grace of a wheezy, asthmatic hippopotamus with three legs carrying a heavy bag of shopping over a cobbled street covered in marbles. We laughed so hard it hurt or was it just the extreme cold causing the pain? Either way we had a great time but eventually the presence of a hungry looking polar bear licking his lips in Cai's direction forced us indoors.

What to do now? Time to play our trump card. In the boot of the car was our secret weapon, a donation from an Okehampton family – a Scalextric racing car set. We hand picked a few of the reliable older boys under the pretence of allowing them the honour of helping us to put it together but in reality it had more to do with the fact that we had no idea how to construct it and thought the boys might be able to work it out quicker than us. Between us we soon had it up and running and the boys were absolutely blown away with it. They were mesmorised and couldn't believe that they were actually playing with a Scalextric. One of the boys grabbed me, gave me huge hug and said thank you over and over again. Slowly we invited a few more boys in to play and they had the time of their lives. Eventually all the boys drifted in and one by one they experienced the thrill of car racing. It really was a big hit. Only one thing seemed greater than the thrill of playing, that was the realisation that we were leaving it there and they could continue to play even after we were gone.

Then it was time, time for my personal favourite moment. We still had the Fireworks and 'Champagne' and we were determined to use them. So the staff sent the children off to get cups so that we could crack open the bubbly and give them a New Year Celebratory drink. Every now and then something happens which brings a dose of reality to proceedings. Amidst all the noise and excitement of children clamouring for a drink of 'Champagne' came the revelation that the Orphanage did not have enough cups for each child. I was very moved to witness the older children take a back seat and allow the younger children to have several drinks. Once we spotted this we were able to encourage the sharing of cups and I think we managed to get a drink to everyone.

Then it was outside for the fireworks. We had bought three 'cakes'; one with 50 shots another with 100 shots and a third with 16 shots. Adrian took responsibility for letting the fireworks off and I grabbed a camera to photograph the children. Then I had my moment, the one which was easily the highlight of my trip. I didn't even see the fireworks as I was transfixed by the watching the children's faces. The joy and delight on their faces was just brilliant and a treasured memory for me. The 16 shot cake was the finale and each shot was spectacular and loud. Once the show was over the children ran over to Adrian and gave him a hero's reception. It was simply fantastic.

Later that evening, after discovering 'our' restaurant was closed along with every other eatery in Provadia, we decided to drive to Varna (35 miles away!!) to find a place to eat. Naturally we headed straight for the Happy restaurant but were gutted to find it closed. So we were forced to make a choice between McDonalds and Subway (hardly traditional Bulgarian fayre). Subway won as it had free toilets!! It was nice and warm inside and we had a good feed so left feeling very content.

Before we knew it the last day had arrived. We went to the shop to stock up on supplies for the return journey – more unidentified meat products which didn't reveal their true colours until we were well into the journey home and the overpowering smell which engulfed us each time we opened our supply box forced us to dispose of what remained.

But we still had one more visit to the Orphanage. More craft, more Scalextric, more table tennis and once again the boys tried to teach me to break dance!! Will they ever learn? Every time I go there I have another break dancing lesson. I'm sure they only do it so that they can laugh at me and laugh they did but it didn't matter I was happy to be their stooge – again! Is it called break dancing because every time I do it I break something? My poor broken body is only just recovering.

Most of the older children had gone to the winter camp in Kichevo today so we had time to devote to the younger ones which they enjoyed.

All too soon it was time to say goodbye and another trip was drawing to a close. It's hard to leave but leaving is made easier in the knowledge that we have had a great few days and the children have made some happy memories to keep them going through the tough times. However, although we go to give, we always receive so much more in return and our own memories will be just as precious to us.

But we had one more wonderful duty to perform. Before we left, Exbourne Primary School had spent the previous few months collecting enough equipment to fill 80 pencil cases—that's one for every child in Barzitsa. They delivered a big box containing all the goodies which we took with us. The presence of the box in the room in the Orphanage had aroused the interest of the children and I was fully engaged in protecting the contents from an early appearance. So our final activity of our visit was to distribute the pencil cases. What a privilege for me, I felt like Father Christmas as I was besieged by excited children keen to get their hands on the gifts. It was lovely to see the delight on their faces and the pleasure they had in showing their gifts to each other.

Thanks so much to the students of Exbourne School, you brought so much joy to the children of Barzitsa Orphanage.

You might be asking yourself, "but what about Fawlty Towers?" If you have a good memory you will recall there were a few oblique references to Fawlty Towers earlier and the promise of another story so here goes.

There was only one place open where we could get something to eat that night. It was a new restaurant in Provadia and we decided to give it a try.

Alex helped us to work through the menu and we decided on an omelette for mum, chicken stew for Adrian, Cai & me and salad for Alex. The waitress approached to take our order which Alex duly gave her. After a brief exchange in Bulgarian the waitress disappeared and returned with the news that there were no eggs so the omelette was off the menu. She also informed us that there was not enough Chicken for three stews. I happily changed my order to a 'meat' (again undefined) stew. Another Bulgarian exchange revealed there was no potato so all stews were off. Alex asked if there was any meal they could make up for us. The waitress disappeared again and returned with a man who between them came up with an idea for a meal based on the ingredient they had left and so we sat back in excited anticipation wondering what would arrive.

Whilst waiting a toilet trip was in order. The toilets were in the stock room but one was out of order, after washing my hands I discovered there was no towel. We later found out I should have used the box of tissues nearby.
After a long wait the first meal arrived – Alex's salad. We were amazed to see it contained eggs and to rub salt into the wound it was the wrong salad and Alex doesn't like eggs! If only they could have used the eggs to make the omelette.
We suggested Alex send the erroneous salad back but she couldn't face it given the farce so far.
The wait for the mystery meals seemed to go on forever and this wasn't helped by the staff sat at the bar continually staring at us.
Eventually the wait was over and three pots of stew arrived. We looked and saw they contained chopped up chips, tomato and something which looked and tasted suspiciously like chicken.
Our appetites had been sharpened by the wait and by the knowledge that there was nowhere else to get a meal in town so the stew went down quite well. Adrian and Cai graciously gave mum their slice of tomato so that she had something to eat. We will never know what we actually ate but there seemed to be less street dogs the next day.
Then, as if from nowhere, the owner appeared in a ridiculous bright blue beret and matching scarf and with flamboyant gestures timed so perfectly with the background music we thought he was actually dancing, tried to explain to Alex why we had experienced such poor service.
Not satisfied with his first attempt he returned and danced part two of his musical interpretation of the excuse which Alex tells us was due to the fact that they had been unable to buy supplies over the Bank Holiday.
Then in a final attempt to absolve himself of all guilt he attempted to explain to us in English. Now I'll be the first to admit that my Bulgarian is very limited so perhaps laughing at this man's English explanation is a little unkind but what he actually said was, "I am lazy man, it not my fault". We can only guess at what he meant to say but these words have given us enough laughs to last us a long, long time.
For my idle amusement I decided to get a translation of Fawlty Towers (or to be accurate Faulty Towers) and it translates thus дефектни кули i.e. Defectni Kooli. Fans of Fawlty Towers will know about the anagrams on the hotel sign so you might be interested to know that one anagram of Defectni Kooli is 'I Look Infected'. If you have any good ones please let me know.

So that's how our Bulgaria experience ended, with a laugh and a story which we will no doubt share over and over again at future family get togethers.

There were a few loose ends to tie up. We gave Alex the supplies for Krivnya Orphanage which we had been unable to deliver as it was closed for Christmas/New Year. Fortunately the children were sent to Barzitsa for the holidays so we saw them there. Some of you will remember that last time we went there the entire inventory of outdoor play equipment extended to two deflated footballs. So we were delighted to be able to deliver footballs, volleyballs, basketballs, tennis balls and various other bits of kit for the children to play with.

We had previously decided to bring forward our departure time so grabbed a few hours sleep before setting off at midnight. The story of the journey home was mostly one of weather (apart from a strange incident trying to 'break out' of our hotel in Austria at 5am). The temperature dropped to minus 11 and for a few moments the thick fog reduced visibility to zero (it also appeared to reduce the size of the brain of the van driver behind us to zero as he overtook us). High winds and heavy rain made the journey hard work, the presence of the roof box was a bit of a nuisance as the winds made keeping a straight line something of a challenge. We were very conscious of the fact that the roof box was empty for the return journey and we wondered if we could take it off and put it in the car. But that would have meant putting Cai on the roof and he would have had trouble sleeping up there so we persevered. We worried about the impact of the weather on the Ferry (or our tummies to be more precise) but it didn't cause us any discomfort (although we were entertained by the staff trying to push a trolley of crockery through the restaurant and the intermittent crashes from behind the scenes).
We got back to Okehampton at midnight where I was pleased to go to bed while mum, Adrian & Cai drove the final two hours to Cardiff.

I was interested to turn on my radio the following morning and hear stories of floods, trees down, debris in the road etc. When they listed the roads affected/closed I was amazed to hear many of the roads we had travelled on and so I offered up a prayer of thanksgiving for our safe passage.

And it's on that note that I conclude this report – a note of thanksgiving. We were really blessed during our trip and I can look back and see God's hand on so many aspects of our adventure. Thanks to everyone who supported us with donations, cash and above all prayer.

4355 miles and God was with us every inch of the way. Thanks be to Him.

Andrew

CHAPTER SEVEN
Rain, Delays & Wheelbarrows
May 2012

Why do all these trips have to start at such ridiculous times? 00:45am saw me standing outside my shop waiting for my lift to Exeter.
This time we were going to prepare facilities for a Summer Camp for the orphaned and abandoned children in the Varna district. Our team consisted of:
Elliot 'Wheels' Maltby,
Barry 'GPS' Gee,
Phil 'Wheelbarrow' Dennis,
Heather 'Card Shark' Dennis,
Matt 'The Dustbin' Dennis,
Ryan 'Where's My Coat' Dennis and
Me (insert your own nickname here _____).

And so it was that in the early hours of Saturday morning Julian and David kindly sacrificed a few hours sleep to transport the team to Exeter Bus Station. It was a two leg bus journey to Luton Airport which, thankfully, went without a hitch.

We had a few hours to kill at Luton Airport so there was plenty of time for a fry up, after all it was breakfast time by now. After playing a quiz game we entertained ourselves with the famous airport game of watching the departures board for the much anticipated 'Check In' sign to alight signalling the surge of travellers towards the relevant desk.

I looked at our team and considered we had a good shot at being first in the queue; young, fit, healthy were words that immediately came to mind. With Barry being a rugby coach I felt sure we could beat the other travellers in the inevitable scrum.
Unfortunately, I hadn't allowed for the frailties of Elliot's suitcase. Fairly early in the proceedings Elliot's case began to limp severely as one of the wheels started to lose it's grip on life and on the case. Bathed in all the sympathy we showed I'm sure Elliot must have felt much loved by the rest of the team but the warm glow soon faded when the wheel finally gave up and departed this mortal coil.

I still thought we had a chance of being champion queue beaters but my hopes were dashed by the departure of wheel number two from Elliot's case. Any sympathy we may have had disappeared as we quickly checked that the aircraft wheels were not from the same manufacturer as Elliot's case. I would like to be able to say that the team pulled together and came to Elliot's aid in a demonstration of devotion to each other's needs but we decided that hurling an endless stream of insults was far more entertaining. It was the pursuit of this childish entertainment and the fact that Elliot had to hoist his suitcase onto his shoulder that meant victory eluded us and we had to settle for a lower place in the queue. In an effort to redeem himself Elliot entertained us with his woeful and hilarious attempts to repair the wheels while we waited to be checked in. Thinking back, the whole wheel fiasco may have got the odd mention later in the week too as we extended our sympathies beyond the initial incident.

When we finally made it to the check in desk the presence of hammers, drills etc in our luggage (and maybe the absence of wheels) forced some of the team to take their luggage (and wheels for those who still had them) to a different despatch point. This passed off without incident so why I have I put it in the report? Simply to get in a few cheap gags about Elliot's wheels of course.

The flight went well for those with leprechaun legs but for those of us with normal size legs it was a bit cramped. I guess that's the price you pay for flying budget airlines—that and the outside toilets on the flight!! Nevertheless, we arrived in Varna on time and raring to go. But something was wrong. As we descended the steps from the plane in our t-shirts, shorts and flip-flops we were stopped in our tracks. What's this? Rain! Cold! Had we just done a complete circuit and ended up back in Luton. No, Luton was bathed in sunshine and boasting high summer temperatures. When I checked the weather forecast the huge sun symbol over the UK was looking very smug and I'm sure it was laughing at the dark, black cloud over Varna. This wasn't supposed to happen! We must have looked quite a sight wearing our beach clothes in the pouring rain, baring our knees so that the whole of Varna could see them knocking together in the cold.

We were met by Didi and Stanislov in the minibus which we donated back in December 2010. The appearance of the minibus was a very welcome sight as it had proved to be a task of monumental difficulties to get the bus operational in Bulgaria. Several times we had come close to giving up but persevered against apparently insurmountable odds. Our faith in adhering to what we believed we were led to do by God was rewarded and it is nothing short of a miracle that the bus is now on the road and fulfilling its divinely appointed purpose. For those who remember the 'minibus delivery trip' you will recall that the journey itself was punctuated with several miracles – if you are not familiar with that story please ask for a copy of the report. It's amazing.

Our travelling was complete on our arrival at the Guest House in Kichevo rented by The Hope & Future Foundation (HFF). The Guest House had been used to trial the idea of taking the children away from the Orphanages for a time of rest and play during which HFF could help them with their education and equip them with vocational based skills. A winter 'camp' in January and a spring 'camp' in April had been a major success with Orphanage Directors and children alike. The Director at Barzitsa was so impressed with the change seen in the children returning from the camps that she told all the children that in order to 'qualify' for a place on the Summer Camp she wanted to see an improvement in both school work and general behaviour. The improvement was both instant and remarkable. This was a fantastic incentive for our team and added real value to what we were here for.

Here at the Guest House in Kichevo we saw more of the donations we had previously made – the car, the quilts, toys and games. It's a really lovely place and provided us with a good home for the week. We settled in quickly and retired for the night ready for a busy day tomorrow.

Sunday provided a full program of activities starting with a site visit. This was the first time that the rest of the team had seen the site and it was gratifying to see that the Bobcat had been working and much of the groundwork had been done. There was a lot of head scratching and chin rubbing but overall the grunts sounded positive so I breathed a sigh of relief.

Next stop was the Church in Varna where we were invited to the main service and a wedding service to follow. Barry and Elliot decided they would like to explore Varna while the rest of went to Church and so we parked the minibus under a very tall building so that there was an obvious and easy to spot landmark to help them return to the right point. As we waved goodbye to Hansel & Gretel I wish I had checked that they had enough breadcrumbs to mark the trail home but I was so sure the enormous building rising majestically into the Varna skyline provided sufficient security that I let them go with a cheery, "see you back here at one o'clock".

The service was great. Lively worship music followed by a good word reminding us not to rely on our own strength but to allow the Spirit to work through us. A timely word given the amount of physical activity which awaited us on site. The sermon was interpreted into English and transmitted through an electronic gismo which we wore in our ears.
Somehow we managed to get press ganged into removing a keyboard from the front of the Church and loaded it onto the minibus for The Hope & Future Foundation. I shudder to think what it must have looked like when five complete strangers walked up onto the stage and took away the keyboard which a few minutes earlier had been used in worship!!

As we were about to leave the Service there was a sobering moment. I was showing Heather where the Church toilets were when we were approached by an older gentleman saying, "edin lev, edin lev." "What is he saying?" Heather asked. "He's asking for a Bulgarian coin" I replied. "Oh, do we have to pay to use the toilet?" asked Heather. "No, he's begging" was my sad response.

And so the time came for us to meet up with Hansel & Gretel as arranged. We returned to the minibus at the foot of the government building (you remember, the huge, unmissable one standing proud above the skyline of the city) but there was no sign of Elliot or Barry. Time ticked on so Phil and I left the warm, dry comfortable minibus and wandered around in the cold, wet, miserable weather engulfing the district but still the wanderers could not be found. Our efforts to contact them by phone proved fruitless. We got seriously bored looking for our colleagues so we went to look at the shops; sorry I mean concern for our friends set in so we widened our search to the shops (yes, that sounds much better). We left a note on the minibus saying we would meet back there at 2pm. Our second deadline came and went and still there was no sign of Elliot or Barry. As our deep concern increased to panic we decided to find a place to have lunch and so another note was left on the minibus telling the guys where we were. We tried valiantly to turn our attention away from the fate of our friends by carefully studying the menu, after all what good were we to them if our stomachs were empty. How would we summon the energy to trawl the city without food in our bellies. In deference to our missing friends we ordered extra food and ate it on their behalf, the situation was becoming increasingly difficult for us to bear but we persevered and ate and drank all we could for them.

Then, suddenly, Phil's phone rang. It was Barry. With no thought for ourselves or our lunch we stopped eating long enough to take the call and play a game of telephone rugby. Barry explained to Phil that he was in the police station with Elliot as they were completely lost and had no idea where they were. Phil, being new to the area, passed the phone to me to explain where we were. Barry, not trusting his inbuilt GPS or his eyes to spot the huge building, passed his phone to the policeman. So there I was with my limited Bulgarian speaking to a policeman with limited English; a recipe for disaster if ever there was one. This is what I heard, "We are second police station in Gobbledigook Street. You come here" I politely pointed out that I didn't have the first idea where that was and that I was going to pass the phone over to a Bulgarian speaker to improve communications. A brilliant spin pass saw the phone relayed into Kremi's hands but it was too late the policeman had rung off. A few moments later and a quick press of the redial key got us back in touch with the police station and Kremi was able to arrange for the officer to put our friends into a taxi and send them to our restaurant. And so the group was restored once more and all would have been well except for the fact that Phil felt obliged to offer our returning friends what was left of his dinner. He was polite about it but we could all tell that deep down he was livid when they accepted.

Kremi is one of the older children from Barzitsa. I have known her for some years and have always been impressed by her determination to escape the fate that so many of her fellow orphans face. She has worked hard at school and focussed on learning English. This trip presented me with the perfect opportunity to reward her for her endeavours and boost her confidence by asking her to work as translator for the day. She was delighted to have the opportunity and really rose to the occasion. If she had not been with us in the restaurant and had the confidence to ring the police station we might still be looking for Elliot & Barry now.

We also had George with us. Another teenager from Barzitsa and he provided us with another sobering moment. While we were all revelling in the joys of selecting our meals from a comprehensive menu we kept saying to George, "pick anything you like" but something was wrong he kept shrugging his shoulders. We kept emphasising that we would pay and he could have whatever he liked but still he just shrugged his shoulders. As the focus of attention turned more and more in George's direction the horrible truth dawned on me – he can't read. I felt very embarrassed for him but thankfully Kremi came to our rescue and helped him select something from the menu.

George is such a vibrant and cheerful character it was strange to see him so subdued but fortunately once his food came he was back to his bubbly self and he thoroughly enjoyed his treat. If gratitude can be measured by the number of times you say thank you he was very, very, very grateful. However, the pleasure was definitely all ours.

Less of a pleasure however was George's attempts at DJ'ing with the minibus Radio. At least by the end of the journey he will know the English for 'Turn it off', 'Rubbish' & 'Headache'.

Next stop was Krivnya orphanage. Followers of my reports will know that I have felt called to work in Krivnya for some time now but to date all efforts to meet with the director had been thwarted. For a while I thought I might fail again as by the time we left the restaurant it was 2:45 and my appointment was 3:00. The journey to Krivnya would take at least an hour. Then, to make matters worse, the road to Krivnya was closed and we had to take a detour. It didn't seem wise to ask Elliot or Barry to navigate so it was left to me as I was driving. Again, followers of my reports will now be trepadaciously awaiting a story of inept navigating, wrong turns and backtracking but I will have to disappoint as for once I negotiated the detour with aplomb (and a quick shout of "Provadia is that way" from Heather).

We were late for the meeting but it didn't matter and we were made very welcome. I presented my letter translated into Bulgarian explaining the reason for our visit but the director already knew why we were there and we soon got down to business. We were introduced to Mladin who spoke some English and he took the team on a tour of the home. As we looked around we saw so much that needed doing:

The walls were bare and cold
The dark brown curtains made no effort to cover the windows
The beds were just like Z-beds and the mattresses so thin and worn
The toilets left quite an impression on the nose

Everywhere we looked we saw a job which needed doing so imagine our surprise when we asked, "What would you like us to do?" to receive the response, "everything here in the home is OK, we really need your help in the school." The unspoken thought we all had was if this is OK what's the school like?

As the home is specifically for children with special educational needs the school is extremely important and our Charity is keen to support any improvement in the children's education as we see this as being one of the key tools for breaking the poverty cycle. It is doubly important for those children who struggle at school. The school is a two minute walk from the home and so we set off to see what we could do there. Somehow, when we got there the children we had just been playing with were already there, clearly there was a back way and they had run round to greet us.

We were taken to a rather small classroom and the problems were quite clear to see. There was a damp patch on the wall which was a symptom of a leaking roof. The floor was in a state of collapse, the windows let in more than just light and the high ceiling contributed to the problems of keeping the room warm during the hard winters when temperatures regularly fall below -10.

And so our next project was birthed there in the classroom, several conversations followed and the project began to take shape. I sensed a good relationship building with Mladin and I am very hopeful that he will facilitate the project his end.

We walked the short trip back to the orphanage where we spent some more time playing with the children. Matt and Ryan quickly had a game of football on the go, cameras were clicking and new friendships were being formed all over the place. More discussions and another quick trip to the school to look at the roof sealed the deal and we agreed to return Easter 2013. The Director gently pushed for an earlier date (as clearly it would be even better if they didn't have to spend another winter in those conditions) but we had to politely decline as we need a sustained period of fundraising and there are only so many days in one year that the team can take off work.

We agreed on Easter as the Children will be on vacation and the school will be empty (the children all transfer to Barzitsa during school vacations). The Bulgarians follow the Orthodox calendar and generally this means their Easter is different to ours which is good as we won't have to travel over our Easter. The Director will not be told until September what the actual vacation dates are but Easter Monday is 6 May so we have a good idea when we will be going (In the UK it is 1 April).

I left Krivnya with a great feeling of having taken a huge step towards fulfilling the call on me to improve the lives of the children who live there and go to school there. The time spent with the children was the cherry on the cake.

There was more pleasure to come as we arrived at Barzitsa. Surprisingly another game of football soon broke out and once again I had to suffer the grave indignity of being 'English' in the international game between Bulgaria & England. (I do it for the kids) You will be delighted to know that England won what turned out to be the first leg. As usual I deluded myself into thinking I was Ryan Giggs but after several embarrassing attempts on goal I coyly hid myself in defence where, in reality, I know I belong. Still that won't stop me from going through the same delusion and embarrassment next time we play.

It was a victorious UK team which made the long journey back to the guest house in Kichevo. We ended day one very happy indeed and looking forward to starting work tomorrow.

And so Monday dawned as did the beginning of the slow realisation that they do things differently in Bulgaria. In the UK building trade everything is done to strict deadlines even to the point that some contracts are agreed on the basis that any delays are subject to fines. I don't know what the Bulgarian for procrastination is but I suspect the root of the word is 'builder'.
Builders Merchants in Bulgaria have a somewhat more laid back approach……..!!!!!!!!

In the UK our builders are used to phoning the Builders Merchant, ordering their supplies and receiving it later in the day. The merchant simply loads their lorry and drives it to the site for delivery. Easy.
In Bulgaria you phone the Builders Merchants to book the materials. Then you have to find a lorry driver to deliver them. Then you have to find a fork lift & driver to load the materials onto the lorry and depending on what you have ordered, a fork lift & driver to unload them on site. If you fail on any one of these parts you fail on them all.

We were a little frustrated that the materials weren't on site given that I had spent the last few months emphasising over and over the importance of this. But apart from all the problems I have just described, ordering materials in advance is futile as there is no guarantee that the merchant will have them on the day of delivery. They all promise but supplies are so variable they may or may not have it on the day.

This led to a very frustrating day simply waiting for the stone to be delivered. To make matters worse a monsoon had set in and it was simply too wet to do anything useful on site.

However, it did give us the opportunity to closely observe the all too familiar battle of man against technology. Now Phil might be a great builder and able to manage all manner of diggers and power tools but give him a simple CD player and those small, fiddly, delicate buttons are just too much for him. It was highly entertaining to sit back and watch him try to get a CD to play. I could have watched for hours but Matt, driven by a mix of embarrassment and exasperation, put an end to his dad's misery and we were treated to some proper entertainment of a musical variety.

Stung by his shameful inability to master the intricacies of a highly complex machine Phil decided to restore his masculinity by returning to a subject he knew better, "We need wheelbarrows, lots of wheelbarrows." And so it began, with the monotony and timing of Westminster Chimes, every 15 minutes we had to endure the somewhat Neanderthal grunts of '"wheelbarrows!"

Could anything get more annoying? Oh yes. Do you remember we 'removed' a keyboard from the church in Varna? Well the keyboard was in the guest house and proved to be a temptation too far for the budding pianists in our group. By 'budding pianists' what I actually mean is 'totally useless keyboard players'. There are only so many renditions of Chopsticks that any man can endure and for this man the number is two. After the 33rd rendition my nerves were frayed, my nails were bitten to the quick and the last hair on my head pulled out. The main culprit was Ryan who had clearly not inherited his mum's mastery of the keyboard. I had to fight hard to suppress my desire to place my hands round Ryan's throat and squeeze until something more tuneful than Chopsticks came out of his mouth but just as I was losing the fight salvation came in the form of a tennis ball and three chairs. Just how many games can you play with a tennis ball and three chairs? It would appear to be an infinite number as Matt & Ryan passed away the time with an endless display of creativity.

As you might have gathered we were slumping into a pit of boredom. Every now and then we would rush to the window at the sound of an approaching lorry to see if it was our materials but disappointment was the inevitable conclusion of each futile window trip. Desperation was growing and we would rush to the window for almost any noise. I first realised we were suffering with cabin fever when we ran to the window on hearing a tiny bird cough.
However, we were beginning to notice that the road outside had turned into a river. There is no drainage whatsoever in Kichevo so all the water simply ran down the road often taking half the road with it. I could say that there were no potholes in Kichevo but this would be misleading as they were actually craters. Huge pieces of road were simply missing and lakes formed where there used to be road. There was one alleged sighting of a blue whale but it was never proven.
Things grew beyond desperate and became a serious assault on our sanity when we began to look forward to hearing Phil's desperate cries of, "I want a wheelbarrow". By now his cries were accompanied by tears – ours!!

Imagine then our excitement when the lorry actually turned up. We could barely contain ourselves and must have made a very sad sight as we lined up outside the guest house and practically drooled at the lorry before us. Unfortunately our excitement was premature, we had no idea of the saga which lay before us.

Kichevo is a lovely village but it simply is not designed to receive a large juggernaut carrying 12 Ton of stone. I'm sure the driver was full of hope when he pulled up outside the guest house as this is on the 'main' road through the village but all hope was dashed when he was directed to turn left then right to get to the site. Having negotiated the left turn there was no way he was going to make the right turn. The turn was simply too tight and there was a grave danger of losing the lorry into the great abyss that masqueraded as a former road.
The driver said he would dump the stone outside the guest house and we could take it to the site by hand. Hmmm 12 ton of stone, by hand, half a mile – if only we had a wheelbarrow. Seriously though this was a stupid suggestion and we told the driver exactly what we thought. OK so we

didn't tell him, in an act of great bravado, pathetically excused by our inability to speak Bulgarian we told Didi to give him a piece of our minds. Even collectively, the pieces of our mind didn't amount to much so this had very little effect. But cometh the hour cometh the man, Galin. I'll tell you Galin's story in a little while but so as not to disturb the flow of this epic piece of writing you just need to know he was our new Bulgarian friend who could speak some English.

It's a sorry fact but women hold no sway in Bulgarian building circles and Didi could have protested all day but would have got nowhere. Galin, being a little larger than Didi, provided a better place for us to hide behind and yell at the driver. We told Galin to tell him to take the next left turn as the right turn at the end of it was much wider and any idiot could get round it. He countered with "But there's no way I can turn back round to get out after I get to the site". This appeared to be a very good point and silenced us for a few seconds but we weren't going to be put off by a blindingly obvious problem. With heightened bravado provided by Galin's robust frame we increased our volume (cos that always works) and pointed a lot (that always works too). We prodded Galin and fed him the lines to say, we could only hope he was translating accurately and not saying, "I apologise profusely for these ignorant English people, when you have gone I will give them a sound beating". Whatever was said the driver was not budging, the stone would be deposited outside the guest house and the rest was our problem. The driver gestured to the fork lift driver (who, by the way, had arrived many hours earlier and had been patiently waiting. No doubt patient waiting is a key skill in his line of work) and the pallets of stone were deposited alongside the guest house. We continued to berate the driver whenever there was sufficient cover and little hope of him hearing or understanding us. "This would never happen in England". "We have paid for a delivery so you will do as you're jolly well told". "You have a contract to deliver to the site". "I'm gonna tell your boss", "I'm gonna tell your wife", "I'm gonna tell your mum!" Nothing worked and before we knew it the lorry was disappearing over the horizon, as we peered over the pile of stone in front of us all we could see was the top of the lorry getting smaller and smaller in the distance. The distance of the lorry seemed to be inversely proportional to the increase in our courage to come out from behind the stone, our voices getting louder and louder as the chances of him hearing us diminished.

However, the silence was deafening when the horrible truth was revealed. The driver was delivering for free to help the charity. He had just driven all the way from Sofia (at least a 9 hour drive) with a full load for the Merchant from who we ordered the stone. As an act of kindness he agreed to keep our stone on board, do a large detour and drop it off for us before he started the long trek back to Sofia. We could have curled up and died at that point as we learned a very humbling lesson.

There was only one way we could respond to our shameful actions – go and buy a wheelbarrow. As designated minibus driver I was forced to accompany Phil (by now beside himself with excitement) on the great shopping trip. I don't know why the others chose to come (maybe the fear of the lorry driver returning) but the whole team set off on the wonderful wheelbarrow adventure. I have previously alluded to the fact that there may be a minor issue with my navigational skills (please don't tell Barry or Elliot because I have ribbed them remorselessly for getting lost in Varna) so I followed Galin in his car who needed to pick up some supplies and then go off to another job. This trip provided us with the first of a hundred occasions to pass the huge building that featured so prominently in the earlier story of Barry & Elliot's hapless wanderings. Oh how we laughed to such classic comedic comments as, "what's that enormous building there?", "building, what building, I can't see any building" "There look the huge, enormous, massive, skyscraper piercing the skyline" "Oh yes, that would make the perfect landmark for anyone daft enough to get lost in the city" It may not seem so funny now but at the time it was hilarious, and the time after that and the time after that and………………… you get the picture.

We eventually arrived at the Builders Merchants which was akin to taking children to Willy Wonka's Chocolate Factory. The air was full of gleeful exclamations of "look how cheap this is", "do you know how much I pay for this at home", "I want one of those". Galin was buying some plasterboard and gypsum which needed to be loaded onto the minibus. The minibus needed to be moved to the loading bay around the back of the building. It was hammering down with rain outside but muggins here had to venture out into the rain and move the minibus. Now the rain was so heavy there was a virtual waterfall cascading off the roof of the building so it was important that I backed the bus right up to the door as wet plasterboard is useless plasterboard. This might not seem too difficult to the casual observer but the amount of room available to swing the bus round in was limited. Limited, in fact, by the presence of an unguarded 5 foot drop onto a railway line. I waited for my colleagues to come to my rescue and see me safely round and avoid the death plunge onto the electrified rails but it was raining and they couldn't be bothered. However, once the bus was loaded and they realised that the next time I moved it they would be on board, they pushed Phil out into the rain and he waved instructions which looked a bit like he was swatting an irritating fly and I manoeuvred to safety.

The observant amongst you will have noticed the distinct lack of wheelbarrow references. Surely after all we had endured that day we wouldn't be leaving a builders merchant without a wheelbarrow. Regrettably this particular merchant didn't sell wheelbarrows so we set off on another tour of Varna for another builders' merchant. Eventually we arrived at 'Practiker' (a sort of B&Q type place). It seemed like a bit of a busman's holiday to me but the team were having a ball looking at all the tools. I went off in search of wheelbarrows which I found and reported back to the others. Unfortunately there was a choice which meant more time deliberating but worse was to come. Galin suggested that they were too expensive and we could get cheaper ones a bit further down the road. I could have kicked him! He offered to go and check it out and said he would be back in 10 minutes. An hour later he finally returned to tell us the ones in Practiker were better and we should buy those. Arrggghhhhhh!! But at least we could finally buy the wheelbarrows (three in all) and finally stop Phil banging on about them; or so I thought.

The 'entertainment' for the journey back to Kichevo was provided by Phil planning a wheelbarrow competition. They needed assembling and so a race was being devised. It was now that I wished we had George back in the minibus as even the multi decibel distortion which passed for Radio entertainment in George's world would have been preferable to even more wheelbarrow talk.

In an act of kindness to you the reader I am not going to regale you with stories of wheelbarrow assembly, I will simply say that eventually three wheelbarrows were parked in the shed and ready for use – if it ever stopped raining. I can't be completely sure but I reckon I heard Phil creeping down stairs when he thought we were all asleep and spending the night in the shed with the wheelbarrows!

Tuesday brought glorious sunshine and a chance to start work at last. Thankfully Galin had arranged for a smaller lorry to come and take the stone to the site which was a great relief.

Ironically, the stone which we had was the dressing stone and so there was a limit as to what we could do with it as before it could be laid we needed rubble and sand. It had all been ordered but had not arrived. The rubble was due but the lorry driver had cried off due to a problem with his eyes. And so we had to start again with trying to arrange a merchant, fork lift driver and lorry driver to coordinate a delivery.

However, we managed to put in a full day's work redistributing the stone we had around the site. It's approximately 2 acres and so we spent the day placing the stones in strategic piles to save time when we needed to lay them. In case you are asking yourself, "how did they do that?" we used wheelbarrows of course.

The rubble eventually arrived and so we were able to start shifting that too and lay the foundations for the paths we were to lay.

It actually felt really good to do a full day's work and by the end of it we all felt quite fulfilled. A reward was in order and so we decided to go to the Happy Restaurant. I had been promoting the values of the Happy Restaurant and was determined to get the team to enjoy their fayre. I marched confidently through Varna town straight to the Happy with my entourage in tow taking care to glance back occasionally to make sure Barry & Elliot were still with us. I gave a triumphal shout as we rounded the final corner, "here it……….." But all we saw was an empty building which was once home to a Happy Restaurant but was now, most definitely, closed down. I was crestfallen.

However, this bad fortune turned to good fortune when we discovered a new Happy Restaurant right on the beach. It was fantastic, we sat on the beach overlooking the Black Sea as dusk fell and had a great feed. A brilliant end to the day.

Oh, one other discovery at the Happy; Matt's capacity for food. It soon became apparent that Matt has that rare condition 'leftoverfoodaphobia'. His deep rooted fear of seeing leftover food drove an insatiable appetite to hoover up every last morsel. Shares in Bulgarian waste bins have plummeted since all left over food was now simply thrown into our own human dustbin. I was amused by the ritual we had to go through before the dustbin would open. No foot operated pedal here, oh no, it was a much more complicated psychological battle. It went something like this:

"Matt, do you want this food"

"No, you eat it"

"It's OK, you have it"

"No really, you eat it"

"I'm not sure I can, I'm getting quite full"

"I don't want it, you eat it"
30 seconds later
"are you gonna eat that?"
But before anyone could answer the dustbin was open and the food gone. It was all we could do to save the plates.

Wednesday saw the rain return, once again it was monsoon like and the roads suffered even more abuse as the bits which were left finally drifted away on the waves of water running down the street. It was impossible to work in these conditions and so we turned our attention to making sure the sand was delivered as this was the next job. We couldn't quite believe our ears when we were told the sand couldn't be delivered because it was raining. The team were incredulous, what difference does it make. They even pointed out something which I never knew, that merchants profits go up in the rain because sand is sold by the ton and so a pile of wet sand is much more expensive than a pile of dry sand. So no one could understand how rain could stop the delivery. Galin eventually explained why. None of the merchants had concreted yards, all the yards were simply standing on bare earth. If they allowed lorries onto the yard it would turn into a quagmire and ruin trade for many days. Further, most of the drivers would not risk getting their lorries stuck in the mud and so wouldn't enter the yards anyway.

So another frustrating period of imprisonment in the Guest House was on the cards. In an act of inspired foresight I hid the cable for the keyboard but was not quick enough to hide the chairs and tennis ball. Maybe the computer would provide a way out of the boredom. Unfortunately the computer had been made by Fred Flinstone and no one had the patience to wait long enough for it to boot up. Worried about how I could rally the troops I dug into the dim and distant depths of my mind to recall a game my parents taught me back in the dark ages. I grabbed the deck of cards and announced a game of Newmarket. I took the blank looks as a declaration of ignorance of the game. I have fond memories of spending many an evening with my family playing Newmarket and thought this would be a good game to teach the team. Sneakily I thought to myself, "I'm bound to win, I've been playing this game for years". But I had no idea that I was to face the mighty Card Shark, Heather.
I confidently shared out the cable clips which were to act as gambling chips secure in the knowledge that they would all soon be heading my way. I tried to keep the instructions to the game as vague as possible just

in case one of my opponents should get lucky, I needed to stack the cards in my favour to ensure victory. I couldn't believe it when every round ended with Heather playing the one card which meant she cleaned up. Before I had chance to make up some new rules Heather had completed the whitewash and the game was over. This is not how I remember it from my childhood. Now I'm beginning to question if my parents had been soft on me and let me win. Heather had not only beaten me at my own game but had trashed my childhood memories. I will be sending her the bill for all my counselling.

At 4pm the sand finally arrived. You would have thought we just won the Lottery as we leapt around cheering and shouting. "Quick everyone on the bus." This is when it started, a cry which would become all too familiar as the week went on – "Where's my coat?" Now if Ryan's coat had been made of camouflage material we might have understood why he could never, ever find it but it wasn't. Heather & Phil made a mental note to go to whatever shop Barry had bought his lovely lime green coat from. You simply could not miss Barry's coat (if only we had hung it on top of that huge building in Varna on Sunday!!)

With the sand came the sunshine so we were able to get to work, a huge relief from the preceding boredom. But the sunshine was living in fear of being eaten by Matt if it hung around too long and so after two hours it saw Matt look up and lick his lips and decided enough was enough. The rain returned with a vengeance and once again drove us indoors.
Panic set in, what would happen now? Another drubbing at cards with chopsticks playing in the background to a backbeat of 'thud, thud, thud' as the tennis ball bounced off the chairs. Or another wheelbarrow assembly competition which would have to wait while Ryan found his coat and Barry & Elliot found their way to the dining room. It was simply too much and I needed to take evasive action. So I proposed we went out to find a restau….. before the word had left my lips Matt had run upstairs, showered, changed, grabbed his wallet and was beating down the door to the minibus. "Where's my coat?" Nothing happened quickly where Ryan is concerned and once again Heather had to come to the rescue. After a quick accusing look in Matt's direction who had a suspicious piece of material still protruding from his lips, the coat was found, peace restored and we were on our way.

On Thursday the sun dared to appear again and so we went straight to work. It seems that we wanted to work much harder than the sun who was on a work to rule and couldn't seem to manage more than a few hours a day. Even Galin commented that the English men were strange as they got so grumpy when they couldn't work compared to the Bulgarians who got so grumpy when they had to work.

We decided to go back to the guest house for something to eat (once we found Ryan's coat) and sit out the rain. Unfortunately the rain didn't abate and so Heather took the opportunity to increase her booty at the card table. I made a mental note to take Heather to the Casino when I got home and gave thanks that we were only playing for cable clips and not real money or I might not have been able to get home.

After a little research we learned that there was a restaurant on the outskirts of the village and so plans were made to go and check it out. An early search for Ryan's coat and a determined effort not to let Matt know what we were planning meant we left in a fairly calm fashion. I had a pretty good idea where the restaurant was and managed to find it straight away. I acted nonchalantly as if it was normal for me to navigate so brilliantly but secretly I was very relieved to have found it. My relief was short-lived though; as we pulled up outside the establishment there was an eerie silence. Everyone looked in through the window into the darkened room and had the same unspoken thought, "Get out of here, quickly". The rundown shack that masqueraded as an eating establishment contained two plastic picnic tables, a few three legged chairs, two men and 431 cigarette butts all still releasing their poison into the atmosphere. Maybe if we could have seen through the grime on the windows and through the plumes of nicotine inside there might have been a nice restaurant in the back but we weren't about to hang around and find out. The staring eyes which greeted us as we peered in through the gloom turned red, the head in which they were set started spinning round violently and a bolt of lightning ripped through the place accompanied by a deafening peal of thunder. Maybe our memory of this event is not as accurate as it might have been but we saw enough to know this was not the place for us.

We decided to drive on a little and try and find somewhere a little more….. well…… hygienic . Our luck was in when we stumbled on the Loza Restaurant. What a jewel this turned out to be. Elliot and Phil decided to order the mixed grill but never could have anticipated what they had done. As the waiter struggled in with the largest plate known to man you

could see him looking at Phil in a way which said, "Where's your wheelbarrow when I need it". As Elliot pushed his knife and fork apart to make room for his plate Barry looked worried as he was sat between him & Phil and you couldn't have got a gnat between their massive plates. He needn't have worried, his 'Hunter's Rabbit' arrived and the waiter skilfully managed to wedge it in and Barry's eyes grew nearly as large as the two plates flanking him. We all had wonderful food and plenty of it. Matt was kept busy as food defeated man. There was much groaning and holding of bellies but somehow we all heroically managed to do our bit for the local economy and selflessly ordered pudding. It was the only polite thing to do as we had received such wonderful service.
The minibus creaked a bit on the way home and couldn't seem to get above 25mph but no one could care; actually, no one could move. It was a truly wonderful experience.

With only one full day remaining more prayer was offered for a dry day as we were desperate to finish the job. God answered our prayers with a glorious full day of beautiful sunshine which allowed us to put in a full day's work and complete the main job.

We eventually finished moving 12 ton of dressing stone, 28 ton of large rubble, 28 ton of small rubble and 33 ton of sand. This was done with 6 men, one woman, 6 shovels and 3 wheelbarrows. In my opinion we should have had an extra wheelbarrow but Phil was having none of it. Despite all the difficulties we managed to turn all the stone, rubble and sand into a car park, drive and pathways which, I must say, looked rather good.
There were a few other jobs we would have liked to have done but we left the site satisfied and in a state which meant the prospect of it being ready for the Summer Camps was very good indeed.

That evening we faced a tough choice; of all the restaurants we had been to which one would we frequent for our final meal of the week? It came down to a toss up between the Happy Restaurant on the beach or Loza Restaurant. I can't recall the reasoning but we eventually settled for Happy on the beach. This should have been a celebratory event in which we all shared in each other's success but unfortunately, sharing was not a word in Elliot's vocabulary as a new and sinister side of him was revealed. Shockingly it transpired he is a food thief. It started with Phil's mushrooms; despite already having mushrooms on his plate he declared that the side order of mushrooms was his as well. We were prepared to let that one go but a trend had started and more and more of the food ordered by other members of the team ended up on Elliot's plate. Naturally, we all accepted this with good grace and it hardly got a mention at the table, on the way home, back at the guest house or most of the next day. It would have been awful if we had added to his severe embarrassment by going on and on and on about it so we gently laid it to one side and forgot all about it. I'm sure he appreciated the way in which we dealt with his misdemeanour.

And so the last day dawned. The unanimous desire of everyone on the team was to return to Krivnya and Barzitsa and spend our last few hours with the children. On the way to Krivnya the minibus started to play up a little. I couldn't quite put my finger on it but something was not right and we were losing power. I decided to stop in Provadia as it was much more preferable to break down here than in Krivnya. Provadia is a medium sized town with garage facilities and I know a few people there who I could call on for help. If we got stuck in Krivnya that would be a much bigger problem. In the back of my mind was the fact that we had a plane to catch in a few hours and it wasn't going to wait for us if we were delayed by a breakdown.

What followed was one of those comical scenes which is played out so many times in 'machoville'. We were men, we were supposed to know about engines and all things mechanical, ignorance was not an option or our masculinity would be in question. So seven men stood around the minibus staring at the engine. Apparently staring at engines is a very manly thing to do. To add to the illusion some mutterings were heard in voices now a little deeper than normal, "maybe it's the manifold", "It could be the big end", "one of the cylinders is gone" We kept throwing in words we once heard in a garage but had no idea of their meaning. Slowly men skulked off and the starers became fewer. Decisive action was required so I took the lead in poking things and emitting knowing noises. It felt good to be poking an engine so I poked some more and made deeper, more manly noises even nodding my head from time to time. Just as I was entering my swan song of engineering brilliance someone asked, "What are you doing?" "er, um, oh you know, some technical stuff" It was no good my bluff had been called and I deflated quicker than a balloon in a porcupine enclosure.

However, when we started the minibus the problem had gone. I leaned over to Phil and said, "someone at home was praying for us". Phil knew what I meant as I recall him telling me that several years ago he felt a great urge to pray for a missionary friend of ours in China only for her to reveal on her return that that was the exact time she found herself completely lost in a very undesirable backstreet but God had intervened and helped her to escape a very dodgy situation.

At Krivnya we made another inspection of the jobs we promised to do next year. There was great excitement when we learned a ladder was available for some of the men to get up on the roof and look for the cause of the leak. However, the excitement quickly turned to fear when we saw the ladder. It would have been a better sight to see a few bamboo sticks held together with chewing gum than the so called ladder before us. Phil looked the ladder up and down. Heather looked his life insurance policy up and down. There was a rush of people to hold the ladder in a sort of 'I'll hold it you climb it' way. Once the rush was over the slowest on the team were resigned to the fact that there was no more room for anyone to hold the ladder and knew that they had lost this particular lottery and had to face the reality of climbing the collection of rotten sticks and rusty nails they called a ladder. There were some vain attempts at quoting Health & Safety regulations but they fell on deaf ears and so the slow, painful ascent began. Once they were on the roof the rest of us helpfully went off and played with the children. We were so desperate to look busy and avoid any calls to join them on the roof that we played football with no ball. For a while we entertained the children with an imaginary ball but this could only last for so long. Matt eventually came to the rescue with a pine cone and managed to keep the game going long enough for the threat to have passed and the call to go back and hold the ladder for the men to come back down to earth.

It was time to say goodbye to the children which, as always, took a little while and make our way to Barzitsa. We took a decision to cut our time shorter than planned in case there were any further problems with the minibus but there's always enough time for a game of football. The second leg of the Bulgaria v England international kicked off and another great game ensued. With just a few minutes left the shout went up, "next goal wins the game" and things got a little more serious. Once again my shooting boots let me down and at times it was difficult for the casual observer to know which way I was playing so I was back in defence again.

Peshko got the ball and went on a dazzling run down the left wing and fired the ball across the face of goal. Ryan, in an heroic attempt to save our blushes, clashed with Kiro, both tumbled to the ground but Kiro just managed to stick his foot out and poke the ball into the goal. As Kiro jumped up to celebrate with his team Ryan was left nursing a cut to his hand. Shedding blood for your country is laudable but not at the cost of losing a game of football. As Alf Ramsey once famously said, "Football is not a matter of life and death, it's more important than that".

Actually the games are always played in the best of spirits and the boys at the orphanage are just so glad to have someone to play with, winning or losing is irrelevant but winning does feel good and we were glad to see them so happy.

Once again we had to say goodbye and once again this took a little while as we had to explain to the children that we would not be back tomorrow. We drove away from the orphanage a little sad but secure in the knowledge that not only had we brought a little joy into the lives of the children but they had brought a lot of joy into our lives too. No doubt at least some of the team will be back again someday and we can try to restore our honour on the football field.

The time had come to leave Bulgaria and reflect on a difficult but successful week in which some great new friendships had been made. We had completed the core work we had set out to do and made arrangements for our next project in Krivnya. We are very eager to get back to Krivnya and start work but before we can do that the difficult task of raising the funds must be undertaken.

The journey home was uneventful but once again found us travelling through the very small hours. We were a little delayed on our coach journey from Luton to Exeter but Bob & Chrissie were patiently waiting for us at the bus station ready to drive us home for some well earned rest.

I end this report by offering thanks to the team who travelled with me and made the week both profitable and fun. The spirit in which the team worked was one of hard work and tomfoolery, the perfect combination of industry and comedy. Also thanks to everyone who supported financially and prayerfully. But most of all thanks to God who watched over us every step of the way and made all of this possible.

Andrew

Earlier in the report I promised to tell you Galin's story:
When he was just a small boy Galin's parents experienced some difficulties in their lives. His mum was an alcoholic and his dad ……… (Galin just shrugged his shoulders and looked at me in a knowing sort of way at this point).
They placed Galin in state care for two weeks while they sorted themselves out but never returned for him and so he stayed in various orphanages for the rest of his childhood. Despite all the difficulties he faced in life he became a Christian at age 14. When he was told he would be transferred to an Orphanage in Varna he knew that this would be a huge test of his faith and would compromise the standards by which he chose to live so asked if he could go somewhere else. Amazingly, this was agreed. As with all children in state care he was ejected from the Orphanage at age 18 but he managed to find work as a plasterer. The company he works for does a lot of work in the Netherlands and so much of his life is spent there but during the periods when there is no work he has to return to Bulgaria. He has no home in Bulgaria and so stays at the Guest House in Kichevo owned by the Hope & Future Foundation in return for undertaking general maintenance duties.
While we were there we made good friends with Galin who had a great sense of humour and regularly made us laugh. He was such an asset to us with his knowledge of the building trade, his English language skills and his enthusiasm to help us help the children currently in state care in the area.
We are very grateful to Galin and all that he did for us. We hope that we will be able to work together again soon.

CHAPTER EIGHT
Okehampton College Trip
July 2012

There's no way it's gonna fit!!

As we surveyed the bonanza of gifts and donations filling the classroom in Okehampton College we knew we faced quite a challenge to fit it all into our luggage.
Lego, crayons, pens, toys, paper, jewellery, scissors, crepe paper, footballs, tennis balls, hockey sticks ……. The list was endless as was the generosity of those people who had gifted all this bounty for the children of Barzitsa Orphanage.
Fortunately, we had all come prepared with space in our bags to accommodate everything which we needed to give the Barzitsa kids a week of joy. More and more was crammed into our bags and each time we thought we couldn't squeeze one more thing in we had to undo our creaking and groaning zips for just one last item.
Then just as were on the point of giving up the lorry arrived which was to save the day. 16 men and a fork lift unloaded 'Godzilla' – the biggest, baddest monster you have ever seen. It was Neil and Abby's suitcase. I say suitcase but to do it credit think 'Albert Hall' We had to open it with care as the vacuum it created was in danger of sucking us all in.
Suffice to say that Godzilla swallowed up everything we needed to take with consummate ease and emitted a mocking cry of, "is that all you've got?"

Somehow we managed to load Godzilla into the boot of the coach but with the boot full the rest of us had to take our bags onto the bus with us. We were off; our journey to Bulgaria had begun and everyone was in good spirits. There was a minor hiccup when the bus driver got confused at the airport but we were given a personal escort by the airport vehicle to the drop off point.
As we unloaded Godzilla Airport Security became confused with their monsters as images from the film King Kong flashed across their minds. You could just overhear them discussing the scene where the monster was swatting aeroplanes from the top of the tower as they looked nervously at the control tower above them. Luckily it was lunchtime and they soon lost interest as the prospect of cheese sandwiches and a flask of

hot tea drew them away from their thoughts of airport carnage and into a dream world of culinary delight.

Talking of culinary delight we took the opportunity to bathe ourselves in the last vestiges of traditional English fayre before we left for Eastern Europe with a trip to MacDonalds !!

We enjoyed a game of pass the passport as we confused the poor check-in clerk by the size of our party. As always in such a situation there were howls of laughter as we trawled through everyone's passport photo. There were varying degrees of shame and embarrassment but it helped to pass the time and increase the camaraderie in the team through such well meaning banter.

Soon enough we were on the plane where a great surprise awaited us. We had no idea that Neil had gone to such great lengths to secure a cabaret for us on the flight. With absolutely no expense spared Neil had booked several acts including 'The Stag Party', 'Grannies on Tour' & 'Mouths Bigger Than Brains' to entertain us on the journey. All the acts were on excellent form as they competed for top billing but it was impossible to separate them. Simon Cowell would have had a field day if only he had been there. Maybe next year Neil?

Just before midnight we arrived in Bulgaria. We made our way to the bus which would take us from the plane to the arrivals lounge and discovered a new approach to air conditioning. The air conditioning machine on the ceiling of the bus looked normal enough but instead of emitting cold air it spat out cold water. The full entertainment value of this unique machine didn't fully reveal itself until the bus started to move, throwing the water in multiple directions. People who thought they were out of reach soon had their smug grins literally washed off their faces as the bus lurched from left to right. And so the great 'air conditioning dance' was born as people did their best to avoid the unexpected shower.

There was one last show from the cabaret as we waited for our luggage but despite the location it was no 'Carousel'

The next stage of the journey saw us travel through the night to the Guest House in Provadia. The minibus audibly groaned when it caught site of Godzilla. Seeing the panic on the face of the driver, Neil took responsibility for loading Godzilla onto the bus. Much puffing and panting and three large tubs of Vaseline later, Godzilla was on board. Unfortunately this meant six of the students had to travel on the roof .... (Don't panic parents who are reading this I'm only kidding – we put them in the trailer on the back!!)

2:30am we arrived at the Guest House. Our hosts Veselin and Gala were there to greet us. They are truly wonderful people who always make sure we are very well looked after. Arrival is generally quite a fun time as we grapple with language barriers to work out which rooms we have but this year Veselin had a trump card up his sleeve – his bilingual daughter. However, I don't think she knew about this plan as she was dragged out of bed at 3:00am to tell this tired group of Brits where to go. It took about 30 seconds which may have seemed futile to her but it saved us hours of pointing, room swapping and confusion.
The Guest house is a lovely, modern, air conditioned home from home although at 3:00am we would have been happy in a cave.

One interesting feature of the rooms is the bathroom. Whilst it is quite common in Bulgaria, the wet room was a new concept to some of the students. The shower was simply hung on the wall of the bathroom and soaked the basin, toilet and anything else you might have forgotten to remove (towel, clothes, toilet paper!)
But, this new discovery simply awoke the ingenuity of the students in one room. In a flash they analysed the situation and came up with a simple but brilliant plan that would have impressed the scientists at NASA. If three of them used the bathroom at the same time they could stay in bed an extra 10 minutes. So as one sat on the toilet and another stood at the sink the one in the shower could effectively spray them all thus saving precious minutes which they could devote to sleep instead.
Now there were other toilet related stories to come out of that room but the stories are more vile than the resultant stench so I will spare the delicate reader any detail. However, hold that thought as later you will learn how one of the boys (oh yes, in case you haven't guessed it was a boys room) devised a brilliant and cunning plan to deal with the assault on his nasal senses.

SUNDAY 8TH JULY

Eventually the time came to go the Orphanage and there was a buzz of excitement in the air. Some of the students were returning for their second visit and were looking forward to renewing old friendships while others, on their first trip, were wondering what to expect.

Arriving for the first day of a trip is one of my favourite moments. As word gets out that we have arrived so more and more children congregate at the entrance to greet us. It brings such joy to hear the children spotting people they remember from previous trips and calling out their names. There are no inhibitions and children throw themselves into your arms desperate for the physical touch of someone who cares. It only took a matter of seconds before 'returners' and 'newbies' alike had children hanging off them and a brilliant week started to unfold before us.

We hadn't organised any formal activities as we only had a few hours on our first day and we wanted time to reacquaint or get to know the children. As always a game of football quickly broke out and the first of many Bulgaria v England matches took place.

There was a token effort to re-name our team Britain as I, a Welshman, must confess to struggling with representing the English team but to no avail and once again I became a token Englishman for the week. If only I could learn to embrace the idea of being English for a week like some of the children who are desperate to dump Bulgaria and join the English team, they consider it a privilege; but I can't, I guess only another Welshman could understand.

Indoors a craft session was underway and children made all sorts of wonderful, vibrant creations with the materials we laid out before them.

Everywhere you looked there was a group of college students engaging with a group of Barzitsa kids, the picture was very heart warming, the soundtrack was even better as squeals of joy and excited chatter filled the air. Any concerns about a language barrier melted away in the universal language of fun and laughter. Better yet, we had a whole week of this to look forward to – fantastic. With appetites whetted the students couldn't wait to get started on the organised activities.

Strangely, one major theme of the week was shopping. There were regular visits to the local shop to stock up on vital supplies. The first trip was not completely successful though; Gareth was seduced by a large block of cheese which he purchased with a sense of eager anticipation. He rushed back to the Guest House salivating at the lips desperate to taste the delights of this unusual looking cheese. Unfortunately, there was a reason why it looked unusual, it wasn't cheese it was pastry, raw pastry, raw filo pastry. His room mates gathered round him to offer support during this distressing time, to the untrained ear it might have sounded like hysterical laughter and abuse but I am assured it was a moving display of empathy and group support. However, Gareth had the last laugh; as if one rush of genius in a week was not enough (i.e. the bathroom/sleep eureka moment) he immediately connected the 40 degree heat with the clay roof tiles and came up with a rudimentary griddle. Tearing off strips of pastry and putting them on the red hot roof tiles he was able to serve a gastronomic delight to his friends who had to eat their words and savour some humble pie before they could sample the delights of our new pastry chef.

During the massive sort out and organising of all the equipment and materials we had taken we found a beautiful pink floppy hat which would have looked smashing on a seven year old girl. But before it found it's true home it was 'borrowed' for a higher purpose. Everyone agreed that it would make the perfect award for 'Idiot Of The Day' together with a comedy pair of glasses. Whoever won the award would have to wear the hat and glasses at the restaurant for our evening meal. We hadn't quite anticipated the wealth of nominations that would crop up during the week. Day one brought several nominations; Rach for opening a bottle of fizzy pop. "That's not so stupid" I hear you say but she had just dropped it down the stairs and so the resultant eruption would have put mount Etna to shame and everyone's lunch got covered in orangeade. Second nomination went to Harry, who, engaged in a discussion on identifying the different meats on the lunch table asked, "What colour is human meat?" But the winner of the inaugural 'Idiot Of The Day' award was Lawrence for falling off a child's scooter at the Orphanage. The full idiocy is only revealed when you know that Lawrence is a rather strapping lad and he had wrestled the scooter away from a tiny orphan child in order to show off his wheel based skills. The child was not initially impressed but tears of sadness turned to tears of laughter as the man mountain hit the dirt. A very deserving winner of the award we all agreed.

Lawrence got to wear the hat a little longer than anticipated in the restaurant that night as the tedious wait for meals to arrive stretched long into the evening. Ultimately, three people were left wishing Gareth had some more 'cheese' in his bag as their meals never arrived. We decided to cut our losses and get to the shop before it closed to feed those who had gone without. Fortunately, Neil decided to send the students on while he stayed behind to pay the bill. Legend has it he is a Business Studies Teacher but this was cast into doubt by his miserable failure to tackle the simple task of paying a bill. There was a mix of embarrassment and laughter (Neil's embarrassment, my laughter) as the waitress had to tell him he hadn't given her enough money. How difficult could it be – as difficult as putting up enough meals maybe!!

We were relieved to know that we had booked a different restaurant for the rest of the week, not just because of the food shortage but we weren't sure if we would be allowed back after Neil tried to short change them.

MONDAY 9th JULY

After a good night's sleep Monday morning arrived and after proving the value of the 'share-a-bathroom' scheme everyone gathered to wait for the bus to the Orphanage.

The bus arrived and we wandered over to board it. After a few minutes something appeared to be wrong; the driver had a colleague with him taking up one of our seats. We needed all the seats, we had booked all the seats. It turned out the extra crew was a conductress (remember those?) who was asking Neil to pay individually for everyone's tickets. This wasn't the arrangement, we had agreed that we would pay one lump sum at the end of the week. After last night's bill paying fiasco Neil needed to prove his competence. Regrettably he got it sorted fairly quickly and efficiently and avoided an early nomination for Idiot Of The Day.

As an aside, by the end of the week the driver who dropped us off and collected us from the Orphanage each day was touched by the work we were doing with the children and so gave us a very decent discount on the final bill.

We made it to the Orphanage on time and were greeted by a sea of excited faces. You really have to experience this to know how it feels, I just can't put it into words. The children can't wait for us to get in and block the gateway calling out our names and asking if we are going to play football (fortunately 'football' is the same in both languages – It suddenly

occurs to me that maybe that's why we play so much football, I guess they don't know the English for Crown Green Bowls).
It's virtually impossible to carry your own bag as there's always a little pair of hands desperate to carry it for you.

The fun kicked off immediately with games breaking out all over the place while some of the team prepared the room with the art and craft activities. We soon learned to start the day with football as the heat was very difficult to cope with in the middle of the day (at least that's the excuse we used when we lost the football match). Our first match of the day was delayed while we waited for Gogo to put on his shin pads. Obviously, children in an orphanage don't own such things as shin pads but they do own fantastic imaginations. Gogo had fashioned a pair of rudimentary shin pads out of corrugated cardboard and string. They took an age to put on but he was very proud of them.

It's a real mix of joy and sadness to see the talent of some of these boys on the football pitch. If they were in the UK they would be spotted by a talent scout and given the chance to play at professional level. Their prowess for all sport is amazing. During the week we introduced them to Rugby, Cricket and Hockey and within minutes they were playing like pro's. I realise it's entering a dangerous arena to single anyone out but there's one lad called Metin (he's 16) who really shines and with a humility that would shame many sports stars he truly is an athlete of immense talent.
For me, this was epitomised later that day when it was very hot and we had started to flag a little. We set up a game in the shade of the trees we dubbed 'Crossbar Challenge' in which we had to throw a tennis ball at the crossbar of a metal frame. About five Barzitsa kids and three Oke Students got involved and after 20 minutes or so no one had managed to hit the crossbar. Up walks Metin who takes the tennis ball and with one effortless throw hit the crossbar with his first attempt. He grinned broadly and quietly walked off leaving us all spellbound.

About 1 o'clock the children have to go in for lunch (well a chunk of bread and sometimes an apple) followed by a siesta so we retire to the craft room for our lunch break. Once the food has been eaten there is a little time to kill so we fill it with educational games. We never forget that these are students and they are hungry for knowledge; it is the responsibility of us adults to ensure that we prepare a carefully constructed, curriculum orientated platform of learning through the medium of entertaining games. One of the more popular educational games is 'how many dry biscuits can you eat in two minutes'. Last year's record holder, Aby Sampson, retained her crown with an impressive 3 ½ biscuits. I'm sure the students will have learned some valuable life lessons from this creative game.

Now it was time for Neil to make a bid for Idiot Of The Day. The stage was set, Neil V Agnes in a serious Connect 4 grudge match. The tension was building with the clink, clink of counters falling into the frame. The game swayed one way then the other but Neil had a master plan and eventually had forced Agnes into a corner and triumphantly announced to the surrounding crowd that with the next counter he would win the game. In a flurry of grandeur he dramatically raised his counter into the air before placing it into the slot. There was a pregnant pause followed by a blood curdling scream as Neil realised he had put the counter into the wrong slot and failed to deliver on his promise to win the game. Not only had he failed to win but he had set up Agnes to clutch victory from the jaws of defeat. Neil had lost; now that would have been bad enough but the pathetic excuse he gave to try and cover his ineptness was weaker than a wet paper bag. "It's so hot my fingers are sweaty and it slipped into the wrong slot" Honestly Neil, you really need to do better than that.

I must confess that I wasn't exactly covering myself in glory with my hopeless attempts to string a guitar. Previously I had claimed to be a guitarist so surely restringing a guitar should be child's play for me but it wasn't. At one stage there were three of us trying to string one guitar; me, Gareth and Neil. You've heard of the three wise monkeys, well we were like their three inbred cousins with six fingered, webbed hands fumbling with all the grace of a sick, land locked walrus over this ill fated guitar. When our hands wouldn't work we tried employing teeth (hey, if Hendrix can play with his teeth we can string a guitar with ours) but even the simplicity of tying a knot evaded us. Men don't do failure so we needed a way out. A quick glance through the window confirmed that some of the children had awoken from their siesta and in an act of great sacrifice we knew that we must stop our self serving guitar activities and rush out to entertain the children; after all that's why we were there. Their needs must come first. So we didn't fail we simply sacrificed our pleasure for the good of the orphans.

It wasn't obvious at first but as the week went on it became clear that Lawrence quite fancied the 'Idiot Hat' and decided that if he could win it three times he might actually get to keep it (it worked for Brazil in the world cup). Earlier he had seen Neil's attempt to claim it for the day with the connect 4 failure and began to panic. So he carefully engineered a cunning plan. He skilfully and patiently drew a crowd around him and just when everyone was looking threw himself up some stone steps in a way which would have made Coco The Clown very proud. A theory was put forward that maybe he just wanted to win the attention of two nurses who were with us for a few days but we knew his eyes were firmly on the hat, not on the nurses.

More games, more fun, more laughter, more delighted kids and the afternoon was complete. Back to the guest house for a shower and rest before making our way to the 'new' restaurant. This turned out to be a brilliant move and we had Alex (our translator) to thank for it. The food was amazing and Alex was brilliant at making sure everyone got exactly what they ordered. She went to extraordinary lengths to ensure we were all delighted with the experience and we most definitely were.

Part two of Lawrence's master plan worked out very nicely as he won the 'Idiot Of The Day' award for the second time and the first inkling that something suspicious was afoot had birth.

TUESDAY 10th JULY

Tuesday started with the sad news that Becky's second pair of sunglasses had expired. It was an innocent enough piece of news but we could never have expected the debate which exploded from it. She announced the sad news with the following statement, "The leg of my sunglasses has fallen off". Neil and I roared with laughter at the use of the word 'leg' when clearly the proper name for this part of the glasses is 'arm'.
We couldn't wait to share Becky's humiliation with the rest of the group and randomly grabbed anyone who would listen to tell them about the 'leg' of the glasses.
"Hey", we shouted, "what do you call this part of a pair of glasses?" Oh the hilarity which awaited us as the chorus of "arm, of course" went up; but it didn't. Various names were offered and much to our disgust some even agreed with 'leg' but several had no idea (and I suspect no interest). Neil and I weren't prepared to be wrong and leaned heavily on our

expertise of being glasses wearers. We weren't any of these fair weather sunglasses people, oh no, we had been wearing prescription glasses for many years and this entitled us to be right. We actually went to opticians for real glasses not Poundstretcher for a cheap pair of sunnies with faulty arms so we knew what we were talking about. But despite our best efforts we were losing the crowd so we rallied round for more support but it just wasn't happening as the debate grew and the list of alternative names for the 'arm' grew inversely proportional to the level of interest.

We never did get a definitive decision but as Neil is head of 6th form I was happy to let him have the final say and trusted that the students' respect for him as their leader would carry sufficient weight to conclude the argument in our favour.

I did consider researching the matter for this report to prove that we were right but decided against it as the risk of being wrong was just too great. You the reader will have to decide for yourself.

Any pressure we had been under from the great 'arm' debate was soon set aside by the first attempt to get the 'Idiot Of The Day' award when Abby Sproats entertained us with her gymnastic fall off the bus. The boards went up but the scores only showed a 5.5, 6, 5.5, 5 & 4.5. Abby would have to do better than that if she wanted to stop Lawrence from getting the triple. Luckily she held an ace up her sleeve which she was holding for later.

Once again we were greeted at the Orphanage gates by a sea of excited faces which was like a trigger for all the students to switch into 'giving' mode. Immediately they sprang into action and focused entirely on being great friends and play partners to the children. Once again the small hall was converted into a craft and music room while outside a game of rugby was being arranged.

Now Bulgaria isn't famous for its rugby and most of the boys didn't have the first idea of the rules – to be honest I'm sure I didn't either so imagine the fun we had trying to explain them through an interpreter. But as I suggested earlier in the report these boys are very quick to learn and a game was very soon underway. One lad, Roman, just couldn't grasp the concept of passing backwards in order to go forwards and the bemused look on his face gave away his confusion every time he threw the ball forward and got penalised; but no matter 'cos this was always followed by a smile which confirmed he was just glad to be in the game.

Just in case all the references to football and rugby have created the illusion of a luxurious grassy pitch I need to help you understand that this is not quite the case. I could describe it as a concrete playground but even then your image might be too luxurious. It's true there was concrete but when Noah originally laid it in BC3012 he promised to come back and finish it the next month but got called away to build an ark and never returned. However, despite the failings of the ground I was secretly pleased. In my youth I used to play a lot of football (no, not with Noah – how dare you!) and somehow the students and Bulgarians had formed the impression that I was quite good. Just between me and you, despite playing for 30 years, the best I ever achieved was just below average but I enjoyed the kudos of the erroneous assumptions that I might be quite good and didn't want to lose it. So the awful playing surface was to come to my rescue and took the blame for every failing of my talent.

Anyway, now that I've put you straight on the playing surface you will understand why we insisted on playing tag rugby (i.e. non-contact). This was a huge relief to me as another myth had begun to develop based on the stereotypical assumption that all Welshmen are passionate rugby players. Oh no, how could I admit that I have never played rugby; could I really be a proud Welshman and not play rugby. I was in deep water, if anyone cared to check they would also find out that I don't sing in a Male Voice Choir and my father wasn't a miner. Before I had chance to concoct a story about an incident with a sheep rendering me unfit to play rugby the game was underway and I was in way over my head. I ran around a lot shouting things which I heard once on Grandstand but I don't think I was convincing anyone so I had to take drastic action and announce a change in the rules.

I pointed out that the speed which people were running was dangerous and that a simple fall could have catastrophic results so a rule change would slow people down and make the game much more safe. They fell for it and I was now able to keep up with the game and pretend I knew what I was doing. A masterstroke even if I do say so myself.

Eventually rugby gave way to lunch and we hauled our tired, overheated bodies into the 'craft' room for a well earned lunch. With temperatures touching 40 degrees the rugby had taken it's toll and we needed a break. There was a very weak attempt to get the Idiot Of The Day award from Harry who, in trying to clear a chair for his poor exhausted body, managed to tip an entire Mecanno set over the floor. I glanced over at Lawrence but he had a look on him which clearly said, "You're gonna have to do better than that". Clearly I wasn't the only one who saw the look, Abby (Sproats) had seen it as well and began to hatch a plan to come up with an idea that even Lawrence would struggle to beat. It took a lot of planning and cropped up later in the day. Abby neatly engineered the conversation onto the work of The House Of Rachel Charity which was brilliant because she knew this was a topic which I could talk about for hours as it is so close to my heart. I was waxing lyrical about the difference between good charity and bad charity saying how sometimes even the best intentioned charitable acts can have an adverse effect when she seized her moment. "You mean it's like that old saying, 'Give A Man A Bucket'" There was a momentary silence as we wrestled with the statement, whatever did she mean? But Abby knew that if she were patient her investment in 14 years of marriage to Neil would mean he will eventually twig and enlighten us. "Do you mean 'Give A Man A Fish'?" asked Neil and so it became clear that Abby had mixed her metaphors and misquoted what should have been – 'Give a man a fish, feed him for a day. Teach him to fish, feed him for life'. Well we rocked with laughter and fed off this unfortunate mishap for what seemed like an eternity. We couldn't understand why Abby wasn't more upset with the relentless barrage of abuse coming her way; it turned out she was plotting the perfect addition to her faux pas in a flagrant attempt to ensure Lawrence had nothing to offer by way of competition for the now cherished Idiot Of The Day Award. In a blaze of glory she stated that it was a direct quote from the Bible. A few nervous glances were cast in my direction as I am a Christian and it was assumed I knew my Bible passages well, I was able to confirm that it was most definitely NOT a quote from the Bible.

However, it might be worth me pointing out at this juncture that the Bible does say this in the book of James, 'what good is it if you see someone in need and simply say, "God bless you, I wish you well" but do nothing about it. Faith without action is dead' (paraphrase). The same book in the Bible also says, 'true religion is this, to look after orphans in their plight………' (paraphrase). Inspirational words which have encouraged me in my journey.

And so it turned out to be not so much 'give a man a bucket' as 'give a woman a hat'; an Idiot Of The Day hat. Poor Lawrence was beside himself.

The rest of the day panned out pretty much as planned with plenty more activities for the Barzitsa kids. This was followed by a short rest and then another trip to the restaurant where once again Alex ensured we were very well looked after with some excellent food.

WEDNESDAY 11th JULY

At the request of the Director we arranged a day of indoor activities as it was simply too hot to be outside. I offered to organise a Table Tennis competition; we had packed all the necessary equipment into Godzilla so had everything we needed. An intricate competition was devised where groups fed into quarter finals and so on. We had a fantastic response with loads of students and Barzitsa kids entering which meant we could keep the competition running all day. Kids were running in and out of the Table Tennis arena plaguing us with shouts of "'am I on yet?", well we assumed that's what they were saying as they pointed frantically to their names on the list.

After all my embarrassment in the football and rugby I was enjoying a little success in the Table Tennis but clearly I had made a terrible error of judgement in organising the competition. As I progressed through the group stage and into the semi final someone made a salient observation. "Does anyone find it suspicious that Andrew went to such great lengths to plan a competition that he is actually good at?" came the first of the accusations. "How strange that long before we even got here he thought to bring table tennis bats and balls across the whole of Europe." The crowd was turning ugly and to make matters worse I had seen the Barzitsa Table Tennis champion and he was very good. I could see a humiliation on the cards at the hands of a 15 year old lad (Milen).

It was then that I saw my way out, in an heroic act of selfless charity I gave up my place in the semi final to one of the Barzitsa boys and thus avoided the probability of meeting Milen in the final and being soundly trounced. In a double victory for me it also silenced the critics who by now were baying for my blood. I don't know if the history books will record my action as a wonderful charitable act or a cowardly way out of a potentially life threatening and most definitely ego threatening situation. We shall have to wait and see but I fear the truth will win the day and I will be outed as a coward.

There were no surprises when Milen made it to the final; his opponent was Okehampton's very own Digs. National pride was at stake. As the final approached so the crowds gathered. As this was a home tie for the Bulgarians they outnumbered the Brits but it wasn't about numbers it was about volume and we had a noisy bunch with us.

Digs was brilliant and took the game to three sets but eventually Milen clinched the final game and the match. The Bulgarians went wild and whilst we feigned misery in defeat, secretly we were delighted that one of the Barzitsa kids won the competition. The day had been a great success.

It's just possible that when Neil gets to this part of the report that he will breathe a sigh of relief and quietly say, "I got away with it". Sorry Neil, you didn't.
During the early stages of the competition Neil made his bid for Idiot Of The Day. He was playing one of the Barzitsa lads and decided to show him what he was made of. It was Neil's serve and in an effort to look serious he crouched menacingly over the table and stared at his opponent. He took the ball and started bouncing it up and down on his bat in preparation for his serve. You could cut the tension with a knife. Bounce, bounce; up and down went the ball on the bat. Up and down went Neil's head as he glanced from bouncing ball to opponent. It was important that he kept one eye on the opponent and one eye on the bouncing ball so important in fact that as he got out of sync the ball flew up off the bat and hit him right in the eye.
It was hard to see from my position of rolling around the floor with laughter but I just about caught sight of him trying to coolly carry on as if nothing had happened while he squinted like Quasimodo and streams of water poured from his injured eye.

You would have thought that would have been enough for one day but while the competition was running there was plenty of other activity.
Today there were two birthdays among the students, Bren 18 & Sandy 17. The craft room was also running a competition to design a Birthday card. This was a very popular activity and an array of beautiful cards was displayed along the table ready to be judged. One of the Orphanage staff were called upon to do the judging which she took very seriously, taking her time to pick the eventual winner. The children never cease to amaze me with their wonderful imaginations and talent, so many of the cards were just brilliant.
There were a few very difficult moments to come during the day as a few of the boys tried to give our lads birthday presents. One wanted to give the apple which was his dinner while another wanted to give his tin of deodorant. How can you take from boys who have nothing but how can you say no and destroy their act of goodwill. I guess that's an

unanswerable question but it is very, very humbling none the less when someone wants to give you all that they have.

Today also heralded what I hope will be the beginning of something special. For about two years I have longed to set up a Jewellery Project but haven't been able to find the right person to manage it for me – then came Abby (Sproats). Abby has taken on responsibility for the project which after much planning started today.
The project basically works something like this:
We provide the materials
The kids make the jewellery
The kids package the jewellery
We bring it home and sell it
We buy more materials and start again
We hope that we can make a little profit which can go back to the kids in the form of something useful for the Orphanage.
For example, while we were there one of the staff brought in a bike for the children to play on. It was interesting to note that they all had to learn to ride it first as even at 15+ the kids had never ridden a bike before. The bike was is in constant use as they took it in turns to ride around the Orphanage, there wasn't a single second of the day when that bike wasn't being ridden by a very excited child. Such was the success of the bike that after three days it was literally worn out and was taken away for repair.
Now if the profits from the jewellery went towards buying an Orphanage Bike for the children………. Well, it would be brilliant.
Aside from this incentive, the purpose of the project is to equip the children with vital skills to improve their lives. This cottage industry would make a very good addition to any CV and could make the difference between getting work and ending up on the street. The project will teach them basic skills in manufacturing, marketing, budgeting, team working and many more work related skills which will impress a potential employer. It may seem small on the surface but it's massive to these kids. Even on the most basic level of being involved in a project where someone is saying, "I value you enough to want to include you" is a huge boost and if what they make is valued enough by someone to buy it the message is made even stronger.
And so it was today, Wednesday 11th July 2012 that the first items of jewellery were crafted and the project became reality.
If you are interested in buying any of the jewellery or if you have the desire to help sell it, please do get in touch with Abby. This is a very

tangible way in which you can help the Charity make a difference to the lives of these wonderful children.

After the rigours and emotions of the day we were refreshed by rainfall of monsoon proportions. The idea of drainage doesn't seemed to have reached Provadia where we were staying and roads turned to rivers in the blink of an eye. There was one advantage to this; you could no longer see the potholes in the road. I think potholes must be the national emblem of Bulgaria as they are everywhere and this is despite much of the route between Provadia and Barzitsa having been resurfaced. The rainfall also provided an opportunity for me to make a bid for Idiot Of The Day. However, I think the fact that I even tried for it on the day when competition was at it's fiercest qualified me for the award more than the act itself. As we made our way to the restaurant the rain had eased off but had left some pretty awful mud slicks in it's wake. Armed only with a pair of flip flops I managed to slip in one of the slicks and in a scene reminiscent of Bambi on ice I struggled but eventually regained my composure. One of the students helpfully pointed out that there was an enormous puddle on the other side of the road where I could wash off all the mud which was now plastered over my legs. It seemed like a good idea to me so I indulged in a little personal bathing on the side of the road. Somehow, and I still don't really understand it, this was even more stupid than the mud slip in the first place. Sadly though, the award was not coming my way, despite very strong competition it went to Abby Sampson for a Freudian slip which is not going to be repeated here. In her defence the remark was made in all innocence but was of catastrophic proportions in our politically correct world.

Lawrence was really suffering now and that third award seemed like it might never be his. Lawrence reacted in the only way he knows how by re-igniting his favourite debate, 'Capitalism v Socialism'. The discussion was in full flow as we all aimed to impress each other with our knowledge of political regimes around the world. After a while Neil sensed the intellectual interaction had peaked and was in danger of fizzling out so determined to ensure that the cerebral battle would not falter by introducing a high brow topic of his own. "Why is it so difficult to fit the rooster chorus into the Old Macdonald song?" Now you would have thought that this would have been an instant conversation stopper but on the contrary, one by one, people started to sing, "with a cock a doodle doo here and a cock a doodle doo there" only to find it was a very valid question. I regret that it was a question which never got answered but at least it meant Lawrence's failure to win the award was forgotten for the time being.

We celebrated the birthdays with some ice cream desserts which were delicious but had a very strange effect on the team. If we hadn't known better we would have thought it was laced with alcohol but I guess it was just the joy of the cooling ice cream on our severely overheated bodies.

THURSDAY 12th JULY

Another blisteringly hot day limited our activities so we decided on a game of quick cricket in the shade of the trees. You will have gathered from the report so far that the Barzitsa children are an absolute delight but naturally in any group of kids there is at least one who challenges even the most patient person. I'll refer to him simply as G and he really did try the patience of the whole team with his antics and unbelievable volume! Things were no different during the cricket and several Saints left as their patience was tried leaving the Oke team to play with him. One of the students whom I shall refer to simply as G …. - Oh, that doesn't work does it. I'll refer to him simply as Gareth - may have allowed his frustrations to dictate his actions when he took a 30 metre run up before launching a torpedo bouncer straight at G. There was never any question in Gareth's mind that G was going to walk for a duck which is exactly what happened as the ball smacked into the wicket. The rest of us managed to stifle our glee with disapproving looks in Gareth's direction which must have had the desired effect as next time it was G's turn Gareth's desire for retribution was sated and G enjoyed a longer period at the crease.

However, the quick cricket gave me my personal 'moment of the week'.
Let me introduce you to Teergut. I've known Teergut for many years and he is the owner of the most endearing smile known to man. That smile is a permanent fixture on his face and nothing can remove it. Teergut spends much of the year in an Orphanage for children with special needs a few miles down the road in Krivnya but during the school holidays Krivnya closes and the children are transferred to Barzitsa. Teergut has a few problems which would make a lot of kids struggle in life and as a result he is often excluded from the activities of the other boys and if he is allowed to join in it's not long before the others lose patience with him and he is unceremoniously removed from the activity. Even so he keeps on smiling,

it's so infectious. A few years ago we were running a football skills school for the boys and Teergut was the most enthusiastic student and coined the phrase, "Football, tomorrow?" that is still used at the end of every single day at the Orphanage.

This visit saw Teergut have to face another struggle, he had a badly infected, septic big toe but even this couldn't stop him from joining in the games; even football – which he played in flip flops!!!! (Many of the boys play in flip flops as there aren't many trainers to go round).

Although he struggled he kept smiling and laughing, our nurses eased his struggle a little by dressing his toe.

And then it happened, it was Teergut's turn to bat. He stepped up to the crease with his trademark grin and without a care in the world. He had the bat and nothing else seemed to matter. The first ball was tossed up for him and he smacked it, he could hardly believe it. He was so stunned he forgot to run, we were all shouting and gesticulating, encouraging him for all we were worth to make the run. Teergut just stood there laughing and bemused at all the fuss until eventually he twigged and ran, everyone cheered. Then the second ball, which he also whacked, then the third and fourth soon he was playing like a pro and the run count was going up and up. On this magical day, in the shade of the trees in Barzitsa Orphanage, Teergut was on top of the world. He passed all the top scores of the other boys until he reached an unbeatable 28 runs. Teergut was the Quick Cricket champion, fantastic. Oddly, Teergut seemed oblivious to this accolade he was simply thrilled to been able to join in all the fun.

An enduring memory for me and hopefully for many others too; especially Teergut.

We had hoped to run a Football competition during the week but the heat meant that the Director was not too keen. However, the forecast was cooler for tomorrow and so we were actively encouraged to hold it then. Digs stepped forward and said he would enjoy making the arrangements and to leave it all to him. We thought it would be a great idea to select the teams by drawing players out of a hat with all the kids present to soak up the excitement. So Digs set to work on complicating this apparently simple idea beyond the comprehension of most human minds. I couldn't begin to try and describe the process Digs went through to set up the draw as I gave up trying to understand it in favour of learning the principals of thermo dynamics which seemed like the easier option. Eventually the time came for the draw. Digs had decided to go hi-tech with several plastic cups and torn papers, the non-sticky sticky tape might have been a mistake though. Poor Alex, our interpreter, had the unenviable task of being Digs' glamorous assistant, whilst she is unquestionably glamorous she had no hope of assisting Digs. Even Derren Brown would have struggled to conjure up some magic from this fiasco. Clearly Digs had been studying his football draw organisation skills at the Sepp Blatta School of Footballing Fiascos.

In fairness to Digs there may have been extenuating circumstances concerning his failing health but we don't want to spoil a good story with the truth so we'll stick with the incompetence theory. As the story is a long one I'll spare you the detail but the high tech wizardry failed miserably as the labels fell of the plastic cups and it transpired that each of the techno cups did not contain the same number of names. Digs soldiered on in defiance of the ineptness of the system until somehow he had created teams from all the names. Just as it looked possible that he may have achieved the impossible he spoiled it all by saying, "I'll take it back to the Guest House and re-organise all the teams tonight"

Digs had the look of a beaten man, a beaten man with a heavy cold but actually there was something far greater going on here than we could have appreciated at the time. Unknown to the rest of us he was skilfully laying the foundations of a cunning plan.

The woeful draw was simply a ruse to get everyone to notice he had quite a bad cold, stage one complete. This justified the continual blowing of his nose, stage two complete. Therefore, no one was surprised when he suffered a nosebleed. His plan looked a little shaky here as he was whisked off to the first aid room where no one could see him but he wasn't about to be defeated at this late stage. So he just kept on bleeding like he was the donor in a blood transfusion for a blue whale. This kept him in the first aid room long enough for people to miss him and ask after him. Once everyone knew he had a nosebleed he felt safe to stop bleeding and put the finishing touches to his plan – two oversized lumps of cotton wool. With one stuffed up each nostril he was ready to return to the guest house and venture into the bathroom for a shower. Apparently things had got so bad in the boys bathroom that Digs had been driven to these extraordinary lengths just to get a shower without the fear of radioactive fallout entering his brain through his nasal passages. It was a commendable effort but simply served to highlight the bravery of the lady who cleaned the rooms while we were out. Seriously, I don't know what the Bulgarian equivalent of a George Cross is but she deserved one. As we left at the end of the week I saw an advert for a new cleaner in the window of the guest house, my Bulgarian is not great but it translated quite literally as 'no nose required'.

There were plenty of other events worth recording on this particular day but I need to limit them to just a few brief outlines. Naomi, who had been suffering with a sore throat, marched up to Abby (Sproats) our first Aid officer and calmly announced for everyone in the park café to hear, "I need more drugs".
Whilst discussing the need for the Barzitsa kids' education, Neil (Head of 6th Form at Oke College) said, "Exam results aren't everything" which provoked an interesting response from his students who may have had a different message drummed into them for the last few years by the same man.
It was Katie's turn to irritate Lawrence by winning the Idiot Of The Day award for some art & craft misdemeanours.
In an effort to suggest that some of the students may wish to find a different place to sit at the restaurant I said to Clara, "Has that chair got your name written on it?" To my amusement she looked to see if it did.
Neil, in a pathetic attempt to get out of playing outdoors in the heat, claimed to have forgotten to bring his trainers. He wished he had kept his mouth shut when Abby sent him out to play in her lovely silver trainers. (Is this the adult equivalent of being forced to do PE in your pants if you forget your kit?)
And it's Neil who will make the final entry on this very eventful day. As we were leaving the shop that night with our supplies for the following day a kindly old lady opened the door for him as his hand were full of bags. To our great amusement she chased him down the street for her tip.
It was an unsavoury scene for which we invented our own headlines should it ever get reported on local TV

FRIDAY 13th JULY

And so it arrived, the day we had all been dreading, the final day.
There was no time for self pity we had kids to attend to and a football competition to organise. By now Digs' health had improved and he was up for the challenge of arranging the football. These boys take their football very seriously. When we are playing our Bulgaria v England friendlies they play in a friendly spirit but put a trophy and medals up for grabs and everything changes. Everyone wants to win and they all up their game. It

proved to be a great competition and a real credit to Digs for his organisation.

The group stages were completed after a dramatic penalty shoot out. The semi finals were a tense affair but eventually the finalists were decided just in time for lunch.
After lunch the finalists gathered for the most important game of the week. Digs' complicated team selection process had paid off and there was a great mix of talent in each team thus giving some of the less able footballers an opportunity for success alongside their more gifted colleagues. Supporters were gathering on the sidelines and the scene was set. The ref's whistle blew and the game began. The heat was intense as was the tension but eventually the final whistle blew and we had a winner. The winning team were made up of Metin, Peshko, Damien, Harry, Rachel & Clara.

We got the Barzitsa kids(Metin, Peshko & Damien) to stand on a bench to receive their medals which were presented by the Orphanage Director surrounded by nearly everyone in the Orphanage that day. We all cheered and clapped and I think I may have got a fly in my eye or something cos grown men don't cry – do they?

With the end of the football came the crushing realisation that our week was nearly over but not without a leaving party. Food, music and dancing were available in abundance and everyone revelled in the atmosphere. Now anyone who knows me knows that I don't do dancing and nothing can get me onto a dance floor – nothing, that is, except the Barzitsa kids. Honestly, your heart just melts around them and it's impossible to refuse when they grab you and drag you up. And so there I was doing my famous 'granddad dancing' surrounded by a sea of smiling faces. I choose to believe that they were smiles of joy and that they weren't laughing at me strutting my stuff.

The final act of the day was the mass T-shirt signing. Armed with felt pens the children spent the remaining time signing all our shirts, creating treasured mementos of a life changing experience.
Then, with the arrival of the minibus came the miserable reality that our time was up. It's heart wrenching to tear yourself away from the children with whom you have created such a close bond. 'Tear away' is a literal expression, not a metaphor, in this instance as hugs and embraces grow

ever tighter the closer you get to the gate. The tears were flowing as we moved ever closer to the final moment which was being dragged out for all it was worth. Final messages were being exchanged as the students struggled with the inevitable question of "when are you coming back?". Given the chance every one of them would have happily united in a chorus of "tomorrow" but in reality all that awaited us tomorrow was the long journey home. For some students there is the hope of a return trip in 2013 while others had to face the reality that maybe this could be their final farewell.

Despite the tears and sadness, through blurry eyes we could see that we were leaving a legacy of joy behind. All week we had been privileged to be involved in helping the children have the time of their lives. We had helped to make enduring memories. We had showed love, a valuable and rare commodity in the day to day lives of the children. We had truly made a difference in their difficult lives.

But, and it's a big but, as always what we got in return was so much more. It's amazing that we go with the intention of giving but receive so much more in return. For most of the students this will have been a life changing experience that they will carry with them forever. They will have returned home with a whole new perspective on life and memories which will last for many, many years.

We have learned that true joy cannot be found in material possessions but in the giving and receiving of love. Love is not an emotion but an action and the students gave this fully and selflessly. Science teaches us that to every action there is opposite and equal reaction but we have discovered that where love is concerned what we got back is so much more than we gave.

Despite the length of this report only a fraction of what we got up to has been recorded. I don't know if those who didn't get a mention will be relieved or disappointed or if those who were cited will be pleased or embarrassed but I urge you to see through the comedy, the drama and the characters to see the true value of what was achieved. And, in case you're wondering, Lawrence didn't win the hat.

So it just remains for me to thank each and every person on the 2012 Okehampton College team, all 21 of you. If you didn't get a mention in this report it is simply because I couldn't be everywhere all the time and I may not have recorded what you got up to. However, I was very aware of the fact that it was in the quiet unnoticed moments that most of the love was given and for the children these are the cherished moments in which they received your personal and undivided attention. A tragically rare event in their day to day lives. So, regardless of this report, everyone's contribution was valued and I thank you all equally.

Andrew

CHAPTER NINE
The Adventures Of A Salzburg Moose
April 2013

SUNDAY 14th
It's midnight, must be time for another trip to Bulgaria! One day I'm going to organise a trip that starts at two o'clock in the afternoon.

Adrian and Cai had already travelled from Cardiff a few hours earlier. While they were travelling David, Mary and I packed the car. When I saw how much we needed to pack I was more than a little concerned; I had visions of Adrian and Cai having to be strapped to the top box. But with skill and patience we squeezed just about everything in, filling every conceivable nook and cranny. Pride of place was kept for the most important item—the box of food which would sustain us on our journey.

And so we were on our way, in howling wind and pouring rain. Not a great start. But soon enough we were at Dover Ferry Port and making our way across the Channel. Once we arrived in Calais the weather changed and we saw something we believed only existed in legends; the sun. 2012 had been the wettest year on record, closely followed by the longest winter on record including the coldest March on record so the sun was a very welcome travelling companion.

We alternated between driving, navigating and sleeping, swapping roles at various service stations across Europe. As the most experienced traveller I felt a compulsion to take the lead during our change overs and confidently led everyone into the service station and pointed out the toilets. Flushed with success (sorry!) I took the lead on navigating to the exit. When will I learn, I actually managed to get lost in the shop and took the others to a door clearly marked 'No Exit'. My inept navigational skills have been well documented in other reports and were well known to my companions so the scene had been set for another tale of woeful calamities. I once again became the butt of the jokes. However, a very unlikely set of events would unfold during the week. There were three navigational errors and I was responsible for none of them. This truly is a first and a very proud moment for me hence it gets a mention on page one of my report.

The first navigational error fell to Adrian who sent David onto the right road but in the wrong direction. We took the next exit but couldn't get back onto our road without a tour of the local town. I felt a momentary nod towards shame as I delighted in Adrian's misfortune but it didn't last long. I was just so grateful it wasn't my fault this time. I waited a polite amount of time after we regained our route before gently alluding to his unfortunate error.

My smugness didn't last long though as I was about to suffer a humiliation beyond any simple navigational error. After 20 hours of driving we arrived at the Germany/Austria border and pulled into the motel I had booked. I strode up to reception and announced to the poor unsuspecting girl on the counter that we had a reservation and threw down my confirmation before her. She looked up and down her list and nervously suggested that we did not, in fact, have a reservation. "We most certainly do", I said and pointing to the paper on the counter before her and added, "it's there in black and white". She picked up the paper with nervous anticipation and cast a worried eye over it before a grin broke across her face and she breathed a sigh of relief with the announcement, "This booking is for Salzburg, you are in Suben". How could this be, I checked and double checked the details when I booked it on-line, the booking even came with a map showing I had booked the motel on the Germany/Austria border which I was at pains to point out. "Look at the map" I said, "It clearly shows this hotel on the road on which we have just driven across the border". I couldn't be wrong, I just couldn't. I was in denial, even the address on the booking form which clearly said Salzburg would not convince me, after all the map was evidence in my favour. At least until Adrian made a very pertinent observation, "maybe there's more than one road on the Germany/Austria border, let's have a look at that map" The terrible truth hit me like a sledgehammer and my weak protestations about the quality and size of the print were crushed by an undeniable feeling of utter uselessness.

Then Adrian decided to really rub salt in my wounds by asking the question to which no one really wanted the answer, "How far away is Salzburg?" I dared to hope that the answer might be "10km along this road" but no, after a moment's thought the girl simply replied "250km away" (that's about 156 miles). To make matters worse, we were heading east and Salzburg was 250km north. The mood of our group hovered between contemptuous and murderous as I frantically tried to negotiate a transfer (as the two hotels were in the same chain). Fortunately, the girl managed to arrange everything for us and the problem was fully resolved. When I went to pay I slipped the girl a generous tip which Adrian spotted and said, "I hope that was at least a hundred"

I was very pleased that all anyone wanted to do at this point was go to sleep and I dreamed that by the morning everyone had forgotten my tiny error. Guess what? They remembered and shouts of 'Salzburg' replaced the cheery 'Good morning' I had hoped for.

MONDAY 15th
At least the morning provided one diversion from my humiliation. I wandered into Adrian and Cai's room to make sure they were ready to leave and what was on the telly? The Make-Up Channel. Adrian only made things worse with his pathetic explanation, "I thought it was Euro Sport". Sorry Ade, extreme lipstick is not a sport. At least I now know what to buy him for his birthday.

Austria was stunning and I never get bored of looking at the mountains and beautiful scenery. However, there was an odd moment when all of a sudden as we passed through a culvert we spotted a moose looking down on us. It was a metal statue but attracted the attention of Cai who was our official photographer for the week. We stopped in a garage for a change of driver but it was just a little too far round the bend for Cai to get his photo of the moose. Now this might seem like an insignificant detail for this report but it becomes very significant later so store the moose in your mind for recall later.

I can barely bring myself to write the next chapter of our adventure as it was a catastrophe of the highest order. Even worse than booking the wrong hotel. Our iPod gizmo broke. Let me explain; last time we did this drive we took a load of CD's to listen to on the journey but hadn't really thought how many we would need to maintain some variety. The CD's we had were worn through by the time we got home and the monotony of the same old songs nearly drove us mad. So, armed with this knowledge we decided to take iPods instead as I had a gizmo which could play the iPod through the car stereo—brilliant. Well, brilliant until the gizmo broke. Disaster! We did a quick count of how many CD's were in the car and calculated that we would have to listen to each one eight times just to get us to Bulgaria. There and then our priority for the trip changed and top of the list was to buy a new iPod gizmo.

To make matters worse, whilst Adrian and I share the same taste in music it's fair to say that David doesn't. Adrian and I were a little peeved that the gizmo had worked perfectly for David's music but gave up the ghost for ours. We had endured several hours of classical piano (which just happens to be an anagram of O pain) but when we wanted to listen to our rock and pop the gizmo was dead. Suspicious? What David doesn't know is that I kept the deceased gizmo which I handed into forensics as soon as we got back and if there is even the slightest hint of malpractice on his part I will have to take serious action.

"I like Croatia", I announced as we crossed another border but I want to put down on record here and now that I had no idea what we would face next. A total assault on all our senses. We made the foolish decision to pull into a lay by for our next changeover. We were pleased to see a few portaloos and sauntered over towards them. Then the wind changed direction and nearly knocked us clean off our feet. No, not the strength of the wind but the strength of the smell but even that could not have prepared our eyes for the sight which lay behind the door. I won't elaborate, you might be reading this over your dinner. Then began the challenge, could you hold your breath for longer than it took to have a wee? And then in some absurd machoistic competition a row began about who had been in the worst loo. Descriptions challenged gag reflexes but no one came out on top; clearly we had all been losers in the world's worst competition.

I think Croatia must have realised that such an assault on our senses needed a remedy so this was provided in their approach to road building. Long and straight & straight and long followed by a bit more straight and a bit more long. Every now and then there would be a small hill hiding the road which lay ahead, providing some hope for what may lie beyond—more straight and more long. We had, in the blink of an eye, gone from an assault on our senses to an absolute numbing of senses. In fact our senses had been numbed to such a degree that we pulled into another lay by at the other border where our senses were very rudely awaken once again. Just how numb our senses were to cause us to even consider using portaloos again I cannot imagine. I can only compare it to being knocked unconscious and being forcefully roused by a dose of smelling salts but believe me, no smelling salt has ever even come remotely close to what we experienced that day.

Serbia didn't offer much relief to the boredom in the early stages. The boredom ran so deep Cai was forced to observe that his headphones fitted up his nose. Interesting.

Our 'interest' in the road was sharpened when David tried to pass a lorry in the outside lane just as we entered some roadworks. There was literally just a few inches either side of us; to one side a lorry, to the other a wall. We all breathed in in a forlorn effort to make the car a bit smaller and just sneaked through the gap—phew!

At one point the weather threatened to turn nasty (some might say British) as black skies loomed in the distance but we managed to outrun them and rejoin the glorious sunshine. At one stop the weather was just so good we really didn't want to get back in the car. In fact Adrian nearly couldn't, complaining of a bad back which was a portent for a run of injuries which would amuse us during the week.

We made the Bulgarian border in good time and although there was a half hearted attempt to delay us the border guard simply waved us through when he discovered that we weren't carrying any cigarettes. Now the pressure was on, not so much to find the hotel but to find the one I had booked. Oh how I hoped I got it right this time. Adrian decided the best way to find it would be to drive at 3mph while we all looked out of the window. After an hour or two driving at Adrian speed we had travelled about a hundred yards but were overjoyed to see the Yubim Hotel come into view. With some trepidation I approached the receptionist and suggested we may have a reservation. To my delight it was confirmed and we were quickly booked in and handed our keys. To my even greater delight the hotel was so much nicer than I thought it would be, at last a triumph for my wonderful internet booking skills.

TUESDAY 16th
Breakfast started off well as course after course was laid before us and very nice it was too. Then, rather strangely, we were presented with a cake. I've never had pudding at breakfast before but I thoroughly enjoyed it. However, just as we were concluding that things couldn't be any better the waiter let the whole hotel down by arriving late with the hard boiled eggs. His profuse apologies couldn't cover up his grave error of serving eggs after cake and so we'll never go back there again. Never mind the 5* rooms, the lovely hot showers, the free Wifi, the £20 price tag, late eggs is unforgivable.

The Bulgaria leg of our trip was a more relaxed affair. We had no deadlines now and had all day to cross from Sofia to Provadia with the prospect of a stop off at The Happy Restaurant for lunch. We were entertained by Cai's endless anecdotes. When I say endless, I don't mean there were lots of them I mean they simply didn't have an ending. So for the rest of the trip if anyone came up with a useless piece of information it was known as a Cai-necdote.

Eventually we reached Provadia where we were pleased to meet up with Alex, our interpreter for the week. Actually, to call her our interpreter doesn't do her justice. First and foremost she is our friend and she does so much more than simply interpret for us, she is our host and takes care of us and joins in all our activities. She loves the kids as much as we do and shares our passion to help them. And so we made our first visit to Krivnya Orphanage to drop off all the materials we had been carrying in the car.
It only takes a few moments after drawing up in the car for the children to swarm over us like an army of ants. Willing little hands everywhere helping us to unload everything and take it all inside. Ah yes, this is why we do it, for moments like this when we are one with the children, serving them and meeting their needs. The joy on their faces had nothing to do with what they were carrying, their joy was in seeing us, in helping us, in anticipating the games we would play. Although the materials we were carrying would make a huge improvement to their quality of life, in that moment all that mattered to them was that we were there and we would play with them. And play with them we did, we had taken some sports equipment and so quickly organised a few games, it was great fun. Our time with the children was short on this occasion as night was drawing in and we had only just arrived after a mammoth drive but we promised them we would return tomorrow. The kids lined up along the fence to wave goodbye while some of them ran to the car in a burst of excitement which simply could not be contained.

Just time for a lovely meal at a local restaurant before retiring to bed exhausted but happy.

WEDNESDAY 17th
I had been looking forward to this day as this was the day I met the new Mayor of Provadia and hoped to get a tour of Provadia Orphanage.

Back in 2010 a team of us went to Provadia Orphanage to undertake essential maintenance to prevent it from being closed. There followed a long period of uncertainty surrounding the future of the Orphanage so we kept up gentle pressure on the previous Mayor to honour his promise of finishing the job and re-opening the Orphanage. The previous Mayor had been a difficult character and often seemed obstructive to our efforts to help.

So it was with great delight that I found the new Mayor to be much more approachable and supportive of our work. We presented him with a gift from the Mayor of Okehampton which was well received and will help to cement relationships. We told him of our intent to work at Krivnya Orphanage to which he responded, "The director has my full support, I am behind everything she asks of you". This was music to my ears as Mayoral support is crucial in Bulgaria.

I asked him about Provadia Orphanage and he confirmed that because of our earlier intervention the home had not only been saved from closure but had also attracted EU funding. Much renovation had been done and the home is currently operating as a rehabilitation day centre for children with physical and mental disabilities and work was underway to complete the residential units as well. It's one thing to hear this but it is something else to see it. We were taken on a tour of the home and I was totally amazed at the transformation. As we approached the building, the view from the roadside did not reveal the transformation on the inside but as I turned the corner I could hardly believe my eyes. And when I went inside I was totally gobsmacked.

The rehab unit is looking great and functioning well. Phase 1 of the residential units is nearing completion and consists of four twin rooms. The rooms are light, clean, airy, large and finished to a high standard. Before long 8 orphaned or abandoned children will find a new home here. Further, in the grounds, building is well underway for a further six twin rooms bringing the number of children who can be cared for there up to twenty.

It's been a long and at times worrying wait to see the fruit of our earlier labour but it was worth it.

The timing of this visit was to have a particular significance later on this day.

That afternoon we were back at Krivnya where we met with Mladen & Ivelina.

Mladen is a carer at the home and has been instrumental in helping me get this project to this point. Ivelina is the director at the home. We were greeted with traditional Bulgarian cheesy bread, biscuits, chocolate and tea, they were clearly pleased to see us. It would have been impolite to ignore the goodies on offer and so we selflessly tucked in, it would have been rude not to.

An interesting discussion ensued during which Ivelina gently suggested we may want to do a few different jobs to which I responded that we had a plan and needed to stick to it. However, I could sense that there was something lying behind Ivelina's continued nudging towards two jobs in particular. The first was to tile the toilet floors, the second was to put laminate flooring in the classrooms. We had already agreed to paint the toilet floor and repair the existing wooden flooring so why was she still pursuing her ideas.

I decided it was time for some straight talking and said, "It's time to stop being polite just because we have the money and the builders, it's time to be honest and say what you want and why". This did the trick and truth came out. The home and school are due an inspection in June and if they fail to come up to scratch they will be shut down. In order to pass the inspection the toilet floors must be tiled and the classroom floors laminated.

That sealed it, if that's what is required then we must endeavour to do exactly that.

Later Mladen confided in me that this is the only home within 200km which cares for children with special needs and his desire for it to remain open was written all over his tear filled eyes. I didn't ask the obvious question of what would happen to the children if the home was closed as I couldn't bear to hear the answer. I just knew we had to help.

It took me a while to put the pieces of the jigsaw together but eventually I began to see God's plan in action. It was over two years ago that I first visited Krivnya and stood in the playground with Adrian and felt the call on me to do something. In what, to the untrained eye, must have seemed like random timing the building team are due to arrive just a few weeks before a critical inspection which I knew nothing about until this very day. And it was also on this very day, just a few hours earlier, that I had visited Provadia Orphanage which we worked at for the very same reason i.e. it was earmarked for closure and saw what great things had been achieved there.

As I say I didn't see it immediately but I eventually recognised God's hand at work. His timing, as always, is perfect and I have the assurance that He will once again accomplish miraculous things through this group of men and women from the UK. A very mixed bag of people with different gifts and with different attitudes towards God but He will use everyone of us in His great plan for these fantastic children.

Then Mladen and I set off to the builders' merchants and stores to pay for and collect all the materials we needed for the work to be done. We left Adrian, Cai & Dave in charge of entertaining the children but without the aid of a safety net. I returned to find that Adrian had twisted his ankle and was incapacitated and David, in an effort to spare his bad back and avoid playing football, had engaged in the children's favourite 'hand slapping' game and was suffering sore hands as a result. Honestly, you just can't leave some people for five minutes! Adrian's injury caused some concern; not that we were worried about the considerable pain he was in but how would he drive home? David and I didn't relish the thought of doing all the driving on our own and it was a bit short notice to put Cai through his driving test.

At least the kids had a great time, the laughing, screaming and shouting was testament to that. Their smiling, happy faces once again provided the reward for our efforts.

Our 'shopping' trip was a success and it was great to have the help of the children in unloading all the supplies. 60 large joists, 20 large plaster boards, bags of plaster, ceramic tiles, loft insulation and much more all unloaded in the blink of an eye by an army of willing helpers. It was very satisfying to see all the materials on site as this was the aim of the trip. It was even more satisfying to have the help of the very children whose lives we hope to improve by our work.

As the week went on a pattern was emerging. The Mayor's wife used to babysit Alex. The director of the orphanage lives in the same street as Alex. The owner of the restaurant we used is a friend of Alex. And so it went on—everyone knows Alex and Alex knows everyone. For a young lady of 19 she is very well connected. We teased her a lot about this but when we jokingly asked if she had a friend in Sofia (hundreds of miles away) who could put us up for the night she calmly replied, "my mother's sister lives in Sofia". And so it went on, there really wasn't anyone in Provadia (or beyond) whom Alex didn't know. I think it pays to be friends with the Angelova family……..!!!

Then followed a trip to Barzitsa for more fun and games (for those who could still use their hands and feet). As the invalids looked on from the sidelines those who had survived the ravages of playing with little children took to the playing field for another game of football.

It's not easy to be injured in a Bulgarian Orphanage. The kids are so full of excitement they cannot contain themselves and however much pain you're in you are drawn in to some game or other and it's virtually impossible to say no to those pleading eyes.

As the day drew to a close it was time to start the long walk back to the car. Not that the car was far away, just that it takes ages to shake the kids off your legs and arms where they hang like little monkeys urging you to play one more game before you leave. In a scene reminiscent of a nature documentary where six hyenas try to take down a buffalo ten times their size, a group of boys decided it would be hilarious to try and get me to fall to the floor. I managed to put up quite a fight for a little while knowing that as soon as my colleagues saw my plight they would come rushing to my aid but they were incapacitated by an attack of breathlessness which on the face of it appeared to be hysterical laughter but they assured me it was not.

Then I saw him, my knight in shining armour striding across the playground with a sense of purpose that filled me with hope. One of the carers was on his way to rescue me. As he closed in on the melee I knew I only had to hold out for a few more seconds and he would chastise the boys for their attack on an innocent visitor.

But I could feel myself going down, I looked over at the carer with a look of desperation in the hope that he would take immediate action. I watched with eager anticipation as he reached into his pocket; was it a whistle, a big stick, a pepper spray. Quick, I'm falling. As I thudded onto the ground I took my last pitiful look at the carer who produced from his pocket—a camera!!!!

As the boys howled with delight at finally felling me my supposed rescuer stood there taking photo's with an air of triumph that his boys had achieved this wonderful victory. My cries of "I know the Angelova family"

were all in vain as no one could understand my muffled cries from beneath the scrum of boys. The situation wasn't helped by the apparent joy with which my colleagues were treating my misfortune.
Battered and bruised I picked myself up and dusted myself down knowing full well that they had had so much fun this wouldn't be the last time I would have to endure this indignity.

Despite my ordeal I still had the use of both my legs which is more than I can say for Adrian who was finding the stairs in our guest house quite a challenge. However, as we left our rooms for the restaurant he discovered that he could hold himself up on the stair rails with his arms and take the weight off his bad foot. Naturally his focus was on his foot as he looked down to ensure all was well. It's a pity he didn't look up because then he would have seen the low headroom. Heaving himself up on his arms, to take the weight of his foot, he managed to bang his head on the underside of the staircase above. Ouch! I think the blow to his head must have done some damage as he would have got away with it as there was no one around to witness it but in a moment of madness he told me what had happened. Maybe he was reaching out to his older brother for some sympathy but I remembered how he laughed at my earlier misfortune as I disappeared under a pack of children in Barzitsa and returned the favour.

As an aside, on the road to and from Barzitsa there were some speed bumps but they only stretched two thirds of the way across the road presenting a tempting opportunity to treat them as a chicane and weave around them. Adrian seemed keen that I should do this but I declined.

So we made our way to the restaurant stopping every 2 seconds for Alex to say hello to everyone we passed which served to help Adrian keep up with us as he limped along on one leg whilst rubbing his head with his right hand. He would have used his left hand but one of his fingers was infected and had swollen to twice it's normal size, which wasn't as bad as his ankle which by now, was three times it's normal size, although it's difficult to tell what is a normal size for his ankles as both had swollen after the long drive to Bulgaria. The vultures had started to circle overhead and we wondered if it wouldn't simply be kinder to have him put down but we decided he might still have some use as a goal post next time we played football with the children.

A few hours later when Adrian had completed the 200 yard walk to the restaurant Cai entertained us with his brilliant idea for an invention which would make him millions. In a Dragon's Den style pitch he tried to explain his idea; maybe it's because Welsh is his first language I don't know but clearly it was a difficult concept as the bemused look on our faces gave away our inability to fathom what he was on about. The best we could come up with was a plastic napkin. It didn't sound like an invention which would set the world alight. Questions such as, "How would you mop up spills?" and "How would you tuck it into the top of your jumper?" were answered with a mix of frustration and distain leading to a chorus of "I'm out!" Back to the drawing board for Cai. Mercifully our meals arrived before he could regale us with his idea for a DIY ferry (more on this later).

THURSDAY 18th
A new day brought a new job. This time we had the pleasure of visiting The Hope & Future Foundation and delivering some donations. We had received a fantastic guitar from Guitar Aid (run by a friend from Riverside Church in Exeter - www.guitar-aid.com please take a look sometime) plus some great accessories from Rock Hens Coop in Okehampton (strings, tuners, harmonicas, maracas and more). I was able to show the others the guest house which forms their base and is the site for the residential camps run for the children from Barzitsa and Krivnya Orphanages. I was also able to show them the outdoor facility for the camp which our team created last year.

We had hoped to see Zuska and the boys we sponsor through college, Plamen & Boyan but couldn't manage to see them all.

We went to the college where the boys are studying and took a tour of the facility which was very interesting. Plamen is studying upholstery and Boyan is studying woodwork. Reports on Boyan are great as he is doing really well but Plamen is finding it more difficult and is starting to fall away a bit. Didi will try to encourage him so that he doesn't lose this opportunity.

Just as it was time to leave the college Boyan showed up. College had just finished for the day so he came to meet us. He certainly looked very happy and proud to be there which was a great encouragement to us. It was so good to see him.

At last we had an opportunity to do the most important thing of the week—buy the iPod gizmo. Unfortunately, Varna was gridlocked due to road works and making our way through the city was torturous but eventually we made it to a suitable shop and after a lengthy search found what we were looking for. It seemed a little expensive but to be honest we would have paid double just to avoid having to listen to the same CD's all the way home. As we left the store we realised that we were in a one way system and would have to go back towards Varna and rejoin the massive traffic queue. Fortunately Alex knew a different road and pointed us in that direction. Well, I say road but really it was just a huge hole with odd bits of tarmac here and there. I've commented on Bulgarian roads a lot in previous reports but this really was one of the worst I have encountered. I recalled a picture I saw once on a Bulgarian friend's Facebook page:

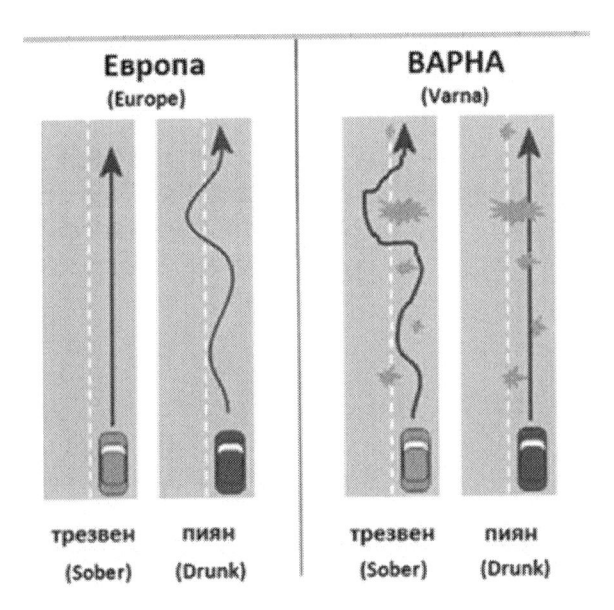

Европа
(Europe)

трезвен (Sober) пиян (Drunk)

ВАРНА
(Varna)

трезвен (Sober) пиян (Drunk)

This truly sums it up!!

I kept hoping that the elongated pothole would rejoin the main road soon but it never did, we had to travel the entire 30 miles bouncing in and out of pothole after pothole. All I could think about was my poor car. I wouldn't have been surprised to learn that the Angelova family owned all the Bulgarian suspension companies but Alex kept very quiet about that one. We made straight for Barzitsa, re-assembled all our bones and embarked on another session of games to round off our day.

Once again Adrian urged me to take the chicane around the speed bumps on the trip back to the guest house but once again I declined.

That night, at the restaurant, we continued our gentle banter laughing at each other's incompetent actions and foolish words when we suddenly realised that David had yet to join the ranks of us mere mortals and say or do even one stupid thing. How could this be? I made a mental note to change the vetting procedures for future team members. Clearly David had read previous reports and knew that the slightest misdemeanour would be pounced upon and reported. I have been accused of exaggerating people's little errors for comic effect in my reports but as I kept telling the team, "I don't let the truth get in the way of a good story". David had taken this to heart and was at pains to ensure that he did nothing to warrant a mention. Now the rest of us were at pains to ensure he did.

I had a serious talk with Adrian and Cai and charged them with the responsibility of setting David up or, if necessary, creating a lie which would show him to be just like the rest of us. They had one night to come up with something.

FRIDAY 19th
Our last day arrived and with most of our jobs done we had a free(ish) day. We busied ourselves with all the little jobs we needed to do to get ready for the journey home (including topping up our box of snacks) and visited the little Pizza store for a hearty feed. You can get a HUGE slice of pizza for 50p and various other equally good value savouries.

After lunch we went back to Krivnya with nothing on our agenda other than to play with the kids. We keep a hockey set out there and so decided to take this along with us. That turned out to be a great decision as it was a big hit with the children. We saw children we hadn't seen on previous visits and some of those who stood on the sidelines for other games wanted to join in. Everyone was of a similar standard so we were all equal which really added to our enjoyment. After a while we managed to get some of the staff involved—one lady in heels!! I'm sure the game would have gone on for a lot longer had time allowed but we had to get going as we wanted to pay a last visit to Barzitsa too.

We offered to leave the hockey set there until we returned a week later. Initially Mladen was concerned but once I assured him that it didn't matter if anything got broken he was keen to accept. I'd like to think that the kids (and staff) have had a great week playing together. If so then maybe we could consider buying them their own set one day.

On the way to Barzitsa Adrian, yet again, implored me to dodge round the speed bumps but I was having none of it and slowly limped over them.

At Barzitsa we decided to open the baseball set we had bought them. Unfortunately it was in one of those impossible to open sealed plastic covers. Impossible that is for the likes of you and me but for an excited child, eyes wide with anticipation, thermo sealed plastic proved to be no obstacle and they tore it off with their bare hands.

I set up the baseball pitch and explained a few basic rules. Adrian was nominated as bowler as after all his injuries about the only part of his body left which was still functioning was his bowling arm and so he pitched the first ball to Angel who had successfully wrenched the bat from the clutches of the other children. Angel is a slight lad of about 11 or 12 but from what happened next must be a distant relation of Babe Ruth. In his weakened state Adrian tossed up a dolly which Angel swung at and made such a sweet contact the ball flew out of the orphanage grounds across the road and into a neighbour's garden. This was bad news as I know from bitter experience the neighbours do not respond very well to the popular childhood plea of "please miss can I have my ball back". Indeed we have occasionally been banned from playing ball games because the neighbours complain so much. However, this story ends well and eventually the ball came back and there were no complaints, we moved the pitch around and carried on.

In an act of amazing courage Alex, deciding that Adrian had taken more than his fair share of physical punishment, put herself in the line of fire and took a direct hit from a full blooded shot. Everyone felt her pain and the boys, to their credit all swarmed around her to make sure she was ok. The kids all love Alex and were quite disturbed to see her hurt.

I'd love to be able to report that this selfless act of courage took the attention off Adrian a bit but no. Not to be outdone he came up with another plan for another injury. After the boys had had about a hundred turns each with the bat we decided it was our go and so David, Cai, Adrian and I stepped up to the plate. I think I went first in a fairly uneventful affair then it was Adrian's turn. Subin pitched the ball to Adrian which he deftly struck with the bat at the perfect angle to skew the ball straight into his head. It was interesting to note that when Alex got hit everyone was deeply concerned for her welfare but when Adrian got hit the concern was more about would anyone die from laughing. By now I think it was only Adrian's left earlobe which was free from injury or pain; the rest of us were suffering from split sides—from laughing so much.

As we were trying to leave (an even more difficult task on the last day) there was a weak attempt at finding something to laugh at David about when one of the boys couldn't remember his name so came up with Mustafa. This amused us a little but was nowhere near what I had hoped for when I asked Adrian and Cai to come up with a devious plot.

Well, all good things must come to an end and so it was that we left Barzitsa and had to turn our minds to the homeward journey.
On the way back from Barzitsa the monotonous cry of "take the chicane around the speed bumps" caused me to respond with, "NO! I'm the sort of bloke who spends his life sticking to the letter of the law only to find that the one time he steps outside the law the police are there to catch him" Oh dear, Oh dear, I wish I had kept my big mouth shut as those words would come back to haunt me later

Time for our final meal at the restaurant and it was here that it finally happened, after five days David finally said something stupid. We were discussing the journey home and commenting on the long, straight Croatian roads when David said, "maybe the Romans built them". We were delighted to point out that it was unlikely that the ancient Romans had built a motorway. It wasn't much to go on but we milked it for all it was worth. If this was going to be the daftest thing David would say we had to make the most of the opportunity and so we did. It was just what we needed to finish off the week, we felt somehow fulfilled and ready to leave.

SATURDAY 20th

After studying the timings for our journey to Bulgaria we decided to bring forward our departure time to 2am and so had an early night. We left Provadia just after 02:00 and began our epic journey home. It didn't feel quite so epic though as we looked at the extensive roadworks on either side of the road, "These roadworks weren't here on the way into Provadia" I said. Spurred on by my faultless navigation on the inbound journey I ventured to suggest that we were on the wrong road as the signs said Ruse but should have said Sofia. In a world first which I am proud to record here, I was right. I'm going to write that again as I may never have another opportunity. I was right, my navigational reputation was restored and we soon got ourselves back on the right road. It would be very unfair of me to mention that it was David who was navigating, so I won't.

Now cast your minds back a few paragraphs and those prophetic words of mine, "The one time I break the law I'll get caught" and you'll have a fair idea of what's coming next. We were in Serbia but I was still in 'Bulgarian Driving Mode' (i.e. the only rule is there is no rule) and was frustrated by the vehicle in front of me doing 12mph so decided to overtake. Unfortunately I hadn't paid attention to the road markings which prohibited overtaking. The bright yellow fluorescent jackets in the distance gave away the reason for the dilatory snail like actions of the car which was now behind me and sure enough I got pulled over.

Although there was limited language between us the policeman explained that I would have to go back to the border to pay a fine. The fine was bad enough but losing all that time to go back to the border was very bad news. However, I was in the wrong so I agreed with all he said and complied with his every request. This was in complete contrast with a lorry driver they had also pulled over who was ranting and raving and arguing for all he was worth. I think this may have played in my favour as it showed me in a very good light by comparison. The policeman took me over to his car to fill out the paperwork for me to take to the border and asked me how many people were travelling and I told him four of us. He asked if anyone spoke Bulgarian so I told him no just as the other police officer appeared from behind the lorry with the driver still arguing vehemently. The policeman dealing with me looked at me and said, with an element of resignation in his voice, "Go and no more overtaking". I didn't need telling twice, I thanked him and got on my way - at a respectable speed of course.

I was very glad to get that episode over but not so glad about the next one. Fed up with the snacks in our box and bloated with poor nutrition we decided to pull over and buy something a little more beneficial to our health. There was a nice display of meat and salad rolls which took our fancy and so we bought one each and made for the picnic tables outside as by now it was 25 degrees (which was quite different from the minus 2 degrees we had experienced in the small hours of that morning). We opened our rolls with some enthusiasm I tore off the label and gave it a quick glance, I couldn't read it but assumed it said something along the lines of 'home grown salad selected by fair maidens from our premium vegetable plot in granny's garden with choicest ham from hand reared pigs fed only on organic caviar—just for you' But one bite was all it took to discover what it actually said was 'using a piece of bread we found in a skip behind Macdonalds we added some unknown vegetation we found in a swamp round the back of a slurry pit together with a de-moulded slice of meat from a roll the last person discarded to create this salmonella riddled treat—just for you'.

And to make matters worse, the others all had perfectly good rolls which they wolfed down with no regard for their poor starving co-driver.

I briefly considered taking it back but with my altercation with the police still fresh in mind I didn't want to risk any further trouble or having to remove a roll from my ear kindly placed there by an angry roll salesman.

So, badly weakened by the early stages of malnutrition I struggled on, you could almost hear the rickets having a party in my bones but it was ok the others just turned up the music to drown out my suffering.

There was one more treat before we left Serbia, we witnessed one of the world's most dangerous jobs. A somewhat worried looking man was actually sweeping the motorway!! Naturally as he was wearing a hi-vis tabard his safety was assured but nevertheless I didn't much fancy having that job.

The tedium of the long, straight Croatian roads (did I mention that the roads in Croatia are long and straight?) was broken by a shower. Unfortunately it was inside the car. Still trying to get the nuclear aftertaste of the rancid roll out of my mouth I reached for a bottle of water—how was I to know it was carbonated?! In a scene reminiscent of the blowing of mount Vesuvius, water cascaded out of the top of the bottle. To this day I'll never understand how an explosion of such magnitude could be contained within such a small area. Despite the confines of the car I was the only one to get soaked, everyone else remained dry as a bone. Still, at least the tears I shed were disguised by the waterfall tumbling from my saturated hair. I think that some of the deluge must have penetrated my ears because the sympathetic concern of my colleagues sounded a lot like hysterical laughter through the water.

Eventually we made it to Austria and a change of roads promised some relief and a change of scenery. Unfortunately, we changed onto the wrong road. Now, whilst I must admit to being navigator at this stage, as we approached the fork in the road I clearly stated' "Go right" but our driver, who shall remain anonymous (but it wasn't David and Cai is too young to drive) thought he knew better. "No, this is where you went wrong last time, we're going left". "It's definitely right" I said, even Cai piped up with "I remember going right last time". "No, we're going left" came the assured retort. The rest of us quietly counted down 10, 9,8,7,6,5,4,3,2,1 and right on queue Adrian, oops I mean our anonymous driver, said, "OK, I've gone the wrong way" Nothing needed to be said, smugness was oozing out of every one of my pores as we patiently waited for a place to turn around and have another go at the junction.

To this point our navigational errors (none of which were my fault, did I already mention that?) had been fairly inconsequential but the next event promised to be a bit more serious. All of a sudden without any warning we met a wall of bollards and our road was unceremoniously closed before our eyes and we were forced onto a road which spurred off in a completely different direction. Now bearing in mind we were supposed be heading back to Suben on the Austria/Germany border where our hotel awaited us and my previous minor error with the hotel booking, imagine my horror when the road signs on our 'new' road all pointed to Salzburg. The irony didn't go unnoticed by my colleagues who were quick to pounce on my misfortune in an effort to distract us from the obvious fact that we were wandering further and further away from our intended destination. We had already been told by the hotel receptionist that Suben is 250km away from Salzburg so carrying on along this road seemed futile. We decided to pull in at the next petrol station and buy a map to navigate our way back onto the right road. Petrol stations pop up about every 20 miles so we knew we would soon be ok. Or at least, they pop up on every other road in Europe except this one. Mile after mile passed and we were getting further and further away from our intended destination and more and more lost. And as if that wasn't bad enough the fuel gauge decided to mock us by pointing out that we were on the brink of running out of petrol. We decided to pull off the motorway and go into a town to look for fuel. This turned out to be a good decision as we found a petrol station quite quickly. Having fuelled up I went to pay and buy a map of Austria so that we were fully equipped to get back on track but to my dismay whilst they had maps of the North Pole and Timbuktu they had nothing for Austria. We needed a plan B so we decided to head for Salzburg as we knew this was on the border and bought a map of Germany so we could find our way back to our original route. David found a local man who could speak some English, well actually a lot of English as he proceeded to describe every inch of tarmac in a set of very complicated directions that could more easily have been covered by 'go back to the road you came in off' How he managed to make 400 yards and one set of traffic lights sound so complicated I'll never know. Perhaps he was a local government minister.

And so we started to consider our new plan of heading for Salzburg and finding a hotel there. Yes, I know, I accidentally booked one there last week, don't think that fact escaped the others and don't even begin to think that perhaps they didn't mention it once or twice. After about the 999th mention of ' Andrew, blah, blah, idiot, blah blah, Salzburg blah blah I cut through the abuse with a shout of "MOOSE!!!!"
I was met with some bewildered gazes but Cai saved me by saying, "Yes, I saw a moose too". We quickly looked to the other side of the road and confirmed that there was a petrol station which gave rise to the impossible suggestion that this situation was identical to one we had encountered on the inbound journey. We agreed that there were lots of similar looking petrol stations in Austria and that the Moose statue was an advertising gimmick which was probably all over Austria.

However, this seemed to really play tricks on our minds as we saw familiarity in the strangest of things. "I've seen that tree before", "That cats eye looks very familiar", "There's that house again" By now we were delusional and took to looking behind us at the signs going the other way to see what they revealed. But the evidence was compelling, our road signs were clearly saying that we were getting closer and closer to Salzburg.

Then Cai spotted a castle high up on a hill, "Isn't that the castle you asked me to photograph on the way to Bulgaria?". He's right, on the inbound journey I had seen just such a castle and asked him to snap it for me but this time we were looking at it from a different angle or was it a different castle? "Look at the photo on your camera" I said, "That will tell us". "I can't, it's in the boot" came the reply.
Surely sleep deprivation and a dodgy roll were playing tricks on our frazzled minds, we were, undeniably heading closer and closer to Salzburg.

"But that toll booth up ahead, it looks familiar too." "Don't all toll booths look the same." "No, we came through this toll before." The excitement was reaching fever pitch as we scrabbled for the receipt so we could find the name of the first toll. Now all we had to do was wait for the receipt on paying for this one and see if they match. "Get the receipt, get the receipt" we cried, "What does it say? Is it the same?" To our complete amazement, somehow we were on the same road as we came in on a few days earlier. It didn't make any sense, nothing added up. But Cai summed it up for us when he said, "God really does answer prayers". There really was no other plausible explanation for what had just happened or the fact that we ended up at our hotel within half an hour of our scheduled time despite everything which had gone wrong.

SUNDAY 21st
That seems like an appropriate place to start rounding off this report but I just need to tell you that David did manage to provide us with one more moment of stupidity when ten minutes into our channel crossing, observing the behaviour of some of the kitchen staff he ventured that perhaps they were about to go off shift. What? In the middle of the channel? Are they going to swim home? We don't think so. Thanks David, you made us a feel a little better with this one.

The final word can go to Cai, who looking out to sea and observing a ferry going in the other direction asked, "is that a B&Q Ferry?" Although tiredness had enveloped us we just about managed to find the last few crumbs of energy to poke fun at him and his absurd suggestion that it was a flat packed vessel purchased from a large DIY chain; it was, of course, a P&O ferry

The journey from Dover to Okehampton (and on to Cardiff for Adrian & Cai) was uneventful and quiet as we were all spent and simply longed to get home and into our own beds.

It was a wonderful journey in which we achieved all our aims and had a load of fun in the process. Playing with the kids is always a delight but the hockey match at Krivnya was a personal highlight for me.

As always God's hand was evident in so much of what we did and the glory for what was achieved is His. His perfect timing in bringing this project to this point is amazing. His guiding hand on our car to place us back on the right road despite all the physical evidence to the contrary was awesome.

So it just remains for me to thank you for your support and to thank God for making all this possible. Now I must go and pack my bags for my return to Krivnya with the team who will start the work on saving the children's home from closure.

Yes, there will be another report………………………..

Andrew

CHAPTER TEN
My Kingdom for a tile cutter…………………!!
May 2013

Andy 'Jonah' Ewen
Barry 'Ronaldo' Gee
Roger 'Peg Leg' Wills
Andrew 'Personal Shopper' Morgan
Nigel 'Pinnie' Price
Ben 'The Kettle' Cook
Eileen 'L plates' Mutanhu
Becky 'Handbag' Howe
Ant 'Germs' Hilton
Tevor 'Scarlet Pimpernel' Colbran

SUNDAY 29th April
I arrived at Exeter Bus Station with Ben & Trevor to find Andy already there. Three more would join us here at Exeter plus two at Gatwick and one in Provadia (plus the unsung heroine of our adventures Alex Angelova our good friend and translator who became the invaluable 11th member of our team).

Amid the chatter we would occasionally glance up to see if the other three had arrived yet. Eventually they appeared on the horizon; do you recall the opening title sequence of Baywatch? The slow motion shots as the handsome lifeguards ran majestically down the beach, blonde locks flowing in the wind. Well it was nothing like that. It was more reminiscent of a scene from Last Of The Summer Wine as Compo, Clegg & Foggy wheeled their suitcases towards the seats in the waiting room.

Had we known what lie ahead we might have taken more time to celebrate the success of this part of the journey. Everyone who should have been at Exeter Bus Station was there and on time, all we needed now was a bus. As it happens there were loads of buses but none of them were ours. Buses came and buses went but we still stood there waiting. When I thought no one was looking I would furtively check the documents I was carrying to ensure I had the right time, the right day, the right station, the right mode of transport. Memories of a minor hotel booking error from my last trip were haunting me. Fifty eight checks later and the documents still said I was right but there was still no bus. Fortunately, the other members of the team hadn't heard about my previous hotel booking debacle and so were blissfully assured that this was a National Express problem.

An hour later the bus finally turned up, it turns out there had been an incident in Plymouth which resulted in the police being called to have a drunken passenger removed from the bus, hence the late arrival. It wasn't too much of a problem as we had plenty of time to wait for our connection to Gatwick at Victoria Street in London so there was no panic (yet!!)

We arrived at Victoria Street with sufficient time for a comfort break and to grab a quick snack. Our bus pulled up on time and we boarded without incident. "This is better" we commented, glad to have got the travelling problems out of the way on the first leg. Just as we were settling down to the second part of our journey and Barry was giving his roomies a taste of what was to come with his loud rendition of The Snoring Song we were rudely awakened from our rest by the driver who radioed into base with these words, "John to base, John to base. I'm on route FJ189 to Gatwick, can you give me directions please as I've never driven this route before". From that moment on all eyes were on the road signs. We agreed that if anyone saw a sign saying 'Edinburgh 23 miles' we would jump the driver and guide the bus ourselves.

Somehow (SatNav I guess) we got to Gatwick in good time. We made for Costa Coffee and started to tuck in to some breakfast. Eventually we were joined by Becky & Ant taking our team up to nine.

MONDAY 30th April
After several hours of waiting we were glad to be on board the aeroplane to Sofia where we would take an internal flight to Varna. Several of the team had planned to take a taxi into Sofia for a bit of sightseeing as there was a long wait for the internal connection to Varna so hopes were high as the plane began to taxi down the runway. The cabin crew gave the safety demonstration and I thought I caught a glimpse of someone paying attention but I could have been mistaken. There was that familiar pause as the plane awaits permission to take off then the equally familiar 'bing bong' that proceeds the captains announcement telling the cabin crew to take their seats for take off. Only that wasn't what the captain said this time. What he actually said was, "Ladies and gentlemen I'm sorry to

inform you that take off has been aborted due to technical difficulties" Mystery flooded the plane as people wondered what that meant exactly. The distant amber flashing lights of an AA patrol man did not fill us with confidence. I'm not sure a jump start was what was required and I doubted his ability to tow us to a local garage. The next message came across the tannoy, "There will be a short delay while we find you a replacement plane". This was received with some relief as no one really wanted to be 35000 feet in the air if the fan belt was going to break.

After some time people started reaching for dictionaries and flicking through the pages to find the definition of 'short delay'. It turns out we could have written the dictionary in the time it took to find a replacement plane. Two and a half hours we sat in the plane going absolutely nowhere. If we had been in the air we would have nearly arrived in Sofia by now.

Three hours, two planes and three pilots later we took off and leg number three had eventually begun. Once again we had the comfort of a long wait at Sofia so the delay was not critical but it put paid to any ideas of sightseeing.

Then, at last, we heard some good news, "This is your captain speaking, please accept our sincere apologies for the delays. We will be happy to serve complimentary snacks courtesy of Easy Jet as a token of our regret for the inconvenience." The beauty of the synchronicity as hands reached forward for the in flight menus was something to behold. Excited chatter filled the air as people selected all manner of baguettes, toasted sandwiches, paninis, soup and other delicatessen delights. With mouths watering we eagerly anticipated the hostess trolley which was making its way up the aisle but I guess the sound of rumbling tummies deafened us to what was going on as row by row people were facing the crushing disappointment of reality. When the trolley finally reached us and we gave our order you could have heard a pin drop when the air hostess handed us a very sad looking Twix and said this was the free snack to which we were entitled. A Twix!!! By now we were so ravaged with hunger we did not have the energy to argue and so took the meagre ration to which we were entitled together with a plastic cup of warm washing up water which they passed off as tea. Thank you Easy Jet; now about those outside toilets……………….!!!!!

In an ill thought out effort to make our ordeal seem a little less awful Andy reminded the rest of the team that last time he came on a trip we got delayed by 24 hours due to the infamous Icelandic ash cloud. Slowly the team started to realise that the common factor on the two ill fated trips was Andy. I watched as grown men trawled their childhood memories for the story of Jonah and then turn to Andy as they recalled the bit where Jonah was thrown out of the ship to banish the troubles which had befallen their fateful journey. Andy's eyes flitted around the plane as he searched for the nearest parachute, panic set in with the realisation that parachutes and rucksacks all look the same to the untrained eye. An unwise choice could see him hurtling towards the ground with sweets, books and jumpers falling out of the pack on his back instead of the reassuring jolt which comes with a parachute. But everything turned out ok, we all had our complimentary Twix's; who could want for more. Our troubles faded as we bathed in the joy of our compensatory chocolate and Andy's terrible fate was avoided.

When we finally made it to Sofia we were greeted by beautiful sunshine and endless blue skies set against a backcloth of snow peaked mountains, it was truly glorious. We got the shuttle bus from Terminal 2 to Terminal 1 which were about a mile apart and I made a mental note of this as it might prove to be critical on the way home when our transfer time is much tighter.
Despite all the delays and problems we were still in good time for our flight to Varna. Now the misery of a potential seven hour wait in Sofia turned in our favour as being 4 hours late had no consequences for the remainder of the journey and we would still arrive at our hotel in Provadia at the scheduled time. Or so we thought……………

"This is an announcement for all passengers on the Sofia to Varna flight. Due to technical difficulties the flight is delayed by three hours"

Surely not! How much bad luck could fall on one group of travellers. Andy looked on nervously as the 'Jonah hunters' gathered menacingly around him and quickly came up with a brilliant distraction. "Let's get a taxi into Sofia and find a restaurant where we can get a good meal" My first thought was, "what, after that complimentary Twix on the flight? That's never gonna work" But I was wrong, it seems that the others still had a healthy appetite despite the generosity of Easy Jet and their complimentary confectionary.

By now the burden of responsibility was weighing heavily on my shoulders. I was the one who had booked the flights (and coaches) and so far just about everything which could go wrong had gone wrong. I rued my efforts to do everything on a budget and wondered if it might have been better to have taken the more expensive and possibly more reliable choices but if I had some of the team might not have been able to afford to come. I consoled myself with this fact and was glad that the others seemed to realise that it was all beyond my control. However, I felt duty bound to stay at the airport and represent our party should any further changes come about or if we were needed for anything. The others took the perilous taxi ride (Formula 1 ride according to some reports) into Sofia to search for a restaurant.

As I sat there and contemplated the lack of feeling in my backside that great voice in the sky which seemed to bring only misery burst forth again, "Bulgaria Air would like to apologise for the delays and are pleased to offer a complimentary meal to all passengers." "Oh, what this time?" I moaned to myself, "Half a stick of Wrigleys chewing gum, an old piece of cheese they found under the fridge or maybe even a left over sausage from the staff canteen" But wait, they definitely said 'meal'. Yes, I clearly heard the word meal. Ha ha, wait til I tell the others that I had a free meal while they paid for taxis (no doubt at extortionate tourist rates) and for a posh restaurant meal. I was going to have the last laugh on this one. I wandered in the direction of the counter serving food only to be turned around and pointed towards the Bulgaria Air check in desk. I thought it a little peculiar that I should collect an Al A Carte meal from a check in desk but was happy just to be walking in the general direction of my gastronomic indulgence. Looking past the tin of Coke and thermo sealed croissant on the counter which was clearly the poor clerk's miserable fayre I enquired after my meal. My heart sank when the clerk pointed to the coke and croissant without any sort of apologetic acknowledgement of the miserable 'meal' before me. The only positive was that it was better than Easy Jet's offering!!

In a display of outrageous decadence I decided to find a different seat in which to eat my meal. Oh yes, I was living it large now, just call me Victor Navorski (ref: Tom Hanks film 'The Terminal').
Thirty seven seconds later a trip to the bin marked the end of my meal and I started to consider the consequences of arriving in Varna three

hours late. I needed to phone several people to re-organise the minibus, the hotel, meeting Eileen (the tenth member of our team) etc etc. As I reached for my phone the little red bar in the corner of the screen brought more bad news, my battery was nearly dead and it was all Dr Who's fault! In an effort to while away the long tedious hours of delays I had used my phone to catch up on Dr Who via the BBC iPlayer, at the time I was marvelling at the wonders of modern technology but now I was cursing Apple's useless iPhone battery. I couldn't help wondering if it's called an Apple iPhone because the battery is made from a Golden Delicious. I needed to charge it but my plug converter was in my luggage which had been checked in hours ago. I returned to the carvery where Egon Ronet was serving the gourmet coke & croissant and asked the clerk if there was any way to have access to my luggage. He started to pull a face that could only lead to a "No, that's not possible" so I quickly reminded him that his airline was the cause of the problems I was seeking to resolve and I drove home the matter by telling him about all the people who would be affected the other end if I could not contact them. To be fair to the clerk his demeanour changed and he was extremely helpful and doing everything he could to accommodate my request but this only served to increase my embarrassment when, presented with my luggage, I could not find the adapter I needed to convert my plug for use in Europe. I don't know how many times I looked through my bag in a desperate act of denial that I had obviously left it at home. I realised this after about the third search but still continued to look over and over again whilst muttering muted apologies to the poor clerk who had gone to so much effort to help me. I could tell he knew it wasn't there too but sympathetically looked on as the hole in the ground got steadily bigger but refused to swallow me up. I handed the bag back to the clerk and skulked away into a dark corner while I considered what to do next.

Then it struck me, I'm in an international airport I should be able to buy an adapter from any number of shops. I thought of Gatwick and could immediately picture about six shops where I could get an adaptor. What I should have pictured was Lundy Island as this would have been a better representation of the shops available to me. Of the six shops in Sofia Airport four were closed. If I had wanted to buy a wooden spoon with the Bulgarian flag on it for £99 or a toy aeroplane to remind me of this wonderful adventure then the two remaining shops would have been perfect. As it was, for someone who needed something remotely useful like a plug adaptor, the shops were about as useful as an ashtray on a motorbike (I bet they sold those).

The look on the clerk's face said it all as he saw me approaching him again. I caught him glancing all around for a colleague who he could fob me off on but he was all alone. He took a deep breath, fixed on his grin and asked if he could help me. "Do you have a USB port to which I can connect my phone? As you may recall the plug adaptor in my luggage has been vaporised" (I blame Dr Who again). "I'm sorry sir but there are no USB ports in the airport as that would represent a huge security risk." This point was so obvious I retreated immediately before I could embarrass myself even further. I was beginning to suspect that they had put some sort of sedative in the meal they served up to suppress the hostile crowd but it was affecting me by reducing my intelligence levels to that of a small worm.

I was glad that I had turned my phone off earlier before the sedative kicked in as the "5% remaining" battery was all I had left to contact the people in Varna & Provadia. As soon as the phone turned back on I knew I only had a few moments to do everything I needed to do. Now if you, the reader, are of a 'certain' age you will understand the hazards of trying to text at speed. With thumbs which for all the world suddenly appeared to be as big as melons punching delicate keys the size of gnats toes it sounded more like I was sending Morse code than text. To be honest I think the Morse code would have made more sense than the gobbledigook which appeared on my phone screen. As you know shouting at your screen is the remedy for every phone problem and this is always enhanced by hitting the buttons even harder. As the battery life reduced 4%, 3%, 2% I shouted louder and punched harder and just in the nick of time got the texts sent but that was it. I had no way of knowing if I received any acknowledgements or responses. I could only hope that my messages got through and that the people waiting the other end could change their schedules to accommodate our delays.

In a moment of calm I considered the earlier revelation that there were no USB ports anywhere in Sofia Airport and began to wonder if that was actually true. I could understand that any computer linked to the Airport mainframe would be USB free but what about all the other computers. The ones in the cafés, the shops, the enquiries counter? I was a man on a mission, there must be a USB port somewhere and I was right, a helpful girl on the enquiries desk plugged my phone in and it began to charge.

There was still over an hour left til our rescheduled boarding time so I sat down to take a breather.
"Will all passengers for the Sofia to Varna flight please make their way to Gate 1 and prepare for boarding" Nooooooo!!!!!! The rest of my team were in town feasting on real food in a restaurant somewhere. I have to ring them and tell them to get back here immediately. Back at the enquiries desk I recover my phone and try to make a phone call while the phone is still plugged into the computer as ten minutes of charging will probably give me about 3.7 seconds of talk time on my Golden Delicious battery. The distance between the computer and my ear was about five feet, the length of the lead about 2 feet. Balancing on tip toe and leaning over the enquiries desk I dialled the number and held the phone close to my ear. "Come on, come on, pick up" Try another number. Then my phone started to ring in my panic I pulled the phone a little too close to my ear and the lead came out. I had enough power to hear Andy's voice on the other end say, "where are you, we've been called to the departure gate". I looked up and there were the team calmly standing in the queue waiting for me, oblivious to the catalogue of disasters I had put myself through in their absence and wondering why I was late for the queue. I couldn't even begin to explain so I didn't try. I simply asked Becky to contact the necessary people in Varna & Provadia as she had a phone with a battery which wasn't made by a green grocer.

Eventually we made it to our hotel in Provadia in the early hours of the morning and Nigel commented that we started our journey on Sunday and finished it on Tuesday thus spanning three days; an astute but unhelpful observation.

On the plus side, despite all the delays, we could still start work on schedule at 9am Tuesday morning. Oh, had you remembered that we were going to Krivnya to renovate the Orphanage there or were you beginning to think this whole report was going to be taken up with the journey?

TUESDAY 30th April
Tuesday dawned and we were raring to go. For most of the team this was their first visit to Krivnya (and to Bulgaria for many). There were two sites

where we would be working, the Orphanage and the school. Because the orphanage is home for children with special needs they have a school just up the road for their education. The two sites are about a third of a mile apart. As designated minibus driver I took the builders to the school first then returned to Provadia for the rest of the team who would be decorating the Orphanage. After dropping off the decorating team I went to the school to see how the builders were getting on and to pick up my tile cutter which I was expecting to be there. I must say I was suitably impressed with progress; already the frame for the suspended ceiling was taking shape and the wall was being marked and drilled to support it.

I was less impressed with the shopping list I was given. I had hoped to start work on tiling the toilets but it was clear that I would need to go and buy more supplies to keep the builders fully employed. As it happens my tile cutter had not turned up anyway so tiling had to wait.

"Where's Ben?" I asked. I wanted to chat with Ben as he was responsible for installing the computers but a minor change to the plans meant this wouldn't happen until the classrooms were ready at the end of the week so I wanted to be sure he had things to do meanwhile. "He's making coffee" came the reply, so I went off to find him. WARNING – if Ben's mum and dad are reading this they may want to skip a few paragraphs.

When I found Ben I wondered if he was conducting some sort of Frankenstein experiment as the equipment he was using bore no relation to a kettle. He had an electric coil attached to an unfused plug with some wire and flappy insulation tape. This was held in a jug of water to bring it to the boil. "What are you doing?" I cried, "Oh it's OK I'm wearing these gloves" he replied as he nodded at the rigger gloves on his hands. "You can't do that" I protested, "It's fine I've made several coffees already" came the assured reply. I got my shopping list and wrote 'new kettle' right at the top.

I'd like to attempt to describe shopping for building materials in Provadia but I don't think it's possible. Let me just say it is the polar opposite of the same task in Britain. Here we might go to a store such as B&Q and an hour later be driving away with everything we need. In Provadia? Well it's very, very different. So when a builder tells me to get him 6 bags of sand but the merchant sells it by the bucket (you have to provide your own bags!!) things start to get a little confusing.

When a builder used to nice straight, planed, correctly proportioned timbers is confronted with wood which looks like it's just been pulled off a tree they can have no idea of the trauma of getting hold of even that.
After a very tiresome morning of trawling builders merchants and DIY stores I commented to Mladen (my guide and interpreter), "I hate shopping", he replied "me too but it could be worse, you could be with a woman" It may not have been politically correct but it made me laugh for the first time in a few hours and brightened up a miserable morning.

In case Ben's mum and dad are still reading at this point, I managed to get a proper kettle which turned out to be a difficult task as apparently everyone in Bulgaria uses the coil of death. I managed another smile after I purchased the kettle as I heard a very British voice behind me ask the shop assistant, "Can I have one of those too". I guess they do a roaring trade selling kettles to tourists.

I dropped off all the building materials (and kettle) at the school and went back to the orphanage to do some proper work. Painting was well underway so I decided to muck in with that. Pleased with progress I stepped back to admire the work and managed to put my foot on a tray of paint which spilt all over the floor. I tried to raise a laugh to trivialise the incident but although my colleagues were polite I felt a bit of a fool.

As the working day drew to a close I was very pleased to see that one bedroom had been painted, the ceiling joists were up in one classroom and work had started on the second. Tomorrow the tile cutter would come and I could make a start on the toilets.

WEDNESDAY 1st May
Well tomorrow came but the tile cutter didn't so I had no excuse to avoid yet another shopping trip. One of the items on the extensive list was new lighting. As we were installing suspended ceilings we needed to 'drop' the lights but the fittings were in such a catastrophic state of repair we decided on brand new ones. The simplest solution was to use pendant fittings to duplicate the existing ones (pendant lights are the ones which hang down on a wire as in most houses). I had a clear picture in my mind of what to buy but couldn't find it anywhere, everything was so …. I'll say ornate but to be honest 'tacky' would be far more appropriate. Mladen and I looked at all the alternatives but, well, they were hideous and definitely not appropriate for a classroom. Strip lighting was available but

I was concerned about running costs, replacement bulbs etc (would the orphanage budget be able to meet the costs) so Mladen phoned the director for guidance. That was an inspired decision as the director was able to confirm that the Fire Officer had visited and had stated that strip lights had to be installed to meet the regulations. So we bought strip lights and bulbs and felt very pleased that we had made that phone call. After another session at the timber yard trying to get some half decent wood we returned with our load to Krivnya and checked on the delivery of the tile cutter. It still hadn't arrived so I made a phone call and confirmed it for tomorrow.

There seemed to exist some sort of paranormal relationship between the absence of a tile cutter and my 'availability' to go shopping or were the rest of the team hiding the tile cutter in order to free me up for the sole purpose of shopping for them.

By now the decorating team were well ahead of schedule and needed more paint as they now planned to paint the main living area in addition to the bedrooms. So once again the personal shopper was called into action and once more I climbed into the minibus to make the journey into Provadia. This shopping trip was a little easier than previous ones as some of the decorating team came with me and so were able to make their own choices. They also provided me with a comedy moment to light up another dull shopping trip. As we approached the footbridge to cross the river someone had made an effort to landscape a little parcel of land by building a well from small pebbles and painted it white. On seeing this Becky commented, "Why would someone build a model handbag in the centre of town?" She tried very hard to cover her error with a myriad of excuses but we were having none of it and milked the 'handbag' gag dry.

When we got back to Krivnya we made a start on painting the walls of the playroom until late afternoon when I wandered up to see the builders to establish which team would finish first and thus get on the first minibus journey. When I arrived I met midshipman Wills hobbling on his wooden leg across the deck of The Black Pearl; at least that's what the other builders would have me believe after a slight altercation with a saw. Fortunately it wasn't a serious attempt at amputation and Roger was forced to work on. He was just a little upset that the saw in question had been one we brought from home and not one of the Bulgarian ones we bought in Provadia as these were incapable of sawing through a half set jelly and would probably have met his leg with all the impact of a slightly damp goose feather.

As usual we ended the day in the restaurant and as we parted company, some to the bar for a nightcap and others to bed, Ant & Becky announced they were going with Alex (our translator) & Karmen (Alex's boyfriend) to find the bright lights and night clubs of Varna. After a moment of incredulity the rest of us thanked our lucky stars that we were 'of an age' that that sort of activity had no appeal and looked forward to a good night's sleep. We were even more stunned the next day to learn that they had got back to Provadia at 4am.

And so a few hours later we were back on the minibus and on our way to Krivnya again (strangely, Becky, Ant & Alex went on the second run this morning)

THURSDAY 2nd May
Everything was still going extremely well, including the game of hide the tile cutter from Andrew which was still eluding me. Concern was growing as days were running out and tiling was high priority as it was one of the jobs critical to passing the inspection. Leaving this job undone was not an option so I decided to make a start anyway as there were large areas which could be tiled before any cutting needed to be done. It wasn't an ideal way to start the job but at least it was a start.

Sadly, Thursday also brought some bad news. Eileen had to return to the UK as her husband was ill and the hospital staff thought she needed to be at his bedside. This was a sad loss to the decorating team. Eileen had started the week a complete novice admitting to no decorating skills at all but as she left for the long journey home she said that she now had the confidence to decorate her own home. We were very pleased to get a message later in the week that she made it home safely and her husband had improved.

Back in the classrooms the team were starting to prepare the floor for laying the laminate flooring. Some old parquet blocks were removed and replaced with concrete. For some reason it was felt that Nigel needed to work a little faster and so the shout went up, "put your foot down" but in his panic he misunderstood and put his foot down in the wet concrete. I'm not sure if he was trying to leave a Hollywood style legacy to commemorate his work but if he was, he failed as he hadn't considered the fact that the laminate would cover it up and it would never be seen again. However, Nigel did succeed in leaving a lasting imprint on the memories of his colleagues by donning a pinny at lunchtime and waitressing for the rest of the team. I think they would have preferred the footprint option.

In preparation for the inevitable daily shopping list I checked the insurance documents for the minibus and was delighted to discover that anyone on the team could drive it. Excellent, someone else could do the shopping run and I could get on with the tiling. So when the shopping list was presented I recited my prepared speech, "I think Barry (the building team leader) should go as he knows exactly what he wants". Barry agreed and I patted myself on the back for getting out of yet another shopping trip. Unfortunately, my self praise was a bit premature as when I handed the keys of the minibus to Barry he dealt his body blow, "Oh, I can't drive the minibus I haven't brought my driving licence" And so I ended up in the driving seat once again but at least Barry was with me and could gain some understanding of the problems of shopping for building materials in Provadia. So we visited a few merchants, shops and the timber yard and hopefully gained Barry's sympathy for the rigours of the dreaded shopping trip. This time we had a little variety as we needed to get some food shopping to top up our supplies and Barry was delighted to find a chocolate bar called 'Roger'. It seemed too good an opportunity to miss so I picked one up for him to give to Roger back on site but Barry wanted to go one better and purchased enough for the whole team to eat a Roger.

As planned we finished a little early today in order that we could go to Barzitsa and see the children. Several of the Krivnya children were staying there while we did the work so it was an opportunity to meet the children who we were working for plus children who some of the team know from previous trips.
I fully expected a game of football to develop but it didn't. This was unheard of. Then one of the boys (Rosin) pointed to a large tree looming over the grounds and there, way up in the lofty branches, was their football. We knew what was required and Andy volunteered to climb the tree and recover the football. We were suitably impressed at the relative ease with which he climbed up but the journey down was little less elegant. However, he eventually made it down and we were all very

grateful to get a game of football underway. Well, actually not all of us were quite so grateful. Barry joined the game a little later and possibly set a record for the quickest injury in a football game: in his first run for the ball he got caught up in his own feet and tumbled to the ground in slow motion. Now normally I would delight in mocking such an event but on this occasion I will resist as it was quite a nasty fall resulting in some facial cuts and a very sore hand; besides we needed him fit for the work back at Krivnya.

Once Barry had been cleaned up a little his injuries didn't look quite so bad but they were much more serious that we could have feared; however, the truth didn't come out until several hours later at the restaurant. To our horror Barry ordered a salad!! Now we knew his knock on the head was extremely serious and we feared the worst. We double checked that he knew what he was ordering and wasn't confused by a Bulgarian menu but he was quite clear he understood it was a salad and he definitely wanted it. We were very worried. However, our concerns were unnecessary as half way through his salad the truth came out, "where's the rabbit?" "What rabbit Barry?" "The rabbit in my rabbit salad" Poor Barry had become confused between Rabbit Salad and Rabbit's Salad. He hadn't, as he thought, ordered a salad with rabbit in it but a salad which a rabbit would eat. Poor Barry !!

FRIDAY 3rd May

Friday dawned and to my relief the builders decided to buy their materials for the day in the local shop before we left for Krivnya giving me hope that I may actually have a shopping free day. While in the shop we asked about a tile cutter, whilst they didn't have the desired electric cutter they had a pretty good manual cutter and so I bought it. It wasn't ideal but it was better than nothing and meant I could make progress.

As the builders were shopping they took the second bus to Krivnya this morning so I parked the bus at the school and decided to walk the short distance to the home. As I was about to leave Ben pointed out a bag which had been left and said, "Alex is going to need that at the home, can you take it?" Sounded like an innocent enough request so I agreed but I soon regretted that decision as I found myself walking through Krivnya carrying a ladies handbag. Try as I might, there was no disguising it and I knew I had to pass the local shop to get to the home. By now I must have made this short walk more than 20 times this week and generally speaking you don't meet anyone so I wasn't too worried but not today.

Maybe the shop had a special offer on cabbage that day, I don't know, but for some reason half the village decided they would be out and about for the three minutes it took me to make the walk of shame with Alex's handbag dangling gaily from my arm. Even the resident goat had a wry grin on his face.
I desperately needed a chance to restore my manly reputation among the locals and hit upon a brilliant idea. I needed the angle grinder which was back at the school so I put my head down to hide my shame and shuffled back through the village. I collected the angle grinder and made sure I held the box with the words 'Ryobi Power Tool' in full view. I marched back through the village armed with the real man tool in order to regain my dignity but where had everyone gone, it was like a ghost town. I slowed down to a snail's pace in the hope that all the people who had seen me with the girly handbag would now see me with the man tool and readjust their opinion of me but all I could see was the goat who mocked me with a look that clearly said, "hard luck mate, everyone will remember you with the handbag".

But better news was waiting for me with the arrival of the electric tile cutter. I was like a kid at Christmas as I tore at the box with an unhealthy level of excitement. Just as I was on the brink of heart failure a horrible realisation descended on me – it wasn't a tile cutter at all, it was a bench saw. In a desperate attempt to salvage something from the disaster I commented that I simply needed to buy a diamond disc to replace the circular saw and I could still use it to cut tiles but my bubble was finally and eternally burst when Barry pointed out that there was no water reservoir and as such it would not be suitable.
I was gutted, the effort I had put in to getting a tile cutter was beyond measure. I had sent photographs of exactly what I required to Mladen and then Galin. I had travelled 4000 miles two weeks previously to ensure everything was available and on site, I had made daily phone calls for the past few days, I had been on numerous shopping trips but the one, single item which still eluded me was the very piece of I kit I required for myself. Fortunately Ant saw my dilemma and volunteered to help me which was a great relief as time was now very short. I admired his fortitude as the toilets presented a very undesirable working environment but he had a bad cold which had fortuitously shut down his nose saving him the burden of testing his gag reflex. We got on well and made a great start to the tiling.

I think I owe a debt of gratitude to Ant beyond his work. His personal germs were so virulent that they overpowered the gruesome bugs of the hideous toilet beating them into defeat before they had chance to infect us both with botulism.

The builders and decorators continued to make good progress too and we were very pleased with the way things were going

That evening some of the team wanted to try a different restaurant so we split up for dinner. Some of you may remember an older report from our New Year 2012 visit when we had an 'interesting' experience at a local restaurant; this was the restaurant chosen.
I was quite amused to hear that some things haven't changed. Ben ordered a traditional English Breakfast but they didn't have any bacon, or sausage, or mushrooms so it turned into egg, chips and beans. In struggling to fulfil another order the waitress suggested an omelette surprise. Then the owner mysteriously drove off in his car returning on a bike with a duffle bag on his back; a few minutes later the meal was served. Very odd. Despite the oddness the food was very good and drew the team back the following night.

SATURDAY 4th May
Saturday was fairly uneventful apart from two acts of incompetence and wouldn't you know it one of them was mine. The curtain rail in one of the bedrooms was hanging off the wall and unlikely to support the weight of the curtains to be hung there so I took it down and re-hung it. It was solid as a rock and would take the weight of even the heaviest curtain now. So I was surprised when Becky came to see me to explain that Alex was having trouble hanging the curtain. It turns out I'd hung it the wrong way round (facing the wall) and it was impossible to get the runners on to the rail. I needed a screwdriver to turn it round but this had been returned to the builders. Becky said she would go and get it so I asked her not to tell the builders why I needed it. She just smiled and gave me a look that let me know she couldn't wait to tell them.
It must have been my lucky day as when she got to the builders they were too busy laughing at Andy to be bothered with my foolish act. Apparently, Andy had started to lay the laminate flooring upside down and was becoming slowly irritated by the difficulties of making it fit until Barry gently pointed out his error. Thanks to Andy I think I may have got away with my curtain rail idiocy.

As I write the closing chapters of this report something has dawned on me. What about Trevor? So far each member of the team has provided at least one moment of foolish behaviour to pad out this report with some gentle mickey taking but I've got nothing on Trevor. To some extent I have been reliant on the building team to provide me with 'tales' of their colleagues as I spent most of my week on the orphanage site so I didn't get to see much of Trevor during the day.

I have made enquiries of the building team, hoping they would spill the beans but they simply said, "Oh, we thought he was in the Orphanage with you?" So where did Trevor spend the week? Did he do any work? "Is he the Scarlet Pimpernel?"

I'm pleased to report that on receipt of everyone's photographs there was clear evidence that Trevor was very busy working with the builders. That reminds me I must look up what it means when the word 'Photoshop' appears at the bottom of a photo.

I'll be keeping a close eye on Trevor next time – not to check he's working (which he did by the way) but to ensure we capture his every error so it can be sympathetically recorded for posterity.

SUNDAY 5th May

Sunday was our last day and we hoped to finish early and get to Barzitsa Orphanage again. It was also Easter day (as Bulgaria follows the Orthodox Calendar) and I reflected on the Easter message of Christ rising from the dead. I couldn't help but draw a parallel with what we had achieved at the Orphanage. New life had been breathed into this home. What better day to finish bringing the Orphanage 'back to life' than Easter day.

We finished off all the outstanding jobs by about 3pm so that those who wanted to could go to Barzitsa. We spent a precious few hours with the children there which was a brilliant finale to a wonderful week. We were able to show some of the Krivnya children the photos we had taken of their home and they were absolutely thrilled. The only sad note (and somewhat selfish) was that we wouldn't get to see the children as they returned to Krivnya but we could imagine their faces as they saw the bright, colourful bedrooms, the clean, sanitary toilets and their brilliant new classrooms.

Ivelina (Krivnya Director), Mladen and some of the other staff were blown away by what we had achieved and delighted with the results – we were delighted too.

Now that's the perfect way to finish this report. There's a few stories to tell from the journey home but I'm going to leave those for now and just savour the satisfying glow which comes from a job well done. No, 'well done' doesn't do it justice, the team were brilliant and we achieved fabulous results. On previous trips we usually reach the midway point with a discussion about what jobs we can drop or scale down in order to meet our deadlines but I knew there was something special about this trip when, from a very early stage, we started adding to the jobs and ended up achieving so much more than we could ever hope or imagine.

My personal thanks to the team who undertook the 'preparation trip' (invaluable), to the team who did all the work recorded in this report, to all the people who donated finance, to everyone who encouraged us and wished us well, to everyone who prayed (wow, the power of prayer!!) but most of all to God who made all of this possible.

Let's do it all again next year

Andrew

CHAPTER ELEVEN
Okehampton College Trip
July 2013

SATURDAY 13th July

How do you fit 1000 cubic metres of toys, games, craft materials, sports kit and Lego into 23 cubic metres of luggage space?
No, it's not a set up for a joke it is the annual dilemma faced by the team of students as they prepare to leave for Bulgaria.
Those who read last year's report will be wondering what all the fuss is about, surely 'Godzilla' will swallow it all up. Sadly, Abby & Neil's enormous suitcase had been retired and replaced by something without 'Pickfords' written on the side. So, armed with crow bars and pots of Vaseline the task of fitting everything in to our luggage began.
Once again we were inundated by generous donations of all sorts of goodies for the children of Barzitsa Orphanage but somehow we had to fit them into our baggage.
Jed, being a rookie, made the mistake of bringing a large bag and so became the focus of attention as anything larger than a pack of cards was rejected by the rest of the team. It started modestly enough with large colouring books rising to board games until eventually Jed's bag even swallowed a scooter. At one point I thought I saw Sandy trying to fit his rucksack in to Jed's bag when he thought he wasn't looking but I may be wrong.

However, we soon reached a stage where the bags were all full and we still had donations to pack so the decision was taken to remove all packaging and empty the contents of boxes in to carrier bags to save room. Somehow, we didn't seem to be making much progress, indeed we seemed to be taking up more room; how could this be? Then we spotted Abby who, blissfully unaware of our 'de-packaging' scheme, was happily packing the empty boxes. With the situation quickly rectified we managed to squeeze everything in. Well, almost everything – for some inexplicable reason Neil felt inspired to buy a 'Limbo' set. His vision of the children laughing and joking as they try to dance under the limbo pole didn't include the bit about how you fit a five foot box into a three foot suitcase. We considered strapping it to his body until we realised that at five foot the box was bigger than him so that plan had to be shelved. It was decided to take it to the airport as it was and see if we could get it onto the plane somehow.

As the madness of the 'Great Pack' subsided there was time for a confession from Adam. Part of the preparation for the trip included putting your name on a T-shirt using an iron on transfer. Adam had somehow managed to iron his name onto the inside of his T-shirt. In a pathetic attempt to excuse this idiotic act he tried to blame his mother but we were having none of it. Adam's mother is a veteran of these Bulgaria trips as his sister has been on three previous occasions and there was no possibility that it could be her fault. However, Adam shamelessly stuck to his story.

Eventually the time came for us to carry our luggage to the waiting bus. I wished I had one of those lovely cases on wheels, Jed wished he had a JCB but we managed to make the short journey and start packing the bus.

Where's Sophie? Neil had just done a head count and discovered that Sophie had not arrived yet.
As it turns out, the answer to the question, "Where's Sophie?" was, in her garden sipping lemonade quietly ignoring the frantic texts and calls from Georgia who was trying to rouse her. After some time Sophie got the message and set off while we patiently waited. We quietly watched a small slug come and go, then a tortoise appeared at the gates and gingerly made its way past us. Impatience was setting in when the three legged squirrel limped past but each of these creatures was more rapid than Sophie. 'Here she is'; at last Sophie made it. While everyone was greeting Sophie Neil whipped out his tape measure to size up her bag but it wasn't nearly big enough for the Limbo set but a bag of Lego was produced and Sophie's dad wrestled it into her case.

So, with everybody accounted for, we climbed on board the bus but someone had stolen all the air; it was so stuffy. It was 33 degrees and the seats were melting so imagine our surprise when we passed a Gritter Lorry on the M5 – only in the UK would you see a Gritter on the hottest day of the year (the hottest day in 6 years I believe). An eager sense of anticipation and excitement was enough to offset the difficult travelling conditions and before we knew it we were at Bristol Airport and standing in the check-in queue – with a five foot limbo pole.

I pretended it was important for me to stand at the back of the queue to keep an eye on our students in an effort to have no part in explaining the Limbo pole to the check-in clerk. To my surprise, after some discussion, Neil persuaded the clerk to allow the Limbo pole to be booked in with our luggage although it was Abby who had to go to the 'Strange Loads' desk to wrap it and put it on the conveyor belt. I don't know if it was necessary to wrap it or if she was just trying to disguise it in an act of embarrassment. I guess baggage handlers see all sorts of weird and wonderful things but a Limbo pole? Nevertheless, I'm sure they treated it with as much care and attention as they afford to all luggage.

We ended up in the check in queue for quite some time as various problems besieged the poor clerk who was a bit more patient than his supervisor who looked as if someone had stolen her sweeties.

Then we played a game of guess who. The clerk had everyone's passport and needed to check them against each individual in the queue. So as names were called we had to step to one side, displaying a wondrous array of nervous grins, and be identified by our passport photo. Now I've seen some of the passport photos and quite how the clerk managed this feat I will never know. Some of the photos were six years old which is fine when you're my age but when you are 17 and your photo portrays you as an 11 year old it presents more of a challenge – particularly when you are trying to do this from 12 yards away.

Next stop was passport control where Katy was looking very disappointed.
"What's the matter Katy?"
"Why didn't they stamp my passport?"
"Because you're still in the UK, d'uh!"

A few hours later we were at the baggage carousel in Bulgaria eagerly looking out for the limbo pole – did it make it? The smile which broke out across Neil's face was a dead giveaway, it was bigger than the pole!! The groaning and straining of the carousel as it slowed to a snail's pace (or, as some may say, Sophie's pace) heralded the arrival of Jed's overstuffed bag and we were ready to take the final part of our journey, the bus ride to the guest house in Provadia.

SUNDAY 14th July

This was the day we had all been waiting for – we were off to the Orphanage to see the children. For some this would be a long awaited reunion, for others it would be the first taste of the joys to come.

One of the joys would be finally getting the Limbo pole into action. But where was it? Oh no, after all the trouble of getting it here someone had left it on the bus which had brought us to Provadia!!! However, all was not lost as it was the same bus which turned up to take us to the Orphanage in Barzitsa; would the pole still be on there? A triumphant Neil announced that it was – phew!

As we pulled up outside the Orphanage some of the children were already at the gate waiting to greet us. It's always a brilliant moment as the children recognise some of the people who have returned from previous years and run to greet them with a big hug or a high five. It always reminds me how important it is to the children that we value them enough to come again and again. It only takes a few moments before the children are embracing the 'first timers' like old friends and more and more of the children appear from all over the home to greet us. I love this bit of the trip.

Regular readers of my reports will not be surprised to learn that after the joy of the welcome the next thing to happen was a football match broke out. The boys love their football and most are very talented. You will also know that there is a direct and inverse relationship between my enthusiasm for the game and my ability to play it on a ratio of about 1:1000. There is a similar relationship between my delusional view of my ability and my actual ability. Deep, deep down I still think I can recapture some of the silky skills of my youth then, bathed in embarrassment at some wayward shot at goal that I try to pass off as a deliberate attempt to hit an imaginary corner flag, I remember that I never did possess such skills in the first place. It's a crushing blow that I subject myself to every time I visit the Orphanage. But not this year. No, this year I packed my secret weapon, not Billy's boots (sorry, you have to be a certain age to get that reference) but a bright red whistle. This year I was going to be a referee. Brilliant, now I could join in all the football without enduring the shame of revealing my ineptitude.

Some time into the game the boys declared 'half time' and so we had a break for a much needed drink. Abby brought a large bottle of water and in an effort to impress us with her football jargon said, "Sorry but there's

no half time lemons". Oh dear Abby, it should be oranges, lemons would not be very popular. We were relieved not to have to suck lemons.
The Barzitsa boys won the game and were very pleased with the standard of refereeing, which I must say was rather splendid. What I didn't realise until later in the week was that praise for the referee was dependant on the result, not on his performance.

At 2 o'clock we stopped for lunch. As always Abby had done a great job of shopping/catering and a lovely spread was before us. She handed Jed a bag of fruit containing a huge water melon and some plums but no one had noticed that the plums had gone soft and when Jed held the bag against his body the plums squashed and leaked leaving him with a large purple stain on the front of his shorts – very fetching.

We hadn't arranged any structured activities for day one as we wanted to spend the time getting to know the children and so the rest of the day passed off with lots of mini games in small groups which developed naturally. Perhaps the highlight was the "Gym-off'; some of the boys showed their gymnastic prowess with leaps, jumps and rolls to impress us all. The pressure was on the students to come up with something to compete with this talent. Cometh the hour, cometh the man and Steve stepped into the breach. Unfortunately, the comedy cartwheel which followed was not so much Beth Tweddle as Beth Tweddle's elderly granddad falling out of his bath chair onto a semi inflated bouncy castle covered in grease.

During the afternoon I started to get a sense that this would be quite a special week. Normally, the older girls simply watch from the side lines and no amount of encouragement can tempt them to join in our activities but there were early signs of interest. Sure enough as the week developed so the girls threw themselves into the activities wholeheartedly which made for a brilliant week in which every child in Barzitsa had great fun all week – fabulous.

Between the Orphanage and our evening trip to the restaurant there is about an hour and a half of time to kill. At the risk of sounding sexist, males and females use this time very differently. The boys chill, the girls queue for the mirror. There are several rooms on each floor of the guest house but apart from the bathroom mirror, there is just one tall mirror on the landing which all the girls have to share. It was my misfortune to share a landing with some of the girls and leaving my room was often akin to running the gauntlet of an obstacle course. It humoured me that sometimes the girls did a good impression of a totem pole with one girl sitting on the floor using the bottom of the mirror another kneeling behind using the middle and another standing using the top. The whirr of hair dryers provided the soundtrack to this comical site as all manner of war paint was being applied to the totem faces.

It's not entirely clear what the boys get up to during this time but it's not a mirror based activity, I don't think they would dare! I think there may have been a parallel between the girls demand for the mirror with the boys demand for the toilet. One story was told about Steve seizing the opportunity of the girls being glued to the mirror to nip into their room and use their toilet. He might have got away with it if the girls had used their make up to bung their noses but a certain 'aroma' gave the game away. Naturally, Steve vehemently denies this but the other boys were adamant.

Whilst on the topic of toilets some of the girls had reported a fault with theirs. Apparently, it would randomly flush in the middle of the night which was a little disconcerting.

As we were all gathering for the restaurant Neil approached the girls and asked, "How's the toilet situation?" Not quite understanding the reason for the question April replied, "Well, Kirsty's had a wee and Rachel has ....." Neil quickly interrupted to save any further embarrassment but not before April could win the 'Idiot of the Day' award for which the prize was to wear a silly hat at the restaurant. Unfortunately, the hat had been left at the Guest House but all was not lost as we fashioned a delightful pair of glasses from a few drinking straws as a substitute award.

MONDAY 15th July

Rocket launching day. Today's activity was to make and launch some rockets. The children were given plastic drinks bottles and asked to decorate them to look like rockets. There were various degrees of resemblance to rockets but the kids had fun making them. However, the best was yet to come; the children looked a little bemused as we led them outside with a large standing bicycle pump and a drum of water. Neil demonstrated how to half fill the rocket with water and pump it up til the pressure was sufficient to throw the rocket high into the air. The kids were thrilled and couldn't wait for their turn. Neil couldn't act quickly enough as the kids bustled him to be next. A few of the boys were

squealing with delight and came to Neil time and time again, there was no end to their enthusiasm. Neil was overrun and falling into a state of delirium when Abby called, "Neil" with a note of panic in her voice, "Be careful" and she pointed towards the rocket he was holding. In order to get the valve of the pump into the rocket he had braced it against a rather sensitive area of his anatomy but he had not seen little Danny frantically working the pump to create the pressure to launch the rocket. Neil moved the rocket in time to save his manhood and Abby looked very relieved. The question still remains – was Abby relieved that her husband was saved from a nasty injury or was she simply relieved that she didn't have to administer first aid.
All joking aside this was a brilliant activity and watching the younger boys having, quite literally, the time of their lives was sheer joy.

The second highlight of the day was the dancing. Our translator/friend Alex is spending her summer as a children's entertainer in a hotel on the Black Sea coast but took the week off to be with us. Using the skills she acquired in her job she led a session of dancing which was great fun. With everyone 'reduced' to the same level all barriers were gone and laughter mixed with music to raise a cacophony of noise that was pleasing to all our ears.

There were quite a few bids for Idiot of the day today, Sophie followed up Neil's 'rocket' mishap; using her newly acquired knowledge of the local dialect she asked, "Is French the main language of Bulgaria?" not surprisingly to the rest of us the answer was, "No, it's Bulgarian!!"

During the afternoon we played baseball. It's the same story every year, the Barzitsa children line up excitedly awaiting their turn with the bat and never seem to tire of whacking the ball all over the playground. Getting out has absolutely no meaning whatsoever as they simply return to the back of the queue and have another go. But the moment we suggest that it's our turn to bat and they must field, they disappear in a trick that would earn them instant admission to the magic circle but this is very useful information which we use to our advantage when the afternoon heat and the endless chasing of a small ball begin to take their toll.
The children of Barzitsa (the boys in particular) are very fine athletes and love to play any sport we throw at them. If there's one thing they love more than playing sport it's winning sport. So often our games turn into a Bulgaria v England competition (regular readers will know that this is a

cause of constant frustration to me, a Welshman, but I learned a long time ago to swallow my pride and become a token Englishman for the week). It must be said that Bulgarian victories seem to crop up more than English ones and the children take great delight in celebrating their victories. Naturally, any Bulgarian defeats are entirely the fault of the referee and I as took that role for the week I was blamed for every loss and branded a rubbish referee. Accusations of bias towards the English led me on another fruitless journey down the dead end street of trying to explain I am Welsh and thus could not be biased – it carried no weight. On the whole it was good humoured banter and any sulking was very short lived as another Bulgarian victory was only ever a few moments away.

So this leads me nicely into a moment of self indulgence where I get the very rare opportunity to share a personal victory. One of the staff was watching my humiliation at the hands of a small boy on the table tennis table and saw an opportunity to add another Bulgarian victory to the growing list; he challenged me to a game. I took the end near the window so that the sun would be in his eyes and give me some sort of advantage. My plan worked and I won the game. His complaints of a rubbish ball and useless bat were all justified but I'll take any victory however cheaply it is won.

Another day at Barzitsa came to an end with new friendships being strengthened by the common bond of joy and laughter.

The great Mirror Battle was on again as girls prepared for our meal at the restaurant. Tonight was going to be a bit special as today was April's 18th birthday. 18th birthdays are special, spending a day with the children of Barzitsa is special so combining the two must be very special indeed. I'm sure that April's memories of her 18th birthday will give her pleasure for her whole life. She had already received lots of fabulous birthday cards made by the children in a craft session earlier in the day.

While the girls were getting ready Steve took the opportunity to put in his bid for idiot of the day. Posing on the balcony in an effort to look like James Dean in his sun glasses, he tossed his head to flick his hair out of his eyes but only managed to launch his sunglasses over the balcony. I don't recall any film starring James Dean where he had to try and retrieve his sunglasses from the canopy of a café. Maybe if he had reached up from the seat of a Honda Fireblade while screaming past at 100mph and wheelied into the sunset with his sunnies firmly attached to face it may have looked cool but unfortunately poking with a long stick just didn't cut it.

We had a lovely meal and sang Happy Birthday to April; I'd like to report that we sounded like a choir of heavenly angels but unfortunately the noise which emanated from our enthusiastic mouths was more reminiscent of the sound that the poor boar must have made which lead to his severed head being mounted on the wall above us.

I can't decide if it was an act of sheer brilliance or stupidity which led Abby to another bid for idiot of the day. As the award had already been made for today this late bid would have to be carried over until tomorrow by which time it's possible we may have forgotten it. Clever? The jury is still out. So what did she do? As part of April's birthday celebration our budget was stretched to buy pudding. The extensive choice laid before us was ice cream or nothing. Abby joined the majority and elected for ice cream. When it arrived she took a mouthful and yelped, "Ooh, that's cold". Who knows what was going through her mind but it wasn't exactly an earth shattering scientific breakthrough to discover that ice cream is indeed cold!

We carried on the birthday celebrations back at the guest house with a few games but common sense prevailed and we didn't stay up too late preferring to keep our energy for the children.

TUESDAY 16th
Oh dear, Abby's plan backfired. Just one short sleep since her 'cold ice cream discovery' and she was at it again. We started the day with a game of hockey. Last year we took a Eurohoc kit to Bulgaria which we leave there and has been used many times since both at Barzitsa and Krivnya. It's great fun and very inclusive meaning everyone gets to have a game. We have six yellow sticks and six red sticks and operate a rolling on/off system so everyone gets a game. Abby rocked up during one of our games and was handed a red stick to which she responded, "Which team am I on?" "Uh, the red one Abby!!"

In the shade of the trees some of our students set up a manicure/pedicure salon which proved to be very popular with the children. It was lovely to see how relaxed this session was as girls patiently waited for their turn and soaked up the one on one attention they received. It was clear that however much they enjoyed having their nails painted this was surpassed by the sheer pleasure of having all this attention lavished upon them. The peace which reigned over this session was palpable.

The fruit of the nail painting session was soon revealed to me in a personal highlight of the week.
I have known Rosanka for many years but she has always been painfully shy. Every time I visit Bulgaria I make an effort to speak to her or to help her join in the fun and games but she always declines. The troubled look in her eyes has always been a concern of mine. I have no idea what her back story is but so many of the children have deeply troubled backgrounds that I have no reason to doubt that something in her past has scarred her. In all my years I have never heard her speak a single word; she will always sit in a corner with her knees under her chin until someone approaches her when she gestures with her hand and disappears.
It was is if the nail painting session had thrown a security blanket over her and all of a sudden she was ready to talk. I don't know which of the students had persuaded her to have her nails painted but what they achieved in this simple act was monumental. Many years ago I attended a mission meeting with my church and first encountered the phrase 'God uses ordinary people to do extraordinary things'. This is a mantra which has been active in my life ever since but perhaps this one occasion was the epitome of all that it means.
The following few hours were just amazing – Rosanka came and sat by me and showed me her nails. I have just enough Bulgarian in my vocabulary to make an appropriate response, "Mnogo Hbovo" (very beautiful) and the most precious smile broke across her face. I was then amazed to discover she can speak a little English so between us we were able to have a chat. She told me about her brother in Italy and her sister who has a baby. She asked after members of my family who she has met over the years. I am aware that Rosanka has learning difficulties as she normally lives in Krivnya Orphanage which is a home for children with such difficulties (Krivnya shuts down during the summer holidays and the children are temporarily housed in Barzitsa) so I wasn't bothered by the fact that we were going round in circles talking about the same thing as if it was new over and over again. These few simple subjects kept us in conversation for several hours. From that moment on I was Rosanka's

new best friend and at least once a day for the rest of the week we sat and chatted about our families.

So often on our trips for every high there is a stark reality check. After years of waiting for this breakthrough with Rosanka I learned that she is 17 which means she is on borrowed time and at some point in the next 12 months she will be ejected from the orphanage and left to fend for herself. It reminded me why we do this work – to stop children like Rosanka from ending up on the scrap heap at the mercy of pimps and criminals.

At this point it's worth pointing out that we have enjoyed some great successes and with the help of our supporters and the work done by the students of Okehampton College we have changed the lives of many children. Not faceless, unknown children but good friends we have known personally for several years. The rewards are amazing and beyond anything you could hope for or imagine but that doesn't stop you from shedding a tear for the ones who get away.

Lunchtime in Barzitsa is always a good time. How Abby puts on such a spread I'll never know but I'm very grateful. I'm considering granting Abby an exemption card for idiot of the day because of her amazing lunches. Now I'm beginning to wonder if someone in the past has given Alex an exemption card; in all the years she has been translating for us she has never 'won' the award. Maybe this is because of the way she singlehandedly takes responsibility for everyone's evening meal. She has painstakingly translated the extensive menu by hand which she produces at lunchtime and then takes orders from everyone which she phones through to the restaurant to ensure that all our meals are prepared and available promptly (it doesn't stop there, at the restaurant she even helps the owner by waitressing for us). Now on this particular day lunchtime conversation naturally turned to the evening menu and some of the 'stranger' delights available. This led to an unusual pact between Jed & Georgia who agreed to choose 'adventurous' meals for each other. With the choices made the pact was reliant on them being honest when it came to their turn to order. Georgia went first and put in her order for chicken livers as decreed by Jed. Jed on the other hand somehow managed to 'forget' the pact in the seconds which passed between the agreement and ordering, a fact which didn't reveal itself until much later.

Jed looked suitably embarrassed at the restaurant when his convenient amnesia was revealed, almost as embarrassed as Georgia was green when her meal was placed before her. It wasn't difficult to read Georgia's face; there was no way she was going to eat that! Fuelled by shame Jed felt obliged to offer Georgia a few morsels from his plate and in return take her chicken livers. I wouldn't like to cast aspersions but I was mightily suspicious of the way Jed devoured Georgia's meal; was the amnesia simply a cover for an elaborate plan to blag two meals? I guess we'll never know.

WEDNESDAY 17th
Today was 'Volcano' day. The morning project was building the volcanoes in preparation for erupting them later in the day. This was very popular as it involved some extremely messy flour and paste glue. The children's imaginations flourished and they created some wonderful volcanoes. Apparently, Neil is alleged to have been very possessive of his volcano and at one point uttered, "keep those kids away from my volcano" but we only have Abby's word for this and she may have been motivated by an overriding desire to ensure someone else got nominated for idiot of the day.
With the volcanoes finished they were put into the sun to dry so that they would be ready for the grand finale later.

The face painting session produced some unusual results but however odd the faces may have looked there was always a huge smile beneath the paint. This is one activity which is popular every year and brings out the 'creativity(?)' in both students and children alike.

I really should have known better but I was so engrossed in watching the skipping games that I let my guard down and before I knew it the kids were dragging me toward the skipping arena. Here two people were spinning a lethal length of rope with a huge killer knot in the middle where two ropes had been tied together. A refrain was being chanted to which children were deftly jumping the rope of death while turning round, touching the ground, raising their arms and all other manner of skilled gymnastics. I had visions of being thrown into the whirling maelstrom and being clubbed to within an inch of my life by the massive knot while children sang a song about a teddy bear who said his prayers. The pressure was really on, girls aged about 7 were dancing in and out of the rope with such ease and abandon that I began to panic and come up with stupid excuses like I had the wrong shoes on or a very rare condition in which I was allergic to being whipped on the back of the head by a rope. It was no good, this was something I was going to have to do. A quick glance around confirmed that Abby, our first aider was within sight, she said she was in training for a half marathon so I calculated she could run to me and administer cardiac massage within 15 seconds. With the risk assessment complete I was prodded towards the rope which seemed to be spinning so much faster now it was my turn. Images of my epitaph raced through my mind, hopes of 'Andrew died rescuing a small child from drowning' or Andrew dies after a lifetime of gallant service to his country' were replaced by 'Fool died skipping'. Argghhh, I was pushed in and jumping for my life. Just for a moment I was in rhythm with the rope and I dared to hope that I might actually be able to do this but as soon as I had this thought I saw the ground rushing towards me and the subsequent thud was all I needed to confirm that I had failed. I foolishly assumed that having achieved my humiliation the children would be satisfied and go back to making this impossible task look so easy. I was wrong, "Do it again" they shrieked. With all my senses deadened by my previous failure I unwittingly agreed to try again. This time I took the precaution of tying my shorts a little tighter in some sort of display which said I only failed last time because my shorts were slipping down. I took a deep breath and dived in, I jumped, I touched the ground, I turned around, I was still jumping. Dizzy with the prospect of success I reached to the sky, I put my hands together for the Teddy Bear's prayer and all the while kept jumping and then in the shock of the century I finished the routine still standing. A group of disappointed children clapped politely as I punched the air, not so much in victory but in relief. Time to retire to a safe distance and bask in my glory.

Meanwhile, Zachary needed to pay a visit to the loo. A simple enough task you might think but no, Zachary managed to turn this mundane procedure into a mini adventure. With his bathroom business complete he discovered he had locked himself in and all his efforts to free himself proved useless. His frustrated banging on the door drew the attention of one of the children, a young man called Plamen. Plamen is quite a big lad and very strong so he immediately leapt into action. Sensing Zachary's panic there was only one course of action available – kick the door down. Given his time again Plamen might have paused to learn the English for 'Stand Back' but this emergency required urgent action and so he kicked the door for all he was worth. Unfortunately the dull thump he heard was the sound of the door hitting Zachary's head as he bent over to look at the lock which was holding him prisoner. The force of the door knocked him backwards and caused him to hit his head on the sink knocking him out for a second.

Where exactly is the line between concern and laughter? At what point is someone's misfortune too serious to be funny? Fortunately, Zachary was OK which we all took as licence to exercise our chuckle muscles. It would have been a real shame if we were denied the gift of laughter by a more serious outcome.

More importantly, we checked that Zachary was sufficiently recovered to be nominated for idiot of the day – he was.

With such a strong pitch for the idiot award Sophie took it as a personal challenge to usurp this pretender to the throne with a couple of weak attempts of her own but they were never going to top Zachary's fine effort.

Firstly, she tried a conversational approach with one of the children. After the child in question had said 'No' four times Sophie was asked why she kept asking the same question her response was, "I don't know if no means no in Bulgarian" Clearly disappointed with this lack lustre approach she tried something a bit more visual. During a game of Dodgeball one of the children was asking for the ball which Sophie was holding so in an act of charity she walked up to the child and kindly gave him the ball (or, some might say, walked into his trap). He gratefully accepted the gift and immediately launched the ball at Sophie who was still stood right next to him thus rendering her out of the game. Sophie's shock and indignation was only surpassed by the lad's sheer delight in having sprung his simple trap. But once again this was not good enough to steal Zachary's crown.

The afternoon brought yet more wonderful moments as the volcanoes were charged and excited children anticipated the eruption. A mixture of water, washing up liquid and baking powder was poured into the volcano chamber then the addition of vinegar was all it took to start the eruption. The kids were thrilled and pushed and jostled for more of the magic ingredients. We could have entertained the children with this for hours but we ran out of ingredients and so this magical moment came to a premature end. A few additions were made to our shopping list so that we would be better prepared for a repeat performance tomorrow.

THURSDAY 18th

A very early bid for the ever popular idiot of the day came from Kaisha who had showered in her sunglasses. When asked why she said "Well I didn't need to wash my hair". Obvious really!!

Chloe had a go too. She had clearly seen Sophie's efforts yesterday and concluded that whilst they were never good enough to beat Zachary's fine effort they might be good enough to see off Kaisha's attempt. So in a repeat of yesterday it was Chloe's turn to fall into the "Please give me the ball" appeal of a doe eyed child during a game of Dodgeball. Once again the trap was sprung and Chloe was out. Once again we all laughed.

Kirsty had a go too. She was just about to lock her suitcase when someone had the presence of mind to ask, "where are the keys to the lock?" "In the suitcase" replied Kirsty!!

Neil had been observing and in his considered opinion none of these efforts was good enough and came up with a plan of his own. As it involved a very inappropriate observation of two of the students and there is the remote possibility that Daryl Chapman (school principal) might be reading this I will spare his blushes and resist the urge to record it here. Whilst it was made in all innocence the remark was none the less not suitable for this report.

But it was Abby who stepped up to the mark with what was possibly the best effort of the week. Little Danny (who is a real treasure and adored by everyone) had a nose bleed so First Aider Abby was called into action. I don't know where she studied her first aid but when I inspected the signature on her certificate I could swear it said 'Crippin' but it was difficult to be sure. So how did Abby treat Danny's bleeding nose? Did she use a cold compress – no. Did she pinch it and lean him forward – no. Did she wrap a large bandage round it – no. Her first move was to reach into her first aid box for some cotton wool to clean away the blood but in reaching for the box only succeeded in punching Danny in the nose. There are many modern branches of medicine which I don't pretend to understand but punching Danny's nose to cure his nosebleed seems way too odd for me.
For anyone who may be concerned at this point, Abby was able to administer a more traditional and successful treatment and Danny was soon running around again, no worse for wear, delighting us all with his engaging smile and enthusiasm for life.

Aside from all these faux pas we managed to fit in a day of activities for the children. We had more volcano ingredients and so set off more eruptions but the main activity was the table tennis competition. Slowly but surely all us Brits got knocked out until three Barzitsa kids were left in a round robin final. Boyan, Rosin & Damien battled it out in a well contested competition until Damien was eventually crowned a very worthy champion.

There were more Bulgarian victories in Hockey & Football although it went to penalties this time but as the lads were keen to point out they would have won in normal time but for the useless referee.
By now we were into a good rhythm and activities were springing up all over the place. Craft, art, modelling, tennis, cricket, dancing, catch, etc the list was endless. The college students were brilliant and ensured that the kids were having fun the whole time responding positively to every request for more and more fun. One of the students accepted a challenge to a game of chess and was soundly beaten in 12 moves by Plamen. The children have a vast variety of abilities and interests but every single one of them was catered for by a fabulous bunch of students – whether it was quietly sitting with Angel and building with Lego or accepting a 'chin up' challenge from the athletic Metin the students covered it all.

It's difficult to interrupt this rhetoric of praise but Thursday also brought us a huge dose of reality. We know that some of the older girls are being groomed and we know some have fallen prey to the scum who traffic them. Yesterday I spotted two pimps talking to a small group of girls while they thought we were 'off duty' at lunch. Today they turned up again in their shiny BMW wearing their bling like a uniform but they got their timing wrong as for some reason the staff changed the kids lunchtime. So they drove slowly and menacingly around the Orphanage leering out of the window. It really does make your skin crawl. The other thing it does is increase your determination to do more to protect these vulnerable kids.
I'm pleased to report that we have had some outstanding success in protecting/rescuing girls from this fate but there is still a LOT to do.

FRIDAY 19th
Our last day with the children. This is always a strange day, the returners know what to expect, the newbies think they know but have a big shock coming. Everyone is trying their best to ignore the fact that in a few short

hours we will have to say goodbye. Extra effort goes in to giving every last shred of energy to make this a very special day for the children. But the grey cloud of leaving is looming and the emotional goodbyes are the shock which awaits our students.

But there's still several hours of fun to be had and we made the most of it. The final Bulgaria v England football match was proposed and I decided to play my trump card. I invited Metin to referee the game. As Metin is one of their best players (and the biggest moaner for every refereeing decision which didn't go his way) I considered it a stroke of genius to remove him from the competition in this way. It also freed me up for the ritual destruction of any ill founded belief I might have that I can actually play the game. At half time England were winning 4-1. This was simply too much for the very competitive Metin to bear and so he gave up refereeing in favour of playing and handed the whistle to Rosin. The second half was a tense affair and Bulgaria made a valiant effort to win the game by adding a further two goals to their tally. Although not refereeing I was still in charge of time keeping and my watch clearly showed that it was full time and with the score at 4-3 to England we should have been victorious but despite pointing this out to Rosin he kept the game going into 'Fergie' time. I remonstrated but his response was to declare 5 minutes of extra time.

Those five minutes seemed like a lifetime in that heat, with our bodies exhausted after a week of intense activity but we held out til the end. The five minutes, which actually lasted seven minutes, at last came to an end and there was no choice but to declare England the winners for the first time in the week. No matter what you may think it is an undeniable fact that England's only victory came when they had a Welsh man on their team – a point I may have mentioned once or twice to anyone who would listen.

The Hockey brought an amusing moment as Georgia bid for the Idiot award. England had just scored and we were walking back to our half for the re-start; Georgia was aimlessly swinging her hockey stick and managed to hit herself in the face with it.

Other bids for the award today:
Sandy – the children found a stray puppy, one of the students said they'd like to take it home. Sandy was worried that a Bulgarian puppy wouldn't understand English

Steve – on being given a bottle of frozen water, "Has this been in the freezer?"

Sandy (again) – chased a child onto the climbing frame and broke it (the climbing frame, not the child)

Neil (to Alex at the restaurant) – don't wait for us, eat before your meal goes cold. She had salad.

After lunch we had a party for the kids which was very well received. Lots of food, dancing and general merriment ensued. The first signal that the end of the day is approaching is the signing of the T shirts. Every child is armed with a felt pen and eagerly goes round signing their name on the student's shirts. Every student wants every child's signature and in the chaos which follows somehow this feat is generally achieved. The signed T shirts become the students' most treasured possession and provides a wonderful souvenir of the best of times.

Then that moment which everyone has been denying finally arrives; our bus pulls up outside and it's time to say goodbye. The tears are flowing and nobody wants to leave. I hate this part of my role, I have to gently push the students towards the bus, the driver has a schedule to keep and another job to get to. No amount of warning can prepare the students for the emotional wrench and they all struggle with having to leave. Strong friendships have been made, the students have begun to understand what life is like for the kids after we leave, some of the older kids might not be there next year and no one wants to think about where they might actually be.

But for all the pain, this moment is key in cementing into their minds the idea of coming again next year. 'Returners' have a very powerful role to play in the lives of the children at Barzitsa. There is nothing quite so valuable and affirming as an old friend coming back to see the children again. The message is simple – "You are special to me, I value you and I want to keep this friendship alive" Not the sort of sentiments that an Orphan hears at any stage of their day to day lives.

So however tough leaving is it is an important part of the bigger picture. We don't just go once and disappear we are there for the long term – going back is one of the most important things we do.

The bus was much quieter than normal on the ride back to Provadia, the quietness punctuated from time to time by soft blubbing. Neil decided to lighten the atmosphere by telling a joke – it was awful but it set off a chain reaction of diabolical jokes each worse than the last. As time passed more and more people chipped in with their worst joke. Mercifully the bus journey is only about 20 minutes and so the torturous joking was brought to an end.

And so another Okehampton College trip drew to a close. As ever it was an outstanding success, the students gave their all to ensure that the children of Barzitsa had a brilliant week to brighten their difficult lives. As usual though, the students, who gave so much, got even more in return. For many this will be a life changing event and they have received an 'education' they would never have got in the classroom. For some this experience will shape their futures and give them a passion for charity work in many different forms. No doubt they will now appreciate the sentiment 'it is better to give than receive'. Hopefully, some of the students will be able to return again next year and carry on where they left off.

I'd like to finish this report with some brilliant news. Some of the students have been so moved by their experience that I have received offers to sponsor two children through college.
This really is a massive deal as it is very rare for a child from an orphanage to get such a golden opportunity. This is something we started last year with three of the children and hope to continue with many more. As I write I'm struggling to put into words how important this opportunity is. It's not just the education (which we see as being vital to our work) but it is also a key to unlocking the poverty cycle and releasing a child into a much, much brighter future.

NOTES
In writing this report I have adopted the journalistic code of 'don't let the truth get in the way of a good story' and it's just possible that I may have exaggerated one or two of the silly stories for comic effect.

My work is driven by my faith and I give thanks to God who makes it all possible.

Andrew Morgan

CHAPTER TWELVE
FUNDRAISER
Men In Tights
Triathlon Nov 2013

All those difficult 6am starts to put in the necessary training had brought me to this moment. It's 7:30am and I'm at Jo's ready to load up the van with kayaks and bikes.

With me is Trevor our 'Support Manager' – it was necessary to give him this grand title in order to trick him into doing this job for us. I mean who in their right mind would want to get up at the crack of dawn to spend the day loading and unloading a van full of kayaks and bikes in the freezing cold. Fortunately, Trevor is not in his right mind and was perfect for the job.

Trevor had received his extensive training in how to inflate the two inflatable kayaks which consisted of, "Here's the kayak, here's the pump, blow it up". The two solid kayaks should prove to be a bit easier. Just in case there are any kayak geeks out there we were using a Sevylor Canyon, a Sevylor Rio and two Feelfree Nomads.

With the kayaks loaded and my bike on board one thing was missing – Rob! Where was he, he was due here at 7:30. I checked my phone and there was a text letting me know that he had problems with his bike and was running 10 minutes late. Trevor and I instantly recognised that this was code for, "I'll be there when I think all the kayaks have been loaded and there's no more work to be done." Sure enough as the last of the loading was complete Rob appeared from around the corner where he had been watching for his cue.

Adam & Neil were making their own way so Rob, Trevor and I set off in the van to Holsworthy where the Triathlon would start. Use of the van was a gift from Gilead Foundations, a good friend of our charity, and we were extremely grateful for their support. We were even more grateful that the van heater worked as it was a particularly cold morning.

Adam had arranged for us to use Holsworthy College as a base for the day and eventually we were all gathered in the car park preparing to start the triathlon. A photo opportunity highlighted something that we hadn't noticed during our car park preparation; as Trevor held up the camera he commented, "You can tell who the professionals are". We looked each other up and down and it became immediately apparent that Adam & Neil looked like Chris Hoy and Bradley Wiggins while Rob and I looked more like Steptoe & Son. Adam & Neil looked resplendent in Hi Vis yellow tops, the tightest of cycling leggings and specialist shoes which clip onto bike pedals. Rob & I looked a little less well prepared in football shorts, trainers and coats. Rob and I consoled ourselves with the fact that Adam and Neil were actually wearing tights and at least we were real men.

And there was another surprise when Adam produced his bike – this wasn't the bike he had trained on with me. When we trained we both had beat up old mountain bikes but today, the day of the event, he produced his trump card and out came a feather light road bike. I looked ruefully at my old mountain bike which was now even more beaten up. At least Rob was stuck with a mountain bike too. Neil however, also had a swish road bike driving the wedge between the haves and have-nots even further. Neil offered us some hope by saying, "You've heard the saying, 'All the gear, no idea'" but sadly it proved to be untrue.

So it was time to get started and we set off in the general direction of Marhamchurch (our first check point) with promises of undying commitment to support each other and stay together as a team. At least, that's what I thought they said but it was hard to hear Adam & Neil as they disappeared into the distance. They mentioned something about a peloton but it made no sense to me.

We made good progress and soon found ourselves at the first check point after 10 miles. Trevor was there waiting for us and we paused for drinks and a various assortment of 'power' foods ranging from Mars Bars to Malt Loaf before getting on our way again.

Rob and I counted our blessings as the men in tights disappeared again, cycling close behind them was not a pretty sight. Honestly boys, get some shorts – please!!

All was well until we reached a fork in the road at Week St Mary and I wondered out loud to Rob if the others had spotted the sign telling them to take the road to the right. Surely they had some fancy GPS built into their helmets or a military grade navigational system secreted away in their manly tights. I volunteered to ride ahead and try to track them down but after a mile of frantic peddling I arrived at the conclusion that they must have taken the wrong road. A quick phone call confirmed this so I rode back to the junction which they missed to point them in the right direction using only the power of my eyes to see the sign pointing right.

The next section proved very challenging as we climbed slowly up a gradual but punishing incline but the reward for our endeavour was great – a long gradual downhill. The village of Trelash was the signal we were looking for as this was the start of the downhill section. For once I was able to hit the front and enjoyed the race down the hill and I didn't gloat at all (well maybe a little) when Adam caught up and said he had been a little nervous on his paper thin tyres of all the gravel and muck in the road. My manly, knobbly tyres took it all in their stride.

But the glory of the downhill section was short lived and once again the professionals set a pace which Rob and I found challenging. Fat tyres are great for grip but hopeless for speed and our moment was over.
Having prepared the course I was well aware that up ahead was an unsigned turning which the professionals would undoubtedly miss. Rob and I had to exercise all the will power we could muster to resist our temptation to leave them to go off in the wrong direction again. I knew that the 'alternative' route would add at least 10 miles to their ride and maybe give us a chance to catch up. But our consciences got the better of us and when we arrived at the junction we phoned them to bring them back. Fortunately this time they weren't too far ahead and had not got very far.

Our next check point was Wainhouse Corner and we were relieved to see Trevor again waiting for us with the van containing our food and drink. As we tucked in to a variety of culinary delights – Jelly Babies, Chocolate Bars, Cakes and the like I couldn't quite believe my eyes when from behind the van Adam strolled into the group with Beef Sandwiches and Hot Cocoa!! I half expected him to put out a table with place mats, cutlery and a candelabra in the middle but he didn't quite go that far.

Suitably nourished we were back on our bikes and Neil commented on the misery of putting on gloves which were cold and damp with sweat. I knew no such discomfort as in my kit bag I had spare gloves which were warm and dry. I revelled in my moment of superior kit, unfortunately it didn't make me pedal any faster.
Any cold induced misery was soon forgotten as we reached the coast road near Crackington Haven. The views over the Atlantic were absolutely stunning. We were blessed with beautiful sunshine and clear uninterrupted views as far as the eye could see. And then came Millook!!! I had tried to warn the team of the steepness of the hills at

Millook but it's difficult to find the words to accurately define what to all intents and purposes is a cliff. It's so steep the downhill sections are as difficult as the uphill ones. Your hands hurt as you grip your brakes for all you are worth to control your speed as you negotiate sharp bends with nothing between you and a very long drop to the rocks below. Just as you think it's safe to let go of the brakes near the foot of the hill there is a hairpin bend waiting to gobble you up if you hit it too fast.

I had decided before the event that I would push my bike up the other side as I was conscious that I still had to kayak and run later on and wanted to preserve my energy and Rob decided to join me. The other two set off and peddled up – very impressive.
The last few miles of the cycle ride took us past Widemouth Bay which is another slow climb which at this stage of the event proved to be very tough but for every uphill there is a downhill and the final mile into the heart of Bude was all downhill. Those who had managed to pedal the Millook Cliff took advantage of a short break while we caught up at the start of the kayak leg.

As we paused before setting off on the kayaks Rob reflected on the fact that his tyres felt a little flat creating extra drag and no matter how hard he pumped them they were always the same. Adam offered a solution by telling Rob all about his specialist high pressure pump which was necessary for maximum inflation and would improve the efficiency of his bike by untold measure. Adam paused for a moment before adding, "I guess I should have told you that before we started". Yes Adam, you should have.

Trevor had got the kayaks out on the canal bank ready for us but he said there had been a problem. I wondered if he had tried to inflate the solid kayaks or used the deflator instead of the inflator. How hard could it be, he had completed his extensive training after all. It turned out that one of the inflatables had a puncture. We spent 20 minutes trying to repair it but nothing was working so we had to resort to plan B. The kayak leg was 2 miles, the halfway point being marked by the first of two locks so a decision was taken for Adam & Rob to do half each. Now before you choke over your cup of tea and start demanding some of your sponsorship money back, the other half had to be walked so these guys ended up doing a quadrathlon and may well be looking to you for additional sponsorship. The other issue here is that the kayak leg was supposed to give us the opportunity to rest our legs a little before the run so it put Adam & Rob at a slight disadvantage.

Time now for a small confession. As we planned this event the rest of the team were well aware of the fact that Rob is a very good runner and we knew that he would shine on this leg and put the rest of us to shame. So without Rob knowing we deliberately made sure he had the slowest kayak (sorry Rob) as it takes up more energy to paddle it than the others and maybe we could use this to slow him down a little on the run.

There was a new excitement on the kayak leg. With the two portages (i.e. getting out of the water to carry the kayaks around locks) there was an increased chance of a 'You've Been Framed Moment' of someone falling into the canal. Disappointingly no one did as we could have earned an additional £250 by getting it on the show although Neil came closest with a bit of a wobble at the second lock.

Kayaking is my strongest leg and I was really enjoying a period of being well within my comfort zone when I stupidly responded to a cry from Neil of 'Sprint finish' and went for it for all I was worth. If Neil was trying to rob me of any running energy he clearly hasn't ever seen me run – it was completely unnecessary.

Once again Trevor was in the right place at the right time and was ready to help us to the van with the kayaks. Here we changed into our running gear and took on more food & drink. Adam disappeared for a while and whilst no proof exists I'm sure he wolfed down some chicken and roast potatoes washed down with red wine.

Time to start the run (and put on another pair of gloves) but despite some decent training I was a little fearful of this leg; this wasn't helped by the long uphill section for the first mile from Helebridge to Marhamchurch. I was encouraged by moans from the others about tight and aching muscles, maybe I could keep up with them after all. Once we reached Marhamchurch we were back on the route which we took on the bikes from Holsworthy and the lead in our legs was starting to shake off.

The team started to stretch out a little as the miles passed by and we all settled into our own strides. I had hoped to run with Adam as I wasn't sure of this section of the route and feared going the wrong way but he simply waved me off with a cheery, "just stay on this road" which was all very well but I clearly remembered taking several turns when we came this way on the bikes.

It was a bit disturbing running past signs pointing left saying 'Holsworthy this way' but I trusted Adam and stayed on the straight road trying to recognise landmarks we had passed earlier. I was very relieved to finally see a sign saying 'Holsworthy 1 mile' and recognised my surroundings. This was a welcome boost for my weary legs which carried me the final mile back to Holsworthy college where we began six and a half hours ago. A moment of smugness overcame me as I crossed the finish line in exactly the time (down to the minute) which I predicted.
I was relieved to hear that the other runners were either already back or accounted for just behind me and before long everyone had finished.

One of the sources of encouragement I drew on during those final few miles was the thought of a hot shower. How grateful I was that Adam had arranged for us to have access to Holsworthy College Showers. This truly was a master stroke and would endear Adam to us for many years to come.
Imagine if the showers turned out to be freezing cold, wouldn't that be funny. Adam might not get his knighthood then. But we didn't have to imagine it because the showers were so cold we were joined by a polar bear and two penguins. The arctic fox ran with his tail between his legs back to the warmer climes of Northern Alaska. I have heard it said that top athletes take an ice bath after a workout as it promotes muscle recovery – are they mad?! I'm happy to wait a week for my muscles to recover if it means I can avoid a freezing shower.

Hang on a minute, it's only now as I write this report that the horrible truth dawns on me. Adam didn't take a shower!! Was it all a huge practical joke on Adam's part, did he know that the rest of us would suffer the indignity of the awful cold shower dance. We can only hope that film of our indignity doesn't turn up on the aforementioned 'You've Been Framed' in an ill thought out scheme by Adam to boost our sponsorship by £250. If he'd only asked us, Rob, Neil & I would have had a whip round and raised the £250 ourselves to avoid the icy water.

A quick trip to the Reydon Inn for a celebratory drink was our final leg before our journey home. In keeping with my Rock 'n' Roll lifestyle I had a cup of tea if for no other reason than to remind myself what hot water was like.

Maybe we had the last laugh when we began to speak of how we might spend our respective day off tomorrow and learned that Adam had to work – in Holsworthy College!! While we are all still tucked up under our duvets supping hot chocolate Adam would be in work. We can only hope he slips in some mud and needs a shower.

All that remains is for me to thank everyone who sponsored us to undertake this ordeal. Although all the money is not in at the time of writing it looks like we will have raised £600.

I hope you had a bit of fun reading this account of our Triathlon adventures but please remember the underlying cause to improve the lives of orphaned and abandoned children in Bulgaria.

Thanks for your support

Andrew

CHAPTER THIRTEEN
No Peeping
May 2014

Saturday 10th May
And so another journey began. This time I started with a drive to Cardiff so that my brother Adrian and I could leave together at 7am the following morning. I was booked in at Mum's in the bedroom I occupied as a boy for a good night's sleep before we set off on our journey. It seemed like an easy enough plan but I hadn't accounted for the Chinese water torture mum had lovingly prepared for me.

In the dead of night it began - drip, drip, drip. It was relentless and oh so loud. The timing was perfectly set up to wake me every time I drifted off to sleep. Why was it so loud? The morning, which had seemed so far away for much of the night, eventually crawled into view and so I got up and tackled mum on the cause of the sanity eroding dripping. "oh yes" she said, "That's the water dripping off next door's roof onto my dustbin." A dustbin! Mum had created a drum kit with devastating effect. However, just as I was about to yell, "Why don't you move the bin!!" it dawned on me that she could return the yell with "why didn't you change bedrooms?" She would have had a point and for some reason (sleep deprivation I expect) I simply didn't think of that in the middle of the night.

Sunday 11th May
At 7:00am on the dot Adrian arrived and in a humble act of contrition mum produced a 'packed lunch'. I looked out of the window for the platoon of soldiers which was clearly coming with us if the amount of food was anything to go by but they were nowhere to be seen. We were only driving for three and a bit hours to the airport so delicately set aside some of the food in order to make space for our modest luggage.

Mum had kindly asked us what we would like in our sandwiches, I suggested ham and Adrian cheese but who knew how this would cause such pain for one of us. On route to the airport we were making good time and decided to stop for a snack and broke out the sandwiches. There before us was all the evidence we needed that I am the favourite child—2 cheese sandwiches and 6 ham sandwiches. Adrian was gutted and refused to be pacified by mum's pathetic texts explaining that some of the ham sandwiches were for him too. By now Adrian's cheese sandwiches were soggy as his tears fell like a waterfall in the harsh realisation that he isn't loved as much as me. My ham sandwiches were lovely.

The banter arising from this kept us going on the remainder of the journey to the airport. As we neared the airport Adrian asked me for the post code of the car park for his SatNav so we could complete the final leg of the journey and arrive safely at our destination. I looked at the paperwork I had printed off and found the post code which was somewhere in Bristol. This was my first clue that something was not right; we were flying from Luton. It turns out that I had printed off the wrong booking form (the June Bulgaria trip is from Bristol Airport—not this one).

It wasn't too much of a problem and we soon arrived at the correct car park from where we were shuttled to the airport. We were travelling Wizz Air which is an Hungarian budget airline so we weren't expecting luxury but what we hadn't realised was that the aeroplane had been designed by Snow White for the seven little men in her life. Whilst Sneezy, Doc and Dopey might have travelled in the lap of luxury, Grumpy Adrian and Grumpy me did not. We would have complained but it's hard to breathe when your knees are in your nostrils.

Well we made it to Varna in one piece and were pleased to be met by warm weather. A trip to the toilet was in order where I managed to humiliate myself at the hand drier. I was pushing my hand back and forth under the drier to no avail amidst a torrent of tired moaning, "it's not working!" Turns out it was a paper towel dispenser. I think Adrian's amusement was very much out of proportion with my tiny error

A quick phone call and our minibus was delivered so we could drive to Provadia where we would find the guest house and settle down for some sleep; unless the guest house owner had left his dustbins under next door's leaky roof. Fortunately he hadn't - instead he had put them under the mattresses which were just a little past their 'best before date' and rather bumpy.

Monday 12th May
The following day we met up with Dobs our translator and made the short trip to the orphanage in Krivnya. We chatted with Ivelina (Director) for a

little while before Mladen joined us. Together we went to view the building which the builders would be renovating in a few weeks time.

Adrian and I took all the measurements we needed and took photographs ready to send to the builders back in the UK. Things were going well until we spied the electrics, Adrian and I exchanged worried glances before I asked Mladen if they were safe. He simply replied, "You have insurance don't you?" and then burst out laughing, we nervously laughed along with him. In case any of the builders families are reading this I have arranged for the electrics to be repaired before we start work there.

While we were there some workmen were attending to the roof repairs. What an eye opener that was as to how far we have moved in the UK under the pressure of health and safety legislation. The workmen simply climbed a very shaky looking wooden ladder onto the roof and walked around the roof without hardhats, hi-vis jackets, scaffolding, harnesses or any of the other paraphernalia associated with modern Britain. Then they removed the faulty tiles and threw them off the roof where they smashed onto the floor at the feet of a man protected only by a brush to sweep up the pieces.

Armed with all our measurements and photo's we made our way back to Provadia where we sat down to convert all the numbers into plans and drawings of the buildings. There are two rooms, one will be a Sensory Room while the other will be a Soft Play Room. We had previously sent sufficient money for the windows to be replaced and it was pleasing to see this had been done although there is a lot of making good required which will involve rendering/plastering the walls around the new windows.

The plan was to email all the drawings, measurements and photos to the builders back in the UK so that they could study them and draw up a list of materials required. As everything had gone so well we managed to complete this task well ahead of time and we had the 'shopping list' in our hands by the end of the afternoon. We celebrated by paying our customary visit to the Happy Restaurant on the beach in Varna. Towards the end of our meal I commented to Adrian that I thought I heard thunder but he corrected me pointing out it was probably someone moving chairs.

After a cracking meal we paid a visit to the toilet where we saw a sign neither of us had ever seen before and called into question the quality of the clientele at the Happy Restaurant. Make of it what you will !!!

As we exited the toilet (having resisted the temptation to look over the adjoining stall) the heavens opened and a monsoon fell out of the sky. Moving furniture indeed, a Michael Fish moment from Adrian there!!! We weren't exactly dressed for the weather as neither of us had any scuba kit so we sat back down in the restaurant and ordered some drinks which we had to make last long enough to keep us indoors until the storm passed. We watched with some amusement as the staff started to run around moving seats and tables as the rain found all the holes in the roof and poured in. We had to move too as the rain grew ever harder and we were getting splashed. I can only hope that the Happy Restaurant was not the previous job of the men fixing the roof in Krivnya. The deluge eventually abated and we were able to get back to the minibus just before the cloud wrung out the last of its moisture.

Tuesday 13th May
This day had to come; it was shopping day. At least we were shopping for building materials so it wasn't as bad as it could have been. We toured the builders' merchants under Mladen's direction looking for the right materials at the right prices. This is where Mladen is worth his weight in gold, firstly a native Bulgarian gets a much different price from a 'wealthy' Brit but secondly because we would have had no hope whatsoever of finding the places he took us to. No bright orange B&Q signs here but alley ways and hidden yards in the most unsuspecting of places. At one point we drove over a bridge, then under the same bridge, turned off the

road onto a stony path past a derelict building, through a wood and into a clearing. I had visions of some Mafia Thriller playing out before us as we drove through a gate hanging off it's hinges into an open yard but I needn't have feared as piles of timber and sand appeared before our eyes and we were in another builders' yard.

One thing on the list was 4 sheets of plywood. Well the builders might just have well have asked for 4 unicorn horns. Several times I found myself trying to explain what plywood is to a timber merchant. I began to think it was one of those childish builders' pranks like telling me to ask for 'a long weight' or 'striped paint' or 'rubber nails'........ you know the sort of thing. But Provadia has never heard of plywood so a trip to Varna was necessary. 45 minutes later we were touring Varna until we found the only 4 sheets of plywood in Eastern Europe. They were literally the only 4 left in the store, probably the only 4 left in the world from what we could tell.
If I ever get asked for plywood again by the builders I think I'll buy it in Homebase and take it to Bulgaria on my bicycle as I'm sure it would be easier. Builders, if you're reading this you had better use the plywood or I might just find a use for it making coffins!!

While in Varna we went to the huge Praktiker store to purchase, amongst other things, an electric tile cutter (here I would refer you to last year's report entitled 'My Kingdom For A Tilecutter'. If you haven't read it please ask for a copy to understand the significance of this purchase). We also got a chop saw and laser level. We paid at the till and were given a receipt which we were told to take to the desk for our guarantee. Mladen had popped out for a cigarette and I needed Dobs to help me at the desk. This left Adrian to struggle through the car park to the minibus with all the purchases. Dobs and I waited patiently at the desk for our turn and dutifully handed over the receipt. The assistant said something to Dobs and I waited for the translation. Dobs hesitated and said, "she needs the tools". With perfect timing Adrian appeared looking pleased with himself for having accomplished his task only to be told he needed to go back and get everything. It didn't go down well.

I just wish to take a moment here to mention a brilliant idea that the folk in Praktiker have come up with (in the vain hope that maybe some of our DIY stores might do the same). After you've gone through the till you are encouraged to take your purchase to another desk (maybe if this was also the guarantee desk this brilliant idea could be a perfect one), plug in your new toy and test it before leaving the store. Simple but brilliant especially for us with a 70 mile round trip to make our purchases.

On the way back to Provadia I was clearly basking in the glory of having found the holy grail (plywood to you) as I was obviously not concentrating on the road. Mladen suddenly shouted, "Turn here" and pointed at the sign indicating the turn off for Provadia.
In response, Mr Condescending here launched an exhausting speech about how I always use the second turning for Provadia. I have used the first turning before and the road is awful, narrow, full of potholes and too slow. The second turning while being further is in fact quicker because it's a better road. So it's right that I should ignore the first turning. Mladen paused for a respectful moment before gently uttering, "that was the second turning". I'm only glad that the next junction wasn't too far away and I could return to the correct road and reduce my suffering at the hands of the mockers in the minibus. Mladen had the final word as we turned at the next junction, having lived in the area for 40 years he simply said, "I've never been on this road before". No Mladen, you've never had me navigating before.

Time for lunch. We know of a shop which sells huge pieces of pizza for 1 lev (that's less than 50p). Also all sorts of other meat/pastry concoctions of epic proportions for the same price. We both had lots of small change which we wanted to use so gathered all the coins together, made up 2 lev and headed for the shop. We handed over the coins and ate the feast which we got in return. The woman behind the counter appeared a little miserable but we thought nothing of it.

We had decided to spend some time playing with the children at Krivnya that afternoon so headed to a shop to buy a few bits. I was doing quite well with my limited Bulgarian and managed to get a football and a small ball but I ran out of vocabulary when it came to a skipping rope so I did the only thing I could and 'mimed' skipping in the middle of the shop like some demented, drunken kangaroo at a charades party. Adrian seemed to find this very amusing but if it had been a charades competition I think I would have won as the woman guessed very quickly and produced a skipping rope from behind the till. Of course it's always possible that she was simply reaching for a rope with which to restrain me and got lucky.

We spent the afternoon with the children playing a variety of games including hockey using the set which we leave in Bulgaria for this very purpose. We had a great time.

That evening we headed back to Varna to meet Didi of the Hope & Future Foundation to make another donation to keep the boys in college. Boyan is still doing very well and has his sights set on University. Kiril is also doing very well but is unlikely to go on to University. We had hoped to see Metin but this didn't happen. We were pleased to learn that he is in a safe house and still makes the occasional appearance in college although there is little hope of him finishing the year. Please continue to pray for Metin who is still at risk of falling into the life of crime which awaits so many of the boys from state care.

Although we are saddened by Metin's situation we can rejoice that two other boys have taken an opportunity which very, very few children from orphanages ever get and are really making the most of it. We are delighted to have been able to make it happen thanks to the generosity of our supporters.

Wednesday 14th May

By now we were ahead of schedule and so decided to go to Varna again to buy laminate flooring. Although this wasn't on our list we knew that it would be needed at some point during the builders' trip so thought we would get ahead of the game. It was on this journey to Varna that we were once again reminded how much Health & Safety has affected the UK.

Imagine, if you will, your local dual carriageway or motorway. You're driving along and you see that dreaded sign. "Roadworks 3 miles". This is followed by further signs counting down the distance, 2 miles, 1 mile, 800 yards etc. Then cones carefully shepherd two lanes into one. You drive past miles of cones protecting an empty lane with no sign of life until eventually, there he is, the man cutting the grass in the central reservation. You know that this is the half way point of the cones and in just a few more miles of inactivity you will be through the road works.

In Bulgaria the only warning we had of the 'strimmer gang' in the middle of the road was a boy stood in the outside lane waving a red hankie on a stick. We laughed but as it turned out this was more protection than the other gangs received (and there were quite a few) who had to manage without a boy and his hankie (unless of course their boy was in the back of an ambulance somewhere). The Bulgarians like their sticks as later we saw one being employed as an extension handle for a chain saw to reach the top of a tall tree. Our Health & Safety executives would go apoplectic if they saw what we saw that day.

We made it to the Praktiker store in Varna without killing any handkerchiefs or breaking any sticks and made our way to the laminate flooring section which was vast. We did some typical 'man shopping' and after a token, cursory glance at a few options alighted on the one nearest us. We worked out we needed 15 packs plus all the extras required to complete the job. We loaded it all on to two trolleys and I racked my brains to make sure I had thought of everything. I asked the helpful assistant if it was click fitting or if we needed glue. I was surprised to hear a snort of derision from behind me as an embarrassed Adrian said, "The clue is in the name". I looked down at the packages we had loaded onto the trolleys and all 15 of them were branded in large letters 'Super Clic'. The helpful assistant, with the patience of a saint, said, "click" and did a little mime just to make sure the stupid Brit understood.

Back to Provadia and it was lunchtime. Unable to resist another huge feast for 50p we pooled all our small change and headed to the Pizza place again. Having made our selection we handed over our coinage only to incur the wrath of the woman behind the till. Believe me we didn't need a translator to understand what was going on here. She started ranting and raving to her colleagues along the lines of, "These stupid men did this to me yesterday. They think they can just come in here and get rid of all their useless stotinkis (pennies). Stupid ignorant pigs" The rant went on quite a bit longer than this but I have chosen to leave out the swear words.

We considered the possibility of returning with a 50 lev note but feared we might get 4800 stotinkis in our change. I checked with Dobs later and sure enough no shop keeper wants small change as it is useless in Bulgaria; we honestly didn't know that but we couldn't help noting that all the small change had been given to us by shopkeepers in the first place (obviously trying to get rid of it).

Whilst eating our meal we became aware of a man outside selling knives, big knives right there on the street outside the cafe. We ran through the potential scenario of having to run the gauntlet of a possible encounter with the salesman. How do you say, "no thank you", to a man waving a 6 inch blade in your face. Oh, I know the words in Bulgarian but I don't know the Bulgarian for "you buy them or I slit your throat". Fortunately, the weather came to our rescue and we had another freak storm which turned the roads into rivers in an instant and washed the knife peddler away. We seized the moment and made a break for it. A minor soaking was a small price to pay for keeping our ears.

Off to the local shop for supplies and Adrian stopped at a section of the fridge which had captured his attention on more than one occasion. There, right between the yoghurts and the meats were various sizes of bottles containing a brown liquid. Adrian had wondered on several occasions if this was chocolate milk shake and asked me if I knew. I didn't and couldn't translate the label which said 'Boza' so wasn't sure, because of its position in the fridge, if it was a milk drink or gravy but I could tell Adrian that the small bottle was less than 25p and so worth a punt. Adrian concurred and bought a bottle. At the till, for some inexplicable reason, Adrian started singing to himself from the soundtrack of Grease, The Musical, "You're the one that I want, ooh, ooh ooh" This was just as the girl on the till was scanning the Boza and she began to laugh. Now, was she laughing at Adrian serenading her or at the fact that he was buying Boza. I think the answer lies in what we found out later when we 'googled' Boza. I quote directly from the internet, "Increasingly popular across Europe and the world for its proved qualities for augmenting women's breasts." We'll never know how it tasted as it was promptly tossed into the nearest bin. At least I now know what to buy Adrian for his birthday, a bra !!

Back to the orphanage to offload the laminate flooring but there was a problem. The caretaker was not around and Mladen didn't have a clue which key opened the door. He studied his bunch and concluded that he definitely didn't have the key and couldn't open the door. But at that one of the boys took the keys off him and made for the door. Mladen looked at us and said, "No chance" just as the lad picked one key from the bunch of 30 placed it in the lock and opened the door. For once it was a Bulgarian who was left red faced to redress the balance just a little. By the end of the week we had nicknamed the lad 'Mr Keys' as he proved his intimate knowledge of the bunch time and time again much to Mladen's embarrassment.

That evening we decided on a return to Fawlty Towers, the restaurant which starred in a previous report entitled 'Fawlty Towers is alive and well' (again, please ask for a copy if you haven't read it). We were concerned that it wouldn't live up to our expectations but we were not disappointed. I ordered pork with a mushroom sauce which prompted a peculiar twitch in the owner as he glanced over the road outside the restaurant. We soon discovered that he was looking to see if the shop was open so that he could buy the ingredients for my meal. It was, so he put on his jacket and went to the shop while we waited. When he returned I went to ask him if we could order drinks but I only got as far as saying, "excuse me" before he pointed towards the drinks cabinet. "Wow, that's impressive" I thought as I helped myself to a coke and a Fanta from the fridge. Turns out he had guessed my request incorrectly and was pointing me towards the toilet.

When it came to ordering pudding Adrian asked for a Banana Split. The owner let out an audible groan as he glanced down at his watch and then looked at the shop only to confirm his fear that the shop was closed. There was a forlorn look in his eyes and a resignation in his voice as he said, "Yes OK". This time in addition to his jacket he got his bicycle clips, jumped on his bike and disappeared down the road. We had no idea if he was giving up and going home or cycling around Provadia looking for a shop which might sell him a banana. Ten minutes later he returned with a shopping bag and disappeared into the kitchen. What came out of the kitchen was the saddest looking banana split ever seen. One banana cut down the middle with a token amount of squirty cream garnished with two small grapes. The amusement value alone was worth the price. It's only fair that I should say that the quality of the meal which preceded it was second to none, it was amazing.

Thursday 15th May
Today we set off for Kranevo where we met up with a few Brits who have homes there. The connection had been made through a friend in my Church in Okehampton and led all the way to Kranevo on the Black Sea coast.

We chatted for ages about the work we were doing and we received so many offers of help. By the time we had finished we had two new team members for our trip in June. Margi & Lynne want to come along and run activities for the children in the afternoons when they finish school. They've got lots of ideas and are very enthusiastic.

John runs a business transporting goods & people between the UK and Bulgaria and has offered to help us get vital materials from Okehampton to Krivnya.

Nigel has a van in Bulgaria and offered to help us purchase and transport materials from Varna to Krivnya.

A very productive morning, hopefully some lasting relationships have been born.

In the afternoon we were due to see the children in Barzitsa but we knew we couldn't go empty handed so it was back to the shop for more sports kit. Once again purchasing a football was easy but we also wanted a table tennis set. After the embarrassing 'skipping' episode I told Adrian it was his turn to play charades and do the appropriate mime. I could tell he was uncomfortable with the idea and while I was arranging for the ball to be pumped up Adrian scoured the shop for a table tennis set, he was determined to find one and avoid the mime. It was like an Aladdin's cave in there and he hunted in every nook and cranny but all to no avail. Eventually the moment of truth dawned and the mime was successfully delivered. The success made Adrian think his performance was something akin to Burt Reynolds but to be honest it was more like Burt of Burt and Ernie fame from Sesame Street.

And so off we went to Barzitsa. Table tennis was first and we opened the table tennis sets we had purchased surrounded by excited, expectant children. I don't know exactly what they were expecting but they managed to disguise their disappointment much better than Adrian and I did. The rubber on the bats was thinner than a layer of butter on a jam sandwich and the wood was about as robust as the bread. In fact, thinking about it maybe that's what we bought, an inverted jam sandwich. Two layers of jam with a piece of bread in the middle. But that didn't explain the balls. If we thought the bats were bad then we hadn't seen anything yet. To continue the food analogy the balls might just as well have been hollow marshmallows for all the bounce they had in them. We tried to get a game going but trying to hit a marshmallow with a piece of bread was never going to be a success. We were so glad we decided to invest in two sets!!! I couldn't help noticing that the quality of the equipment was on a par with the quality of the mime which went before; so maybe it was Adrian's fault.

But cometh the hour, cometh the man and on this occasion the man was Damien. One of the boys decided that enough was enough and went off to get his own personal table tennis set which was a vast improvement and meant we could at last have a decent game. As it happens the younger children managed to play for ages with the food set and seemed untroubled by the lack of quality (or indeed the lack of table as their game seemed to know no boundaries).

Last time I played Table Tennis in Barzitsa it was on my visit with the students from Okehampton College in July last year. There was a huge tournament that took up a whole day and included most of the Barzitsa kids and Okehampton students. The overall winner of that competition was Damien so although we were delighted to see his bats and ball we weren't quite so pleased that it meant playing against him.

But you know what men are like where sport is involved, that competitive spirit kicks in and it's win at all costs. There's no mercy even in a Bulgarian Orphanage. Adrian and I knew that the reputation of the entire Welsh nation was at stake here and nothing but a victory was good enough. We both managed to sneak a very marginal victory and chose to ignore the very obvious fact that Damien was quite clearly taking it easy on us. We didn't care, we'll take any victory even if it is gifted to us on a plate by a young man who was simply taking pity on these two old men with delusions of youth and skill. I've seen Damien play and I know he could beat us both with his hands tied behind his back, blindfolded, standing on hot coals in bare feet and carrying a fridge on his back but hey, we're shallow and are happy with our hollow victory.

Football next so out into the yard we went. Fortunately the football we had bought was OK, we had feared we might have bought a melon but at least we had got this right. We had a good game and it was mercifully cooler than some of the games I've had there.

After the football I was able to chat with some of the children and was delighted to learn of a few adoptions. Adoptions are very, very rare and because of the language barrier it's possible that there may have been some confusion between adoption and fostering but nevertheless one boy had gone to live with a family in Provadia and another was awaiting a decision from a different family also in Provadia. This is such good news and completely changes the future which lies ahead of them from one of darkness to one of light. I thank God for this wonderful news.

Before I left I had chance to chat with Mrs Zlateva (Director) which was a much warmer experience than I'm used to. She's a lovely lady but running the orphanage is such difficult and stressful work it's not often she has chance to simply chat. But today she particularly wanted to see me about something and was very generous in her praise for the work we have done with the children in Barzitsa. I was able to share with her how so many people in the UK are involved in making these things happen and that above all it is God who is in control. So, to you folk who support this charity with so much with time, effort, finance and prayer be assured that it is appreciated, Mrs Zlateva was keen that you should know this.

As we left Barzitsa one of the boys came and asked us, "please bring better bats next time."

That evening our first choice restaurant had some sort of function on so we decided on a return to Fawlty Towers. We were a little concerned that Basil may have peaked last night and the visit would be an anti climax but he didn't let us down. He received our order with his customary glance towards the shop over the road and seeing it was closed seemed unsure what to do. After a bit of dithering and murmuring to himself he accepted our order. As he donned his jacket and bicycle clips and made his way to the door he looked over and told us to help ourselves to drinks from the fridge. He was gone quite a while but eventually he returned with his shopping bag and presented the contents to the chef. Once again the meal was fabulous. After we had eaten the main course our attention turned to pudding. Adrian didn't have the heart to order Banana Split again and send Basil on another shopping expedition so settled for the Sundae. We gestured that we were ready to order and with a triumphant air Basil said, "Would you like a Banana Split?" He looked devastated when Adrian said, "No, please may I have a Sundae?" Clearly when he went out earlier he had bought a banana in anticipation of this moment, his face was a picture as he realised the banana was redundant.
I'm not sure if was an act of revenge or resourcefulness but both our puddings contained chopped banana.

Friday 16th May
Last day today so we went back to Krivnya to make all the final arrangements with Ivelina and Mladen. I had a list of questions for both of them. I ran through everything with Ivelina and asked if I could speak with Mladen. "No" came the reply, "He's broken his leg"

It turns out Mladen broke his leg yesterday while playing with the children and has been signed off work for four weeks. After our initial concerns I was grateful that we had completed all our shopping before his accident as I couldn't have managed without him. Whether I can find the builders' yards again remains to be seen and will no doubt be the subject of the next report after the builders have been.

It was time to go back to the guest house to pack our bags ready for the journey home. I popped into the bathroom to collect my toothbrush and returned to the room to find Adrian with one of the pictures from the wall in his hands, "What are you doing?" I asked. "I was trying to straighten it and it just came apart in my hands" he replied. After much fiddling and exasperated noises a frustrated Adrian finally announced, "I've done it, now to hang it back up" as he placed it on the wall it paused for a second before settling back into the same wonky position it had occupied before Adrian felt the urge to adjust it.
This was definitely the time to leave and so began our journey home. Another flight that even a sardine would have rejected as being too cramped followed by a drive to Cardiff and ultimately a drive back to Okehampton.

All in all it was a very successful trip. We got everything done plus some extras. Everything is ready for the builders to convert a redundant building into a fabulous sensory room and a soft play room. The kids are going to love it and it will be such a fantastic improvement to their day to day lives.

Thanks once again to everyone who supports our work, we couldn't do it without you. I am really looking forward to writing my next report which will be full of exciting news about a new sensory room, a new soft play room and lots of very happy children.

Andrew

CHAPTER FOURTEEN
A Meeting With The Flies
May 2014

Following last year's calamity ridden journey to Krivnya nothing could possibly go wrong this time could it?

Well the car started, that was a promising sign. I made my way to Ben's, loaded him and his luggage into the car and headed to Folly Gate to pick up Bob. I parked outside and waited a few minutes as I was sure that their drive wasn't regularly populated by cars at 1:40am on a Friday morning and so my arrival would have been spotted. It wasn't so I went to knock the door where I was met by Eirlys who was making a cup of tea for Bob who was still trying to drag himself out of bed. When Bob mentioned later that he had been naked when I arrived I thanked my lucky stars that Eirlys had come to the door not Bob as we didn't have a team counsellor.

With Bob (now clothed, thank goodness) and his luggage safely on board it was off to Brightly to collect Andy. Once again I made the foolish assumption that the arrival of a car outside their quiet, remote bungalow would trigger Andy's appearance at the door but it didn't. Blissfully unaware of the panic being played out indoors I phoned Andy's mobile to let him know we were outside waiting in the cool, calm summer night. Cool and calm weren't exactly two words which could be applied to Andy who, moments before, had discovered his alarm had failed and he had about 37 seconds to get up, washed, dressed and fed. The few additional moments we had to wait were well worth it just for the sight of Andy hopping around his kitchen trying to put on a shoe with one hand while drinking a cup of tea with the other and grabbing his bags with his teeth. It would have been polite to offer him some assistance, which I did eventually but not until I had enjoyed this spectacle for a minute or two. Andy made it to the car and just as we were about to pull off Trudy appeared with his wash bag which he had forgotten to pick up.

Only William to go, would he be ready? He was which was a relief at the time but slightly disappointing when it comes to writing this account of our adventure.

We were grateful for a clear run all the way to Bristol, a simple check in at the car park and a successful transfer to the Airport. All eyes turned to the check in board but this wasn't working so we decided to look for the rest of our team who had travelled in a different car but it was quite dark in the airport and it was crowded so we couldn't see them. Slowly we began to put the pieces of the puzzle together; no departures board, no lights, big crowds - something was clearly wrong. There was a power cut. Luckily we had arrived in plenty of time to allow for a minor inconvenience such as this.

However, a minor inconvenience it was not. The hours ticked by painfully slowly and nothing changed. The endless passages of time were occasionally punctuated by the helpful announcement, "We apologise for the delay which is due to an electrical problem, we hope to have it fixed shortly". Unfortunately, the word 'shortly' was not being used in the context of an electrical failure but more in the context of eternity.

To while away the hours the team played a game of 'who's fault is this?' They looked back over previous travelling problems and discovered that there were two common factors to all of them; me and Andy. We were the only two who had been on all of the difficult journeys including a 24 hour delay thanks to the infamous Icelandic Ash cloud a few years ago. In an effort to deflect attention from me I pointed out that I had been on several trips where everything went smoothly but Andy had only ever been on troubled trips and quickly deduced that it was clearly his fault.

With that game over we needed something new to amuse us so up stepped Adam. Adam is a magician and came prepared with all manner of astounding card tricks. Every now and then a small crowd would gather and Adam would entertain them with his magic. At one point the TV cameras arrived (as by now the problem at Bristol airport was big enough to make the news) which was like a magnet to Adam. He was very quick to grab the cameraman to film an impromptu magic show with a brief advert for the charity.

But the most magical moment of all came when the Airport decided we had suffered enough and they needed to offer us some complimentary sustenance to make our ordeal more bearable. The stakes were high following EasyJet's offering last year when, after 3 hours stuck on the tarmac due to a technical failure with the plane we were given, free, gratis and for nothing the most amazing token of their deep regret - a Twix. Bristol Airport would have to pull something very special out of the bag to top that one. I don't know how high up the board of directors they had to go to get the necessary permission but they came up with - a bottle of water. A bottle each that is, we didn't even have to share.

By now people were becoming a bit frustrated and at the thirteenth playing of the recorded message "blah, blah, blah ... fixed shortly" everyone began to search frantically through their luggage until someone found a Duracell AA. Raised high on everyone's shoulders the hero with the battery was passed to the chief engineer who accepted the copper cell with joyous appreciation and placed it into the central workings of the Airport. There was just enough power to run three check in desks but enough excitement to power Birmingham.

More joy followed as when we reached the check in desk we were given a £5 voucher to be used anywhere in the airport. We are seasoned travellers and our expectations of what £5 might buy in an airport were realistic or so we thought. We discussed pooling all our vouchers and buying a packet of Polos to share around but time was running short as having kept us waiting for three hours we were now being urged to hurry to our departure gate. So we pooled our vouchers as planned and a few of the team went off in different directions to buy whatever food might be available while the rest of us gathered our belongings and got ready to make our way to the departure gate.

But with depressing regularity each of the voucher bearers came back with the same news. The shops will not accept the vouchers. It turns out the vouchers were about as valuable as a Zimbabwean dollar. We'd have had better luck trying to pay with a sheet of toilet paper - a used sheet!!!!

We now faced a tough choice, our energy reserves were virtually zero, did we used what little we had left to shout angrily as some spotty oik from Thomas Cook or to hurry to the departure gate. The decision was tougher than you might think as the level of anger was already at fever pitch and we were primed and ready to go after the spotty oik but in a rare moment of lucidity in our starved and angry state we realised that our resources were best applied to reaching the gate.

We followed the crowds all rushing towards the golden gate which would at last send us to our destination and with a sense of eager anticipation we joined the queue of excited travellers……. Wait a minute, a queue? Why was there a queue? Can you believe it, the plane wasn't ready!! Seriously, after three hours of delays and being kept in the dark (literally) the plane wasn't ready. It got worse, when we eventually boarded the plane the captain came on the PA to say that the luggage wasn't even on board and that we would be delayed yet further while we waited for it. If it had just been our clothes I think we would have asked the captain to go without the luggage but most of us had squeezed all our personal effects into our hand luggage (well we are all blokes) so that our main luggage could be filled with tools and materials for the work we would eventually do—if we ever got there.

Well we did get there and much to our relief Alex, Ivelina and our bus driver were all there to meet us. Ironically, they had left Krivnya early so that they would have an hour to look around Bourgas so when I texted them to let them know of our delays it was too late and they were already on their way. So an hour in Bourgas turned into four hours in Bourgas but we were all grateful now to be boarding the bus and starting the two and a half hour bus ride to Krivnya.

One of the advantages of setting off from Okehampton at 1am is that our journey through Bulgaria was during the late afternoon and we got to see the country in all its glory. Bulgaria is a spectacularly beautiful country with great views in every direction (a bit like a very large Devon) and once or twice the view was very reminiscent of Dartmoor. But each time you got lost in the view you were brought back to reality with a violent jolt as the bus hit one of the many large potholes which congregate in Bulgaria. I think that potholes are like sardines, they travel half way around the globe to breed in one small part of the world where they mass in such large numbers they are visible from space. The pothole breeding ground just happens to be in Bulgaria and the breeding season just happens to be when we are there. Some of the bumps had us bouncing out of our seats so that we were airborne on several occasions during the journey.

At last our destination came into view as we arrived at Krivnya. We passed the orphanage and went on to the school just a few hundred yards up the road. This was the first time the team had seen the job. Until now they had been relying on plans drawn up by me on my Fisher Price Etch-a-sketch and photos which I had taken a few weeks earlier. Much attention was given to the stud partition walls in each of the two rooms; a decision needed to be taken to remove them or leave them there. If we left them it made the job of hanging joists for the suspended ceiling much more complicated but if we removed them we had much bigger rooms on our hands and thus a much bigger project.

With a little deliberation the decision was taken to remove the walls. Apart from all the logistical considerations the children would end up with a much bigger space and this swung the vote.

With the end of a long day came the chance of a meal at one of the Provadia restaurants and a chance to relax and rest our weary bones. We went to the closest restaurant which also happens to be the restaurant which has featured in several previous reports thanks to its comical adventures. Two hours elapsed between ordering and being served (no doubt while the owner cycled around Provadia trying to buy all the necessary ingredients) during which time night fell. A slight chill filled the air so William went to his room to get a jumper. Elliot went too but I think he collected his pyjamas as it continued to get darker and later but still no food.

Obviously by the time we turned in for the night there was nothing which could keep us from our much needed sleep after such a long exhausting day. Nothing that is except an express train speeding through our room during a thunder storm or as it turned out, Bob's snoring. If I hadn't been so tired I would have crossed the room and force fed Bob my pillow in an effort to shut him up but exhaustion ruled and Bob survived my alternative plot to fill his airways with expanding foam (besides, we needed it for the building site).

SATURDAY

It turns out that William and I weren't the only ones to suffer a night of sharing a room with an active volcano. Roger had it in stereo with Barry & Andy both hitting decibels that you might associate with a Led Zeppelin gig. It seems that William was worst affected as evidenced by his woeful attempts to prepare breakfast. I had introduced him to my staple breakfast fayre of an Activia cereal pot. It's quite simply a pot of cereal attached to a pot of yoghurt. William was amused that it actually contained instructions in diagram form of how to pour the cereal into the yoghurt. However, there was clearly one diagram missing, the one which showed how to use the spoon to mix the two together as this apparently simple exercise defeated William. Having employed all his skill in removing the utensil from its packaging he failed to notice that the handle was folded into the spoon and tried diligently to use the still folded spoon to mix and eat his breakfast. I waited a few moments so that I could enjoy his suffering and then pointed out his error much to his embarrassment.

With breakfast finally completed it was all aboard the minibus and we set off for Krivnya. No sooner had we arrived than Barry presented me with my first shopping list. He could at least have waited for me to get my shirt dirty so it looked like I had done a little work but no, my work is to do the shopping. I should confess here that I'm not the only one who does the shopping, Alex always accompanies me as with my grasp of the Bulgarian language I would probably return with a cucumber instead of a hammer and three frogs instead of nails. As much as beating frogs with a cucumber might be amusing it wouldn't help much with the work we had to do.

Sometimes shopping with Alex becomes a game of charades subtly mixed with a game of Chinese whispers. The builders give me technical words for what they require with a 50% chance of me knowing what they mean. Generally the English word has no direct Bulgarian translation and as Alex has no building experience it challenges even her excellent command of the English language. I then enter into an Oscar winning performance to show Alex what the item is using my extensive acting skills (I once took a part in a Fairwater Presbyterian Church Panto as one of the Guatemalan Garglers—that's true by the way!). Alex provides the subtitles to my performance for the poor sales assistant who then has to come up with various offerings before finally getting the thumbs up from me who by now is slightly disappointed that my efforts to mime an extension lead produced an air horn for a car in the first instance. Doesn't he know that following my epic performance as a Guatemalan Gargler I was invited back for a cameo role as Phil Mitchell in the following year's panto.

After all these years of doing this sort of work a lot of the shops now know this routine and enjoy watching my performances and trying to guess whatever it is I am trying to buy. Poor Alex, how does she put up with it? I can't help but wonder if Ronnie Barker had seen one of these episodes just before he wrote the classic 'Four Candles' sketch—I wouldn't mind my share of the royalties from that.

Back on site there was a bit of an incident with its roots in last year's trip. Some may recall Andy's efforts to make a pirate out of Roger. No, he didn't give him a parrot, he tried to saw off his leg. As it happens Roger still has both his legs and so Andy hatched a new plan. This year, while taking down the partition wall Andy 'accidently' dropped a section of wall onto Roger's head. Clearly he was trying to remove Roger's eye so that he would have to wear an eye patch like a real pirate but once again his plans were thwarted, this time by the thickness of Roger's head. We are all a bit worried that if both of them make the trip next year Andy might consider ways of replacing Roger's hand with a hook.

With the first wall down work started on the new ceiling. "We need the chop saw and the laser level". That was my cue to spring into action and provide the kit which Adrian and I had bought a few weeks earlier. I knew exactly where it was and marched off ready to impress everyone with just how efficient I was. As you might have guessed by now things didn't exactly go according to plan. Firstly we needed the key to get into Ivelina's office (Ivelina is the Director) which seems like a simple enough task but there is only one bunch of keys and any one of about ten different people might have them at any one time. Then when you eventually find the bunch (usually with the help of one of the many willing children) you have to endure an extreme test of patience while the caretaker goes through every one of the forty keys on the bunch before finding the right one. This was the first of many (very many) times we asked the seemingly obvious question, "why don't they label the keys?"

Eventually we gained access to the office and I pointed to the area where the tools were but couldn't understand the confused looks on the faces of the people with me. So I pointed harder with large exaggerated hand motions to explain to the directionally challenged crowd where they were. The faces looking back at me just got blanker so I bent down towards the spot I was indicating and turned my head to look at it in my final attempt to draw their attention to the tools. But the sight which confronted me was not what I was expecting. Instead of tools there was nothing but a vast empty space of cosmic nothingness. Just to the left of the black hole there were some odd boxes and in a scene reminiscent of Basil Fawlty looking for the duck in a trifle I rummaged through the boxes in a futile effort to magic up the absent tools. (If the Basil Fawlty reference means nothing to you, shame on you! You must immediately locate this episode of Fawlty Towers and watch it before reading on).

We painfully played the 'guess which key' game over and over again outside several doors but still the tools eluded us. I knew they were here somewhere, I had personally bought them and delivered them and I had a witness but unfortunately he was about 2000 miles away in Cardiff and was of little use to me. Besides I had a strong suspicion that if I had called on his evidence in my defence he would have taken great delight in pretending to know nothing about any tools.

I suggested that Alex phoned Ivelina to resolve the mystery once and for all but was surprised to learn that she was in Shumen taking a maths exam. Yes, that's right, as part of her continuing professional development she has to regularly prove her competence by passing exams. You can't help but wonder if there is lesson here for some of the hierarchy in our own schools.

Eventually contact was made with Ivelina in Shumen who sent her mother to show us where the tools were. Ironically they were in the one room which we didn't search. So about an hour after I confidently said, "Give me two minutes I'll go and get them for you", I finally delivered the elusive tools to the team. Armed with the right tools for the job work could start on preparing the main beam and joists for the new ceiling.

It was great to see people discovering skills they never knew they had under the watchful eye of the skilled members of the team who were patiently training them. The unskilled men who had gone with the idea of labouring and making tea suddenly found themselves doing jobs they never thought they could do. I won't go in to detail as I am under strict orders not to reveal their new skills to their wives back home for fear of a rather large 'to do' list being presented to them on their return to the UK.

Saturday morning also saw the arrival of Margi & Lynne, two British ladies living in Kranevo, who had signed up to join us. They turned out to be angels in disguise as apart from helping with the work and running activities for the children they also found the time to arrange breakfast and lunch on site. This was a real blessing as it meant the team could stop for vital refreshment without having the added burden of preparing or clearing up afterwards which meant a big increase in productivity. (Note to self - must book them for next year).

I took the ladies to meet the children who were in the home just down the road as it was a Saturday and there was no school today. Friendships were formed instantly, the children have a lot of love to give and the ladies weren't slow in returning it. Bonds were created in this one simple moment that will last long beyond the week we will be working here.

As the morning progressed Adam was revealing quite an interesting CV. There didn't seem to be a single topic up for discussion that he didn't have an association with. He had worked here, there and everywhere doing every conceivable job. Over lunch Firemen got a mention so I asked Adam if he had ever been a Fireman; he replied, "No, but I've been in a fire".

Then there was a revelation that will haunt me for as long as I live. I was innocently chatting with Barry about music and concerts which we had attended when he revealed he had been to The Rocky Horror Show. Foolishly, as I was confident the answer would be 'No', I asked if he had gone in fancy dress. I was shocked to get a "yes" reply and as if I really needed a mental image Barry regaled me with details of suspenders and stockings. Arrgghhhhh, how much therapy will it take to get that picture out of my mind—and yours now :-)

Back on site things were progressing very well but the day was getting hotter and hotter. One of the boys from the Orphanage was becoming very animated and trying his best to tell me something which I simply couldn't understand. Finally, after the longest game of charades I think I have ever played I understood that he was telling me to move the minibus and put it in the shade. Fair enough, that sounded like a very sensible idea so I found the one tiny patch of shade which existed on the other side of the yard about 100 yards from where we were working.

Now I don't know who the Bulgarian weather fairies are but they were clearly in a mischievous mood that day because as soon as I had parked the bus in the shade the skies began to darken to an apocalyptic black, thunder began to rumble in the distance and lightening forked across the sky. In a scene reminiscent of a Steven King novel rain clouds robbed the sky of all its light and cast an inky black shadow over the building site. As day was turned instantly into night the tools we were using took on a menacing appearance and with the added risk of a lightning strike the team very quickly parted company with any electrical tools which were being powered from a long extension lead running across the open yard. It was five o'clock and so a decision was taken to use this natural break as an excuse to finish work for the day and go home. The team assembled in the doorway and looked at the empty space where the bus used to be. "Where's the minibus?" With a daunting resignation to the inevitable stream of abuse I replied, "over there .... In the shade". As the team peered through the curtain of rain into the blackness beyond, the occasional lightening strike revealed the whereabouts of the bus. I was spared the impossible question 'Shading from what?' but I knew there was only one way I could put things right. I was going to have to sprint across the yard, running the gauntlet of the lightening and recover the bus. I was aware that Usain Bolt could make the 100 metre dash in 9.58 seconds but as I wasn't wearing spikes I felt I may be a little slower (otherwise I could, of course, have made it in the same time). A quick calculation of the amount of rain falling multiplied by the time it would take me to cross the yard factoring in the risk of being hit by lightening left me looking at two options; getting severely soaked or cooked. I ran for my life but these supernatural conditions had played havoc with time itself as after 9.58 seconds I wasn't, as I expected, at the door of the bus but in fact, only about 12 metres from the assembled team who seemed to be enjoying the sight of me lolloping across the yard with all the grace and speed of a wounded slug. By the time I reached halfway all the officials from the British Olympic Committee had put away their stopwatches and were reaching for calendars instead, the best I could hope for now was that they were 2014 calendars and they were still on the June page as this was becoming very embarrassing. After my ordeal I was pleased that I had had the wherewithal to park the bus in the shade as I now had somewhere to cool off before driving the 100 metres to collect the team. There was a moment when the temptation to simply drive back to the guest house without them was almost too much to resist but I remembered that I needed them back on site tomorrow and I wanted to keep all my limbs.

For some reason, during the scramble to board the bus, Roger seemed reluctant to sit anywhere near Bob. It turns out that Bob had been trying to get photographs of the team but when Roger posed for his turn Bob said, "turn around I want your backside". Bob protested that he simply wanted to see the name printed on the back of Roger's shirt but Roger wasn't taking any chances.

That night I was actually glad to hear Bob snoring as that meant he was asleep and William and I were safe in our beds.

SUNDAY
A quick head count at the minibus revealed someone was missing. Where was Elliot? Still fast asleep apparently. Why his room mates decided to leave him asleep I don't know but Elliot managed to haul himself out of his bed and join us, to a chorus of general abuse, in time to leave for another day at Krivnya.
We knew that as it was Sunday we only had a small window of opportunity for shopping so we started the day by drawing up a list and once again Alex and I headed for the shops. This time Barry came with us which added another dimension to the game of Chinese whispers. Barry has a very broad Devonshire accent which I had to translate into English

before Alex could then translate it into Bulgarian but somehow we got the supplies we needed and returned to the school.

When we got back Lynne was attempting to take photographs and in doing so sustained the first injury of the trip. With the rest of the team having survived a day with all manner of sharp and dangerous power tools it was a camera which would bring the inaugural shout of pain. I've never read the book 'Photography for Idiots' but if I did I would expect to see on page one, 'do not walk around while peering into the viewfinder'. Clearly Lynne had never read the book either as she managed to bang her elbow on the door jamb while 'peering into the viewfinder' once again raising the impossible question of why do they call it a funny bone?
Naturally panic ensued as the team expressed deep concern - could she still make breakfast? Mercifully the answer was yes and we were able to pretend that really we were only concerned for her welfare.

Fuelled by another great breakfast and lunch a little later, work progressed at quite a pace. The timbers for the ceiling in one of the rooms was completed and Elliot was busy repairing the reveals on the windows in the other room. Ben was employed to 'assist' Elliot but he was secretly charged with the responsibility of ensuring Elliot actually stayed awake.

During the afternoon Mladen turned up. You may recall from previous reports that Mladen is one of the staff at the Orphanage and normally plays a key role in our work there but had recently broken his leg (playing with the children) and was off work. He arrived in his car which surprised me so I asked if it was an automatic? "No", he replied, "I use my one good leg for all the pedals", a bit taken aback I half joked, "I hope the police don't see you" to which I go the response, "It's none of their business." Another entry in my book 'The cultural differences between Bulgaria and Britain'

By now Andy was beginning to feel the affects of missing his alarm on the day we left Okehampton. In his rush he forgot to pack his toothbrush. Ignoring our efforts to be helpful by suggesting he leave his teeth for the guesthouse owner to clean while we are working he insisted on buying a new toothbrush. After forgetting to buy a brush for the fourth time Ben & Alex decided to help out by offering to buy one for him. His delight in accepting their offer was short lived when they returned with a beautiful Barbie pink toothbrush. Maybe next time he'll buy his own!

Last thing that evening I was in the local shop buying supplies for tomorrow's breakfast when I was stopped in my tracks by a sign which said БОБ you don't have to be able to read Cyrillic script to see that that clearly says BOB; it's even pronounced bob in Bulgarian. Tins of БОБ were available for just 79 stotinkis (approx 35p); having got to know our Bob I couldn't help thinking they were overpriced. Later Alex was able to confirm that БОБ was Bulgarian for bean so naturally enough Bob got the nickname Mr Bean. I couldn't help but wonder if, given Bob's antics over the week, he wouldn't have earned that nickname without us ever knowing about the translation of his name.

MONDAY
Not surprisingly another shopping trip was in order so I carefully recorded everything required into my phone and set off for Provadia - again!! However, I was a little bemused by an entry on the list which said 'waster', what was a waster? Now I know you are thinking that I could make a cheap joke here about one of the team but you misjudge me, I would never do such a thing and frankly I'm quite hurt that you should even think that about me. Anyway, the mystery remained and every time I checked my list 'waster' was still on it. The list gradually got shorter and shorter as I deleted items we had purchased until only 'waster' was left but I was no closer to working out what it was. I was going to have to return without it at the risk of it being a vital element of the work and having to return to Provadia immediately. Then, just as we were passing the last of the shops on the return journey to Krivnya I had my eureka moment and shouted, "Water". Alex looked a little shocked, clearly I had lost the plot but I was quickly able to explain that the mysterious 'waster' was in fact, water. As it happens this was a vital element as with the days touching 30 degrees the team could not have gone on without sufficient drinking water. That rogue 's' had a lot to answer for.

Back on site I managed to take a break from all the shopping and do some real work. Andy needed an extra pair of hands to get some of the beams in the right place for the ceiling in the second room. I noticed that the Square he was using was fashioned from a few twigs a bent nail and a piece of chewing gum. I was a bit confused but said nothing as, after all, what do I know about building. But the rickety Square played on my mind and I couldn't let it go. I managed to keep my mouth shut while Andy took all his measurements and I drew dodgy pencil lines on the walls according to his instructions. When we had finished I found I couldn't help myself and had to say something. Conscious of my own ignorance I ventured, "Andy, forgive me if I'm being stupid here but why are you using the knobbly sticks, wouldn't this be better?" at which point I produced a shiny new three foot metal Square from the pile of tools on the floor beside us. Andy's face was a picture, he didn't know whether to laugh or cry. I thought I would be helpful by consoling him with the idea that he could use it for the rest of the job but this only rubbed salt into the wound as he advised me that he had finished all the jobs for which a square was required. Ah well, there's always next year.

Monday also marked the start of the toilet renovations. The school site only has outside toilets and these have no mains sewerage just a simple pit. The toilet pans, such as they are, consist of a hole which goes directly into the pit. (Sorry, I hope you're not reading this over your lunch). Needless to say the smell is bad enough to curdle milk at 50 metres. Entry into one of these toilets is literally an act of desperation. As William would put it, "I have a meeting with the flies." Well guess who had been appointed the job of official Toilet Repair Man? That's right, me!! I thought I was in charge of this trip but somewhere along the way the others had clearly had a meeting, to which I wasn't invited, where they nominated me to take on the Toilet Roll, sorry I mean Role. These people used to be my friends.

I hatched a plan to get out of it by badgering Barry with questions to make it look like I had no idea what I was doing in the hope that he would pull me off the job. "How do I put this pipe in? How do I saw this wood? How do I open the toilet door? How do I re-house all the flies I will make homeless?" The questions become more stupid and desperate but all to no avail. Barry patiently and calmly answered all my questions until there was nothing left to do but get on with it. There was a limit to how much time I could spend in such a confined space where breathable air was in such short supply so progress was slow. I grabbed the wood I needed to construct the frame for the new floor and piled it outside the toilet, drew a huge breath and entered the room of fumes. I had just enough air in my lungs to take the first measurement before exiting to cut the wood. I couldn't believe the irony when I found that in the few seconds I had spent in the toilet a bird had poo'd on my wood outside. I think there may have been a message here somewhere.

Back inside the toilet I began drilling holes in the wall but as there was no power available here I was forced to use a battery drill which was proving to be about as difficult as drilling into granite with a carrot. Andy appeared at the door and said, "Would you like that drill to spin a little faster?" "It's on the maximum setting" I replied ruefully and pointed as if to drive home the obvious when Andy reached out, flicked a switch on the drill and sent it into warp speed. I don't know which I felt the strongest, the relief that the job would now be significantly easier or the embarrassment of my foolishness. Foolish embarrassment certainly felt like a more familiar friend.

TUESDAY
This morning I set off early for the shop to buy breakfast, unfortunately I was a little too early as it wasn't open yet so I sat on a wall to wait. What a nice surprise followed. Bobi, one of the girls from Barzitsa orphanage saw me and came across to say hello. She took me across the square where I also met Mimi & Damien. In my broken Bulgarian I managed to tell them that I would be visiting Barzitsa with the students from Okehampton College on July 13th, news which they were delighted to hear.

Today's shopping list from the builders included paint which was easily sourced from our favourite shop. Some of their supplies are kept in the shop itself while the rest are outside in a covered yard, on this occasion we were invited into the yard to collect our paint. Arriving in the yard I was most concerned to see the sales assistant climb aboard the fork lift truck and start it up. Oh no, how much paint had I ordered? I thought I had asked for 10 litres so why would he need a fork lift. I was mightily relieved to discover he was simply moving it out of the way to gain access to the paint and watched him collect two five litre tubs for me.

Back on site Bob & Ben (sounds like a pilot for a children's TV program) were working on plasterboarding a particularly difficult area of ceiling around the window. Bob was on the ground while Ben was in the roof space manoeuvring the plasterboard into position. "Move it a few more inches towards me" said Bob. With an exasperated shove Ben pushed the plasterboard saying, "I hope you're standing by the door" as Bob had not factored in Ben's lack of X-ray vision to see through the ceiling and clearly had he no idea where Bob was actually standing when delivering his instructions. Despite this they did a great job and put the finishing touches to the ceiling without killing each other.

Just as we were standing back to admire the new ceiling William arrived with the worrying news that there was an emergency. "I need to borrow someone to help me……. I was coming across the yard ……. I had my beige shorts on ……… the sun was shining …….. It was about 10 minutes after my cup of tea ………. I passed Margi who was going down to the home ……….. The birds were singing …………. " It took so long to tell us what the emergency was it was over before he finished his speech. We were glad that it wasn't a fire or we might have burned to death while he told us about the impending danger. I don't recall ever finding out what the emergency was, perhaps he'll finish telling us in a week or two.

Although we were making excellent progress with the work, today we began to realise that we might not finish everything we set out to do. Having taken the decision to remove the partition walls we had added a day's work to the job. Even then we might have been able to pull it off but we were half a man short. Barry was still recovering from an operation and as such was confined to light duties, sometimes this meant committing two men to ensure he didn't overdo it.
We took stock of the situation and decided on the sensible course of action by agreeing to focus on getting one room completely finished and just doing as much as we possibly could on the other room. The room we would focus on would be the prospective sensory room. Whilst there was an element of disappointment in arriving at this decision it was definitely the right one or we risked ending up with two incomplete rooms and could have compromised the safety of the team. With the team already working extremely hard in demanding conditions it was not possible to stretch them any further without an element of risk which we were not prepared to take.
Our decision was ratified the following day when the Director, Ivelina, came to speak to us and said, "I can see that it won't be possible to finish everything so please will you try to get the sensory room completed?" A no brainer as the decision had already been made.

The evening brought one of the highlights of the week; we had been invited to the children's graduation celebration. At the end of grade's 4, 8 & 12 the children 'graduate' to the next level. Several of the Krivnya children had reached this stage and it was a real privilege to be able to join them in celebrating this at the local restaurant. Unfortunately, this event cost me a fortune as I had to pay several people who took videos of me dancing not to post it on You Tube. I am not a willing dancer and I'm certainly not a good dancer but what could I do when the Director dragged me onto the floor for a traditional Bulgarian folk dance. As someone who cannot master the Shadow's four step shuffle a complicated Bulgarian Folk Dance was way beyond my ability and I looked about as confused as a builder confronted with a line of shovels and told to take his pick!

However, as luck would have it, when I sat down and prepared to receive all the abuse and 'gentle teasing' of the team their attention was diverted by something even more embarrassing than my hapless prancing around the dance floor. Oh thank you Elliot, I will forever be grateful to you for being even worse than I was and selflessly drawing all the scorn away from me and onto yourself. You are a true gentleman. The next time I see a chicken on a hot tin roof I will remember your dancing.

One thing which struck us all was the relationship between the children and the staff. The children freely danced with their teachers and threw themselves with joy and laughter into warm embraces. The staff were free to receive and respond to the hugs with equal joy and love. Whilst accepting the good reasons for why this would not be possible here in the UK it was, none the less, very heart warming to see this in all its beautiful innocence.

WEDNESDAY

Today's shopping list was mercifully short and as Alex was fully employed with Ben attending to the ceiling I decided to take the huge step of going to the shop without a translator. This was a big test, if I returned with a Guinea Pig I might never be let loose on my own again. By now I was very experienced at charades and had amassed a massive vocabulary of at least ten words of Bulgarian. I'm not too sure how the words Tomato and Hat were going to help me in a builders' merchants but I was keen and that was enough. Fortunately, I didn't return to the site with a furry rodent or a tomato hat so I reckon I passed my test.

Interestingly, on a different shopping trip a Bulgarian sales assistant told Alex she spoke excellent Bulgarian for an English girl. As a Bulgarian native born and bred in Provadia she wasn't quite sure how to take that but she was very pleased to be considered as part of our team. She was certainly very proud to be wearing a team t-shirt which may be what fooled the sales assistant.

Having delayed it as long as possible it was time to return to the toilet. Yesterday I had managed to put in the soil pipe and lay the marine ply floor so the area was ready for tiling. I couldn't believe my luck when William asked if I needed any help. Yes, I needed someone to hold my nose or maybe fill it with expanding foam. However, I decided to ask William to help me to cut the tiles.

Did you read last year's report, 'My Kingdom For A Tile Cutter'? If so you will be familiar with the torturous events surrounding my failure to procure an electric tile cutter. If you also read the more recent report of last month's trip to prepare for this week you will know that at last we were the proud owners of an electric tile cutter. The excitement which filled the air was tangible. Unfortunately, it wasn't just excitement which filled the air, the little drops of liquid we could feel on our faces was the precursor for another monsoon. I couldn't believe it, the trouble I had gone to to get the tile cutter and then I had to go through the whole key debacle again to get a room opened so that I could run three in line extension cables to the area outside the toilet where the cutter was situated and I couldn't use it because it was pouring with rain!! Arrgghhh, the electric tile cutter just sat there all shiny and new, mocking me as I trudged to the tool store to get a manual cutter which wouldn't electrocute William and me if it got wet. The storm passed fairly quickly but William and I didn't notice courtesy of a persistent drip directly above our work area. I was inside measuring and marking tiles then passing them outside to William for cutting. All I could see was what I thought was continuing rain falling directly onto William's head. It turns out that the rest of the site was once again bathed in glorious sunshine as the storm had passed. I don't know what William had done to deserve it but all around as far as the eye could see were blue, cloudless skies resplendent in golden sunshine, there was just one tiny spot, in the whole of Bulgaria, where there was falling water and William was stood in it. Somehow and I've no idea how, water was continuing to cascade off the roof of the toilet all over William. While everyone else was in sunglasses and sunhat William was in a poncho and souwester.

Whilst the rain had freshened the heavy air on the rest of the site it had had a very undesirable affect on the basic sewerage underlying the toilet we were working on. After three days working in the confines of that small room with nothing but flies and smells for company it finally occurred to me that every day I had been shopping I had returned with the answer to all my problems - a carrier bag. I simply placed the carrier bag over the protruding soil pipe and hey presto, like one of Adam's magic tricks the smell was gone. I wasn't sure whether I felt elated to have finally beaten the smell or angry that such a simple solution had been available to me for three days but hadn't occurred to me.

Meanwhile work was going extremely well elsewhere on site where the finishing touches were being made to one room to prepare it for laying the laminate flooring tomorrow and the ceiling was completed on room two. We might have got on even better but for one minor problem. Andy was busy plastering around the windows; his head was down as he focussed 100% on the work calling from time to time for a top up of mixed plaster. On one such occasion Bob responded to the call for more plaster, grabbed the bucket and passed it to Andy. Without raising his head from the work Andy applied the plaster, paused, looked over to Bob and asked who had mixed it this time as it was not a good mix. Upon closer inspection it transpired that Bob had passed Andy a bucket of emulsion in error. Either it was genius at work inventing the first self painting plaster to save hours of labouring or it was an act of gross stupidity. I haven't seen Bob and his new invention on Dragon's Den yet so I'm afraid it's looking increasingly like the latter option.

We finished the working day with a wonderful treat; a magic show. Adam delighted and amazed the children with his tricks and illusions. They sat on the steps of the orphanage with eyes wide and mouths agape as the magic unfolded before their eyes. Adam called out children one by one to join in the magic and Alex played the role of glamorous assistant and translator. The team didn't know whether to watch the magic or the children's faces which were lit up brighter than the glorious sun which bathed us again that afternoon. What an amazing time we had with the children, one which will be a lasting memory of our trip.

Later, at the restaurant Barry called into question his abilities as a builder. He had taken some doll's furniture (in kit form) to Krivnya in the hope that there might be some spare time for the children to construct it. While we were waiting for our meal Barry decided to try one out; after about an hour of head scratching, chin rubbing and various grunting noises he finally had to give up and put all the pieces back into the box. It was during this act of defeat that we noticed the directions on the box, "age 6 upwards".

THURSDAY

This was our last day of work so the pressure was on to get all the jobs completed. Elliot was on laminate floor duty and inspected the wood we had on site as having enlarged the room on day one we were concerned there may not be enough laminate to cover the whole floor which we were determined to do. We knew that if we needed to buy more supplies a trip to Varna would be necessary. As official shopper I was very keen to avoid this as I felt it would take about two and a half hours and I still had the toilet to finish. However, Lynne poured scorn on my estimate of two and half hours and reckoned she could do it in half the time. Just for a moment my male ego was hurt as I was sure I was right (of course) but suddenly I saw an opportunity to get out of going shopping and with a few carefully chosen phrases I heard the words of an angel as Lynne said, "Well I could go if you like." I was so overjoyed that I didn't even make a token effort to resist and immediately gave her the shopping list, the money and my eternal gratitude. And so it was that Lynne & Margi set off on their great adventure. Now you might think that describing a shopping trip to Varna for some laminate flooring as 'a great adventure' as being somewhat over the top but believe me, what unfolded next is worthy of the label.

My phoned bleeped with the tone which told me I had a text so I dug in my pocket to read the message. It was from Margi, the car had overheated, please could I take some water to them. The message said they were on the edge of Provadia. Not too much drama there, a 10 minute trip with some water was no problem. I located a few empty bottles, filled them up and set off in the minibus to 'the junction where you turn left into Provadia' as the text said. When I got to the junction I couldn't find them. Strange! It was hardly spaghetti junction more like tumbleweed corner. The odd donkey would saunter by two or three times a day but that was about as busy as it got. The daily passing of our minibus was the most exciting thing which happened at that junction and drew crowds of as many as two people some days. So why couldn't I see the car? I phoned Margi half expecting to hear her phone ring from behind the nearest tree but I didn't. It turns out that the left turn into Provadia which they were describing was not the one from Krivnya (where I was) but the one from Varna from which they were returning. Still that wasn't such bad news as it wouldn't take long to drive to the other side of Provadia and soon enough I had found them. About an hour had passed from the time they broke down to the time I got there with the water so plenty of time for the radiator to have cooled down and be safe for me to pour in some cold water. I slowly poured watching the expansion tank carefully for the rising line of water to reach the 'max' marker but there was no sign of the line. I continued to pour until the whole bottle had been emptied but still the expansion tank was as dry as a bone. Bottle number two followed and still nothing. We cobbled together all the dregs of water from various drinking bottles all to no avail. We could have dipped the car into the nearby Black Sea and it would have gobbled it all up leaving a direct walking route into Russia on the other side.

It was then that I asked a question which was playing on my mind, "Why didn't you go for help at the garage?" "What garage?" came the reply. "The one 50 yards around the corner." The ladies had no idea that help was so close at hand. But for a few tall bushes they might have been in the safety of the garage for the last hour instead of stuck on the busier of Provadia's junctions.

Fortunately the minibus had a tow rope, unfortunately it didn't have a tow hook!! However, we eventually worked out a way of safely attaching the two vehicles and tentatively made our way to the garage in Lynne's first ever towing experience.

Arrival at the garage heralded another false dawn in this mission of dashed hopes. No one spoke English and my Bulgarian might have enough vocabulary to ask if 'Rado cuts fish' (*) but that was of little use in this circumstance. However, we soon established that this garage only served fuel and did not offer any sort of repair service.

Phone calls and discussions followed until eventually Margi and I returned to Krivnya in the minibus while Lynne awaited rescue in the garage. You will be pleased to know that Lynne was rescued and the car transferred to a garage which diagnosed a failed head gasket.

(*) The Bulgarian phrase for Rado cuts fish is Rado Reje Riba and is used as an exercise to teach school children to roll their R's

The one positive to come from this unfortunate episode was that the ladies, who had planned to leave today, spent another evening with us.

Back on site the pressure was on to finish the toilet. As the rest of the team finished their various jobs and one by one began to pack everything away William and I were still putting the finishing touches to the toilet. As jobs were finished so the men began to hang around the minibus in an unspoken request to take them back to the guest house for the final time. William detected the mood was in danger of turning and came up with a plan to defuse the situation. "I still have a big job to finish on the toilet so why don't you all go back and leave me to it, Andrew can return for me later." I knew what he meant but the thought of hanging around while William finished his 'big job on the toilet' was enough to send the men running to the minibus without a second thought for William's selfless act and demanded to get out of there as fast as possible.

And so as the rest of the team left William to perform the ultimate test on the newly installed toilet they reflected on the week and concluded it had been an outstanding success. The sensory room was finished having been enlarged, fitted with a new ceiling, new windows and new floor, all the crumbling walls made good and finally decorated. The soft play room had been similarly improved except for the new floor and final decoration but we were able to leave sufficient funds for that to be done by local tradesman after we had gone.

Luckily I remembered to go back for William who had finished his big job on the toilet and was ready to re-join the team for the final evening meal together. Before we gathered for our meal a few of us with sufficient energy remaining made the trek up to the castle overlooking Provadia. Whilst the castle itself is just a ruin the views are spectacular and well worth the climb even on aching, work wearied limbs.

FRIDAY
The trip home threw one more curve ball at us. As we arrived at Bourgas Airport we couldn't believe what we saw on the departures board; our flight was delayed by five hours. Oh no, we couldn't go through this again, after all we had to endure on the trip out here. We began to consider the idea of going into Bourgas for a while in order to kill some time and avoid the excruciating boredom of five hours in an airport lounge but with the torment of the news and the efforts to contact loved ones back home nothing was being decided. I went inside to try to get some information and spotted some seats in the café so hastily arranged for the team to park themselves there while we considered our options. Slowly the café filled up with other people on our flight and added to the collective moaning. I wandered around looking for a rep for our airline but there was no one to be found, I guess they had made a hasty exit for fear of being lynched so I returned to the café to see if a decision had been made

about leaving the airport and heading in to town. Lethargy had set in and everyone seemed to have resigned themselves to a long, bottom numbing wait when suddenly a fellow passenger rushed in and announced, "It's back on schedule." We never found out, or cared about, the reasons for the change but were extremely pleased that we had not gone into town.

And so we returned to Okehampton at a reasonable hour despite a few half hearted attempts by the M5 to delay us but just as I was about to settle down for a well earned rest my phone rang and Bob had one last mini disaster to play out—he had got home with the wrong luggage! Fortunately it had been a simple mix up between him and Ben and they organised their own swap without involving me any further, much to my relief.

It had been another great week in which so much was achieved. Having taken the decision to spend the first day removing the partition walls we had effectively increased the size of the job and lost a day all in one go but it was definitely worth it. An amazing effort by the team ensured that a huge amount of work was accomplished and we left Krivnya with a completed sensory room, an 85% completed soft play room and a new, sanitary toilet. A remarkable achievement.

However, there is still work to do. We have been able to establish a healthy fund to help buy the equipment for the sensory room thanks to the generosity of our wonderful supporters but buying the kit is proving to be a monumentally onerous task. Oddly, it is significantly cheaper to buy it in the UK and have it shipped to Krivnya than to source it in Bulgaria. However, I could write a book about the problems I have had in trying to buy it. I started back in May but my efforts reached an all time low when having finally, after four aborted attempts, completed my order with one particular company I was told that the order was too big for them to process!! I have never found it so hard to spend money as company after company found all manner of novel reasons to excuse themselves the burden of accepting the order. I took a break from the torturous task while we were in Krivnya and will return to it again in the near future. The target is to have the sensory room fully equipped by September when the children start the new academic year.

Ah yes, the children, the wonderful children for whom we do all this. What a delight they are. Despite all the disadvantages they face in life they bring us so much joy. Sometimes it feels as if the balance is the wrong way round. The joy which we deliver through the work that we do is eclipsed by the joy they give us in receiving it. This year we had the added joy of some of the children being on site to help us; then there was the magic show and the cherry on the cake was to be able to share in their graduation celebrations. Such a wonderful 'reward' for our efforts.

Thanks to all the team - Barry, Andy, Elliot, Adam, Bob, Ben, William, Roger, Margi, Lynne (& me!)
Thanks to all our supporters; those who give financially and those who pray
Above all thanks to God who makes all this happen for the good of His children.

Andrew

CHAPTER FIFTEEN
FUNDRAISER
Running, Kayaking, Cycling and Swan Dodging
September 2014

After the Three Peaks Walk in 2011, cycling the Coast To Coast route in 2012 and a triathlon in 2013 we needed a new challenge for 2014 but it needed to top all the other challenges, something out of this world. However, as the Atlantis space shuttle had been retired in 2011 it was going to have to be something on planet earth.

Having personally recently kayaked the Brecon and Monmouth canal I was idly searching the internet for more canals to kayak when it hit me; there were several canals meandering their way through the South West of England which could be combined to make a decent route. It could be possible to run from the end of one canal to the beginning of another all that was needed now was a cycle leg. The final canal finished in Tiverton so a natural cycle leg would be to ride back to Okehampton and so the Ultra Triathlon was born

I drew a rough map showing the proposal to kayak - run - kayak - run - kayak - cycle from Street in Somerset to Okehampton in Devon to circulate among a few people I thought might be stupid enough to join me. I was very careful to choose a scale of map that made the route look very small, no more than a few inches on paper and emailed it around.

I have already certified several of my friends as insane by virtue of the fact that they have joined in previous challenges so targeted them as well as a few new names who I thought I could fool with my mini map. It worked, two of last year's fools and two new fools signed up for the challenge.

When I finally got round to plotting out the route on a proper 1:25000 Ordnance Survey map I was concerned to discover that it required 5 maps to cover the route and some of those maps were printed on both sides. Last year's triathlon was all contained in one map.
I managed to conceal this fact from the team and only revealed it to the support crew about 7 days before the event. Even rolling the map measurer over the route at 1:25000 was exhausting.

I had a few months to explore the route and make sure that what I thought was possible on a map was possible in reality. I was checking the route in reverse order heading steadily further north with each trip. Each week I explored a new section and all was going well until I finally checked out the first stage (kayaking the old Glastonbury Canal).

Apart from a tricky entry point down a steep embankment the canal was fantastic as it ran through an RSPB nature reserve. The sun was shining and the birds were singing - fantastic.

I was initially surprised that the canal was so straight as traditionally they follow contour lines in order to keep an entirely flat course but then I realised that this was Somerset and flat is something they specialise in. Having grown up in South Wales and then moved to Devon, hills are a way of life which might explain why I have one leg longer than the other (it comes from walking around hills)

The bendy Devonshire Canals do a good job of disguising distance as you can only ever see a few hundred yards ahead but the Glastonbury Canal was dead straight and what looked like a bridge about half a mile away was actually a bridge 2 miles away and took an age to reach. This might have been a problem had it not been for the regular distraction of the swans. Several swans had appeared up ahead and were paddling just a fraction slower than I was (I should explain that they weren't in kayaks) so every few minutes I would catch them up. It turns out that swans are poor losers and frequently took to flying in order to get ahead of me. Well, I say flying but if you're conjuring up an image of a swallow flitting in and out of the reeds to dance on the surface of the water or the flash of iridescent blue that points to a Kingfisher plunging from a branch into the crystal waters below please think again. Think more about what would happen if you put your cat on a bicycle and threw him into a river. I have come to realise that swans bring shame to the bird world as they have still to get past page 1 of the 'How To Fly' instruction manual. I think swans must be God's prototype for the flightless emu.

The energy required to get that mass out of the water would probably be sufficient to power your home for a year. In fact I'm thinking about getting a few swans installed on my roof instead of solar panels as we get more rain than sun here in Okehampton. The launch pad of your average swan is about 200 metres and in that distance they can gain at least 3 feet in height which, coincidentally is about the height of my head when sat in a kayak. At first it was quite comical catching up with the swans and watching them try to take off in front of me. They beat their wings and start to 'run' on the water, the effort this takes brings out a chilling shriek which is amplified through their elongated necks. With the constant thud, thud, thud of wing on water and the intermittent screeching it's like listening to a radio commentary of Venus Williams playing Maria Sharapova at Wimbledon.

However, events took a sinister turn when one of the swans decided he didn't like this game anymore and decided to turn and 'fly' in the other direction, my direction. Funnelled by the banks of the canal the aerially challenged swan only had one route, a route with me in the middle of it. The term 'sitting duck' took on a new reality. Fortunately, apart from being straighter than canals I am used to it is also wider and so disaster was avoided as the swan lurched harmlessly past me. "Phew, I'm glad that's over", I thought to myself and was pleased to see the remainder of the swans disappear down a drainage channel just as we approached the only bend in the canal. Relieved I took time to enjoy the silence and the gentle interruption to the monotony of the relentlessly straight waterway. But my enjoyment was temporary; as the canal straightened once more I couldn't believe my eyes - swans, more flipping swans!! Were these new swans or the ones who had just disappeared down the drainage channel? If it was the original swans they must have got out of the water and run as there's no way they could have flown without me hearing them so I deduced they were new swans. Unfortunately, they had received the briefing from the original crew and so they knew exactly what to do. The remainder of my journey was punctuated by the merciless cries of a swan screaming at me, "Get out of my way, I can barely get this ridiculous body airborne so if you think I can track left or right you are hopelessly mistaken"

With all the grace and manoeuvrability of a Lancaster bomber the swans kept coming but fortunately this little Spitfire managed to dodge them and avoid having to explain a huge hole in my face when I got home.

At least the battle of the Swans made the time pass more quickly and I was soon at the end of the canal. The end was easy to spot as there is a huge building sprawled across the water as the canal comes to an abrupt stop. What was not so easy to spot was any point where I could take the kayak out of the water. I paddled around but couldn't find anywhere and as time was against me had to give up and paddle back to the beginning where I had left my car. You may recall that I started by saying the launch point was a difficult drop down a steep embankment, well, it's not as difficult as using it as an exit point! In the struggle to exit the water with my kayak and haul it up the bank I managed to fall butt first into a bush of stinging nettles and pepper my posterior with little red stings. For that brief moment I was about as graceful as the flying swans I had been lampooning earlier.

I returned to the same spot about a week later so I could walk around and try to find somewhere where a kayak could be brought ashore. I had already got a few ideas from various maps but soon discovered that none were viable due to a variety of man made and natural obstacles. Saddened I returned home and explained to the others what I had found and suggested we might have to drop this stage as the only alternative was the possibility of having to get out of our kayaks and swim to shore then haul our boats up the embankment in the dark, into the unknown. With a mixture of surprise and disappointment the others opted for the latter.

Eventually the day arrived and the Okehampton crew gathered to make the journey to Bridgewater where we would meet the Cardiff crew at 11pm. The Okehampton crew were Neil, Rob, Rhys (who had travelled down from Cardiff the day before) and me who would be doing the challenge, Adam who was driving the van kindly supplied by Okehampton Glass and Claire who was driving the 'athletes'. The Cardiff crew was made up of Wayne who was joining us for the running and cycling and Adrian and Cai who were organising our checkpoints.

Neil, Rob and I had all taken part in last year's triathlon and we were reminiscing about the mountain bikes which Rob and I had ridden that had made our ride so much more difficult. Now we both had new road bikes and were looking forward to an easier ride. So when we arrived in Bridgewater and found that Wayne had brought a mountain bike we exchanged knowing glances and sniggered smugly to ourselves.

When we were all together I took the opportunity to brief everyone and stress that when we arrived at the start we needed to be ready to go immediately and with the minimum of fuss and noise so that we didn't disturb the neighbours and attract unwanted interest in our activities. So we all kitted up and prepared to leave Bridgewater and head for the start.

Well we managed to launch the kayaks without too much fuss and were soon on our way although we were about 20 minutes later than we had hoped at about 20 past midnight. Unfortunately, the outstanding beauty of the canal we were on was lost in the dark and the mist but at least the conditions meant we couldn't see very far into the distance and the far horizon never seemed to be more than a few metres away.

We settled into a steady rhythm and started knocking off the miles. Suddenly Rob picked up the pace and made a burst for the front putting a little distance between him and the next kayak. What was he playing at? All was revealed a moment later when we reached the first check point and Cai's camera started flashing. Rob wanted to be in the front for the photo call. We stopped for a moment to refuel on Jelly Babies and Lucozade before setting off again.

Rob had clearly invested a lot of time in studying the whereabouts of the checkpoints as with another burst of energy he indicated we were about to reach the next one and once again was at the front when the camera started clicking.

I hadn't bothered mentioning the whole swan thing to the team as obviously they would all be asleep at this time of night. Wrong!! Do swans sleep? Not these swans who were charged with night patrol duties. If there's one thing worse than seeing a swan coming at you from 200 metres it's not seeing a swan coming at you from 200 metres. You could hear them all right as the cacophony of noise grew from a distant grumbling to a mind invading tornado of noise before a flash of white sprang out of the darkness just feet away from you. It didn't help that we had turned our head torches off because all they did was light up the mist and make it harder to see but now hands moved like lightening to reach the on switch the instant we heard the first rumblings of swan activity. We didn't know if we were warning them off or creating targets for them but it began to feel like the latter.

Rhys was the first to take a major wobble as a swan stroked his face with the tip of a wing. He was very relieved not to have capsized. I was quietly laughing to myself as on one of our training days I had capsized while ducking to go under a very low bridge and Rhys found this extremely amusing. His laughter, while hurtful, was useful in as much as it distracted the attention of the numerous people in the car park from the indignity of my attempts to re-board my kayak with my shorts slipping down my thighs revealing more of my anatomy than is good for anyone to see.

However, my revengeful amusement at Rhys' misfortune was rudely interrupted by another swan who wanted to make a closer inspection of my head and caused a major wobble in my kayak. My laughter quickly turned to terror as I battled to regain my balance and then to empathy with Rhys as the beating of my heart drowned out the noise of the evil swan.

The swans continued their assault and each time we would fall into silence as we listened for the tell tale splash of an unwanted capsize. Then the silence would be broken by shouts of "are you OK?" back down the line of kayakers. Fortunately, we all survived but our average speed was badly affected.

Eventually we made it to the end of the canal and with one final flurry the remainder of the swans made their last ditch effort to dump us in the canal but failed. And so we had arrived at the unknown, this was the point at which we had no idea how we were going to get back on to terra firma. The feeling of the unknown was amplified by the darkness and the distant barking of the 'hounds of the Baskervilles.' It was Rhys who spotted the wooden posts which presented a potential exit point. The bank was about 8 feet high but the posts gave us some purchase points to grab onto and haul ourselves ashore. Rhys made the first wobbly exit and beat down the nettles and reeds which disguised the bank while Rob and I pushed our kayaks against his in an attempt to make a stable platform from which to make his bid for freedom from the water. Half way up the bank he had to turn and grab his kayak and drag it up behind him. He made it. This was met with part relief and part realisation that the odds were shortening on all of us making it without falling in.

Rob was next while Neil and I tried to steady his kayak. Another clean and dry exit of both man and boat. Neil also made it leaving just me in the water and the odds of success getting ever shorter. As I stood on my boat and prepared to put a foot part way up the embankment I realised that the motion of stepping off would propel my kayak back into the canal. Then as my foot made contact with the bank I realised that the passage of three wet kayaks across it had rendered it extremely slippery and it offered about as much purchase as a bowl of custard. With a helping hand from Rhys I struggled up the bank with my kayak, there was a brief wobble but I made it. Against all the odds and despite the best efforts of the angry swans we all made it to shore as dry as when we started.

The relief of making it to land was short lived as we faced the 'hidden' fourth discipline in this triathlon. Navigating our way across fields to a gate we couldn't see while dragging our kayaks behind us. I had an aerial image of our route in my mind from the maps I had been studying but translating this into directions on ground level was a mystery to me. In an effort to fool the others I marched off confidently in a direction I thought had a more than 10% chance of being right. It worked, they placed their full confidence in me and followed me into the darkness. I strode on in a manner inversely proportional to my failing confidence but was brought to an abrupt stop by the presence of a ditch which on closer inspection was actually a stream disguised by an overgrowth of weeds. I nervously edged closer to the steam trying to find the edge of the bank then using my paddle I gauged the depth of the water but what I couldn't determine was the how far away the opposite bank was. There was only one thing for it, I jumped. There was a painful pause while I was airborne followed by the satisfying thud of feet hitting land. I called for my kayak to be laid across the water and invited the team to come across the makeshift bridge. Each of them traversed the stream and then used their kayak to create a bridge for the next one. Buoyed by my success (and extreme luck) I marched on looking all the while for the twin tracks which I had seen on the map which I knew led to the gate where our support vehicles would be waiting. I could hardly believe it when I stumbled across the tracks and only just managed to disguise my surprise in an effort to keep up the pretence that I knew what I was doing.

"There's the gate" I yelled above the sound of the continuing barking of the hounds. "But where's the van?" came the sharp reply. In all my self congratulating I hadn't noticed the stark absence of the support vehicles. Surely, after all our struggles on the water and in the fields we weren't going to have to abandon the event because we lost the vehicles. But all was well, they were spotted a few hundred yards down the road parked by the wrong gate and any minute now they will turn round and come to us having been roused from their sleep by the noise of the dogs, (which by now in our deluded state were sounding a bit more like wolves) and the flashing of our head torches in the distant blackness.

When we realised that they weren't coming Rob was forced to run and alert them to our presence. It must have been hard for them in those comfy seats, listening to the radio with the heater blowing while we were having so much fun on the water.

Soon the vehicles were in the right place and so began the first transition. Now I've watched triathlons on the TV and so had a very clear image of what a transition should look like. Slick and quick would be a way of describing it. However, what I saw here I have never seen on the TV, bodies lying on the grass gasping for air, men hiding behind the van changing underwear, others rummaging through holdalls looking for trainers. Not so much slick and quick as dishevelled and disorganised. We had scheduled 10 minutes for the transition but it took this long just to change our socks. What with evil swans, land marches, unexpected streams, lost vehicles and a painfully slow transition we were now 90 minutes behind schedule.

Never the less we were encouraged to be joined on the next leg (running) by Wayne. We were less than encouraged to see the heavy strapping on both of Wayne's knees. This was industrial strength strapping that looked as if it might have previously been used to hold together a length of undersea oil pipe. It was hard to tell in the darkness but at one point as the clouds moved across the sky I thought I caught the glint of scaffolding poles strapped to his legs in the moonlight. If we tied a little box around his neck with a slot in it we could place him outside the local shop and collect extra money but we decided to take him on the run with us instead. We needn't have worried, Wayne was quite capable of running and so we headed off. I handed out the laminated route cards which I had carefully prepared and hoped I had recorded every turn. As the miles went by we began to split up and find our own pace and I was pleasantly surprised to find that the running was fairly easy going. Once again the flatness of Somerset was playing it's part and months of training on the unforgiving hills of Dartmoor meant this leg was relatively comfortable.
However, I was very surprised to come across a group of youths on bikes mucking around outside a row of shops bearing in mind it was about 4am. Just as I was beginning to wonder if I should be concerned Adrian pulled up in his car and drove alongside me for a little while; I was very glad of the company.

We finished the run at Bridgewater Marina but it was still dark as we began transition number two which was about as slick and elegant as the first transition. Maybe we should have included transitions in our training program!! While we were struggling with unloading kayaks whilst changing socks with one hand and eating Jelly Babies with the other

(other sugar based sweets are available) Adam's phone rang. It was Wayne who, a bit concerned that he might have got lost, was asking if the route took us past the The George Public House. Surprisingly, none of us had really taken much notice of the surrounding attractions in the dark, at 4am, 6 miles into a run after a 5 mile kayak session and offered about as much help as a snow machine to an Eskimo. After a moments concern that my route card may be to blame for Wayne's temporary wilderness moment I quickly turned my attention to a sausage roll which was far more important. Moments later Wayne came into view and I was able to make a reasonable job of pretending I had been so worried I was forced to eat something to calm my nerves.

Back in the kayaks we set off from Bridgewater Marina which was a little different from our first kayak leg. The natural beauty of the landscape was replaced by high brick walls and tower blocks of flats and the wildlife replaced by beer cans and empty whiskey bottles. At first we moaned about the state of the canal but soon changed our tune when we realised that bottles and cans cannot take off and fly at you through the darkness. However, one thing that did come through the darkness was a voice shouting, "hi, are you ok?" "Well, how nice", I thought to myself, whoever is at the front is aware that I am at the back and taking into account the state of the canal are concerned for my welfare. "I'm fine, thank you" I replied cheerily. Imagine how foolish I felt when I discovered it was in fact a drunken man who was sat under a bridge and perhaps a little startled to see four men in fluorescent clothing with head torches on paddling down the canal at such a ridiculous hour of the night. Not wanting to alert the others to my stupidity I nervously but briefly carried on my conversation with the drunken man in a futile pretence that I had know he was there all along and at no point was I a little tearful at the heart warming concern of my colleagues. I didn't actually see the man as it was too dark but I had images of him looking at his bottle, looking at the sight before him, looking back at the bottle and throwing it into the canal whilst swearing to never touch another drop again. My paddle speed increased quite markedly at that point as I didn't fancy being capsized by a wayward bottle of Guinness. Although I think bottle dodging was marginally more preferable to swan dodging.

Eventually the domineering walls and tower blocks gave way to nature and the more familiar sight of bulrushes, reeds and trees once again became the backdrop for our journey. But there was also a notable drop in temperature, as dawn approached it brought with it a cool chill in the air which was becoming increasingly uncomfortable. Several miles into the first leg we were faced with a very low bridge and decided this would be a good place to take a break for rest and refuelling but by now it was so cold that as soon as we got onto the bank we decided it was much better to keep moving to try and stay warm. However, when I looked back at the water I had an horrific flashback to a previous encounter with a similar low bridge whilst training on The Grand Western Canal, on that occasion I ended up unwillingly swimming under the bridge. At least that time it was mid afternoon on a sunny day, I really didn't fancy repeating this performance at 6am in the freezing cold. So I took the cowards option of dragging my kayak over the bridge and putting it in the water on the other side. I noticed that Rhys, who had seen my previous capsize elected to follow me whilst Neil & Rob, oblivious to the risk, decided against hauling their kayaks over land and took what appeared to be the easier option of returning to the water where they left it and running the gauntlet of the low bridge. Whilst, naturally I was delighted they negotiated the bridge without incident thus avoiding further delays a small part of me was a little disappointed that despite being the most experienced kayaker I was still the only one to have suffered the indignity of the splash of shame.

The next stop was a 'mini transition'. In my preparation I had noticed that two sections of the canal had become clogged with weeds and were impassable. The two sections were fairly close together and so I took the decision that we would take the boats out of the water and travel about a mile and a half on foot past the two obstructions. We were extremely pleased to see the van exactly where it was meant to be and Wayne & Adam loaded up the kayaks while we found some extra layers to keep us warm and took the opportunity for a quick top up of food.

We quickly got on our way again and began walking along the tow path until for some inexplicable reason Rob decided it would be a good idea to run instead of walk. I smirked quietly to myself as obviously no one would run and Rob would be left looking completely stupid. To my horror Neil sort of grimaced and with a look of resignation on his face joined Rob in a gentle trot. My only hope of bringing some sanity into proceedings was Rhys but even he silently and reluctantly started to shuffle in a manner reminiscent of jogging. I don't believe there was any thought process involved I think it was simply a case of being numbed to reality and a lemming like response was provoked so he simply did whatever the person in front of him did. There was only one thing I could do, in a fake act of machoism I declared, "Good idea" and forced my leadened legs to respond. Fortunately I was at the rear of the group and they were unable to see my tears.

I was very pleased to see Adam and Wayne waiting for us up ahead and we were quickly back in the kayaks and heading for the next check point. However, the check point seemed to take an age to arrive; as each bridge approached we kept expecting to see Adrian & Cai which would herald the 9 mile marker and signal the final 3 miles of what was becoming an arduous stage. But that point never came; unbeknown to us Adrian and Cai had gone to the wrong bridge and we never saw them. Even now I cannot understand how this happened. It's not like there are hundreds of canals between Bridgewater and Taunton (there is only one) so where were they? My theory is that they found a bridge, parked up and fell asleep. If they had bothered to look over the bridge they would have seen the 7:22 to Plymouth racing past and realised their mistake. The absence of the check point had a psychological effect on the kayakers who consequently had no idea how far was left to travel. We were really starting to feel the burn now and were desperate to see any sign of our support crew so that we could get a bearing on both time and distance.
Feeling somewhat responsible for the team as the event organiser and being the one with the most kayaking experience I decided to take the front and act as a sort of pacemaker to drag the others along. I completely zoned out the pain and everything going on around me and began to paddle with metronome monotony not looking left or right but fixed ahead begging my eyes to see any trace of our support crew.
On a couple of occasions I would hear a shout behind me, "look, houses. We must be on the outskirts of Taunton." I don't know if it was an hallucination but by the time I registered the comment and sent a message to my neck to crane my head towards the side the houses had gone and all I could see were some bemused cows looking on disdainfully.

But then I saw something in the distance which triggered a vague recognition in my mind. Could it be, could it really be? Yes it was the end of the canal and there was Cai armed with his camera and to top it all I was in the front for the photo call. I yelled back to the others, "That's the finish line" but instantly regretted it as I had images of a sudden burst of speed to overtake me and get to the front for the photo. Nothing was going to deny me my moment, I had worked hard for this and I deserved to be at the front for at least one photo. In the final few hundred metres I paddled for all I was worth whilst practicing my victory smile. With my head down I dug in deep and made sure that no one could overtake me. As I approached the finish I raised my head up high and with the very last dregs of my energy I forced my face into a magnificent smile which said, "I'm still strong, fit and loving this" and pointed it towards Cai. But wait a minute, where is Cai? More importantly, where is the camera? It was nowhere to be seen. I couldn't believe it, Cai had assumed that the finish point was just the other side of the bridge. He didn't know that the only place to get our kayaks out of the water was this side of the bridge and so was in the wrong place to record my glorious victory. And just to rub salt into the wound he had taken all the others with him. Cai, Adrian, Wayne and Adam were blissfully unaware of my triumphant entry into Taunton which consisted of me climbing out of my kayak to an audience of two very disinterested ducks and a robin. I looked back at my colleagues on the water for some sort of acknowledgement but all to no avail, their faces were still etched with misery as the joy of finishing had still not registered. Despondently, I turned around only to see Cai running from behind the bridge with his camera to take photos of the rest of the team approaching the finish. The camera recorded, for all posterity, the finish of this marathon kayaking stage without me anywhere in sight and of course, the camera never lies!!

The end of another leg meant the beginning of another transition. Once again the hope that we would be like the Brownlee brothers was replaced with the reality of being more like the Chuckle brothers. Eventually we were ready and once again Wayne joined us as we set off on foot for the second and longest running leg, twelve miles in total. We arranged with Adrian and Cai to set up a check point at six miles where we could also stop for a drink and to re-fuel as necessary.

Once again we all settled into our own pace and slowly the group began to stretch out. I was very lucky to find a small snail with a limp to act as my pacemaker and with a bit of effort managed to keep up with it. It was very tough and as we got closer and closer to Devon so the hills began to get steeper and more frequent. Judging by the proportion of uphills to downhills by my estimation we should be on the moon by the time we made it to our first checkpoint. However, on reaching the agreed point I was devastated to find a complete absence of Adrian and Cai. Surely they hadn't got lost again. Then a text came through on my phone, "we've moved the checkpoint to 8 miles". Oh no, my water bottle was empty, my energy levels were zero and my legs had been filled with concrete. I relayed the message back to Rhys who had been following me and the limping snail and the news was met with a grunt of disapproval. I'm certain that the next two miles were all uphill and even the snail got fed up with waiting and contacted his elderly granddad to take over pace making duties. I reached Wellington looking dishevelled and broken. I had hoped to have been refreshed at 6 miles so that when I reached the town I could bound through the onlookers like a sprightly gazelle but it was not to be. Instead the onlookers were treated to a sight more akin to walrus on a spacehopper. And as if this wasn't bad enough, in sympathy with my expiring energy the elastic in my boxers also gave up the ghost so every hundred yards or so I had to reach into my running shorts to yank up my boxers. Unfortunately, hauling myself 'walrusesque' with one had shoved down my shorts through the town centre of Wellington was not my lowest point, this would come later around the 10 mile mark.

Finally, I made the checkpoint and was very surprised to see Neil & Rob there as I had assumed that they were so far ahead they were probably home in their respective beds by now but they were taking advantage of an extended break to rest and take on essential fluids. Rhys soon joined us and we were a group of four again. Rob graciously suggested we stick together for the final four miles of this leg but soon realised that it was impossible for him to run as slowly as I do. After all, I have spent many years training at this speed so I had the advantage there.

Then it happened, at 10 miles I hit the wall. I was slowly becoming aware that whilst my legs and arms were in motion my body was not. My legs appeared to be moving but I wasn't getting anywhere. I was on a gruelling uphill climb but was travelling so slowly I thought, "I could probably walk quicker than I am running right now." So I tried it and I was right, my walking speed was now quicker than my running speed so I walked the rest of the hill and only returned to running when gravity assisted. The final two miles were incredibly tough but I made it. Once again Neil and Rob were already at the finish of this leg and Rhys was close behind after an unscheduled toilet stop.

Now it was decision time - we were scheduled to kayak the Grand Western Canal which is 11 miles long and would have taken about four hours but we were several hours behind schedule thanks to a difficult first leg and extended transition times. After that there was another 3-4 hours of cycling some of which would now be in the dark if we kept to plan. To be honest the decision was an easy one partly because we couldn't cycle in the dark as we had no lights and partly because it was inadvisable to add another few hours to an already gruelling event but we managed to string out the decision for quite a while as cover for a much needed rest.

The decision was to cycle the tow path of the canal thus extending the cycle leg from 30 miles to 41 miles. At this stage we were all feeling exhausted and were unsure if cycling 41 miles was within our ability but we struggled onto our bikes and set off along the tow path.
As it turns out, the 11 miles of completely flat tow path served as a warm up for the main cycle leg. We made excellent progress and by the end of the canal we all felt considerably better and much more confident about the remainder of the event. Cycling this leg instead of kayaking had helped us to recover three hours and put us back on schedule thus justifying the decision to make the change.

We stopped to refuel again as energy reserves were very low by now as we had been on the go for about 14 hours and we knew that there was a punishing series of hills ahead of us. We set off again with some trepidation as we all knew that there was a hill about 4 miles in to this section which would be at home in the Himalayas. The approach to the hill was relatively flat and so we got into a good rhythm as we hit the foot of the hill. All the fear for the hill was somehow converted into adrenalin and everyone made it without too much difficulty adding to our growing confidence. After a few more hills we hit paradise; a downhill section which must have been several miles long. It was bliss as gravity did most of the work for us and we flew along the route until we all regrouped again in Crediton. Another brief rest and we took to the road again. Neil, being the strongest cyclist, took the front and set the pace for the rest of us to follow, we were only too pleased to have someone to slipstream and make the going a little easier for us. The next rest stop was Bow which provided us with another opportunity to take on food and water and another phone call from Wayne. Unfortunately he phoned Adrian. The two lads from Cardiff trying to identify where exactly in Mid Devon Wayne was. At one point Adrian triumphantly produced the map to show us where Wayne was but after 20 minutes of turning the map this way and that had to admit that he didn't have a clue.

Wayne eventually managed to find his way back to Bow only to learn that he had been on the right road all along which he would now have to ride all over again.

We could almost smell Okehampton from here and we were keen to get on. Neil wanted to contact Abby to let her know that we would soon be finished so I took on the role of pacemaker and led the team to our next stop at The Countryman Inn. By now there were some seriously aching limbs in the team but the finish line was so close it was just a case of mind over matter. We agreed to regroup at the top of Okehampton so that we could all reach the finish together.

All five of us dropped down that last hill with a final burst of energy and Rhys hit the front for the first time in the entire cycle leg just in time for the finishing photos: Rob was secretly livid. Here we were greeted by friends and loved ones outside Okehampton Baptist Church which was our final destination. 17.5 hours after we started we had completed the event.

It had been amazing. None of us had done anything like it before. 17.5 hours of running, kayaking, cycling and swan dodging; through the dark of the night, the cold of dawn, the heat of the day. Fighting through pain and exhaustion to complete an endurance event which seemed impossible on more than one occasion.

Why did we do it? Well, insanity is one plausible explanation but the real reason was to raise money for The House Of Rachel so that they can continue their valuable work with the orphaned and abandoned children of Bulgaria. Whilst we may have endured 17.5 hours of discomfort some of these children have a lifetime of misery. Whilst we had comfortable beds and homes to look forward to many of these children will end up on the streets. Whilst we might not have been looking forward to returning to work the following day these children have no hope of ever getting a job.
So every painful step, every agonising paddle stroke, every excruciating pedal revolution was worth it as we have seen firsthand what a difference we can make for these children. The money raised will go towards paying for college, paying for vocational courses, paying for safe houses, building better orphanages and creating a future full of hope for these wonderful children.

So to everyone who helped; athletes, support crew, sponsors and everyone else a huge thank you from everyone involved in The House Of Rachel. Because of you we have been able to do amazing things in the lives of the orphaned and abandoned children of Bulgaria.

Andrew

CHAPTER SIXTEEN
New Lungs Please
May 2015

TUESDAY

The 3am alarm heralded another trip to Bulgaria - via Cardiff!
This time I was meeting my brothers, Kevin & Adrian for the trip and as Adrian was driving to the airport we met in Cardiff where they live.
The rendezvous was at mum's house at 6:15 am. This was arranged under the pretence of convenience but really our motivation was to procure some sandwiches and some of mum's famous Welsh cakes. Readers who remember the 'sandwich gate' debacle from the last time we tried this may question our decision but it proved to be a good one and mum came up with the goods.

Part of my long and meticulous preparation was to ensure Kevin & Adrian brought bags large enough to accommodate some extra bits and pieces we were taking out with us (a football kit donated by Okehampton Argyle Juniors and some school jumpers). I managed to get the football kit into my bag and Adrian managed to get half of the school jumpers into his but when we asked Kevin to pack the remaining jumpers into his bag he simply produced what appeared to be his wallet. Unfortunately, this miniscule container turned out to be his luggage. At best it couldn't have contained any more than half a toothbrush and a single sock. Adrian and I quickly did some mental arithmetic, 5 days divided by one pair of pants, we didn't much like the result. I changed to my reading glasses to get a better look at the tiny carrier before me but without the aid of a microscope it was no clearer. Any thoughts of squeezing in even one jumper quickly disappeared and mum's offer to lend him one of her bags was rejected for fear of a pink flowery offering.

And so we set off with luggage which looked like it belonged to two men and a small flea, with mum's words of wisdom ringing in our ears, "make sure you leave the cake box in the car so that you remember to bring it home." Ah, the wisdom which comes with maturity, without it we would probably have taken the cake box on the flight and carried it around Bulgaria with us - maybe we could have swapped it for Kevin's handbag.

On route we decided to open the sandwiches only to find a note from mum (clearly written with 'sandwich gate' in mind) which read, "Andrew, don't eat all the ham sandwiches. Kevin, don't eat all the biscuits. Sorry Adrian, no Jelly babies". Despite our own advancing years we're still being told off by mum like naughty little boys although to be fair, she had a point and it was all in good humour.

It was a fairly uneventful trip to the airport and we were soon in the queue for boarding. We were enjoying following the adventures of Mr Boring (first name Incredibly) doing the rounds of the people in front of us in the queue and watching the faces of the people he was engaging with his riveting conversation change from impatience to blind panic in a matter of seconds. Then the horrible truth dawned on us, Wizz Air operate a free for all boarding system, no seat allocation just grab whatever seat you can and the gravity of the situation hit us hard; what if we get stuck next to Mr Incredibly Boring who in the few minutes we had been observing him changed his name by deed poll twice, firstly to Unbelievably Irritating and then to Completely Obnoxious. What had started as amusing people watching quickly turned into an urgent workshop on how to deal with the unthinkable possibility that we might get landed next to him on the plane. Kevin tried to make a fake hearing aid from his sock and half a toothbrush which he could pretend was broken. Adrian filled a clear plastic bag with tomato sauce and using a black felt pen wrote 'Bloods—Botulism' on it before making a small hole in it and allowing a little of the sauce to leak out. I panicked and it true Black Adder style shoved my underpants on my head, pencils up my nose and cried 'wibble'.
Clearly our education had not been wasted and our efforts worked as none of us got stuck with Mr Obnoxious. Cantonian High School can be proud of its three past pupils and no doubt it's only a matter of time before we are asked to return there and unveil a plaque in our honour.

We arrived in Provadia around 7:30pm and made straight for the restaurant which has featured so abundantly in previous reports for its similarity to Fawlty Towers. I ordered a pork dish to which 'Basil' responded, "We do that dish with chicken as well", "No", I said, "pork will be fine thank you". It was only when Basil got on his bike to go to the local shop that Adrian pointed out he obviously wanted me to have chicken as he had no pork and now he had to go and buy some. It was a very nice meal but we made the mistake of discussing pudding within earshot of

Basil who responded by presenting us with the bill before we had chance to order something else he didn't have and once again send him off to the shops on his bike. We have worked out that there is a direct relationship between the lateness of the hour and the distance he has to cycle to the nearest shop which is still open. Clearly he remembered Adrian's request for a banana split last year which meant he had to do the 'Tour De France' for one miserable banana; he wasn't going to make the same mistake again.

We finished the night off by making arrangements with Alex for the following morning. Suggestions of 8:30 were laughed off as we all said we would be up by 6:30.

WEDNESDAY
We woke the following morning at 7:30! Fortunately, despite our bravado, we had arranged an 8:30 meeting allowing us an hour to make ourselves look presentable so with 55 minutes remaining we went to the local shop to buy breakfast. As a veteran of these trips I had remembered to take a spoon so I bought a yogurt and an apple. Kevin, also keen to select the healthy option, went for two chocolate croissants and a bottle of coke - a traditional Bulgarian breakfast!!!

Suitably nourished we met Alex and set off for the Orphanage to meet the director (Ivelina) and plan the next few days. As we sat down in Ivelina's office I joked, "So what plans have you changed this time?" Alex looked a little sheepish and said, "well, actually………." and sure enough a few jobs we had planned had been changed.

This wasn't a problem and we fully understand that priorities have to change as circumstances change (such as a recent damp problem from a damaged roof which wasn't expected). We took a tour of the areas where work was needed and amended our shopping list accordingly.

We headed back to Provadia to do our annual round of the builders' merchants but with a threatening sky and rain in the forecast decided to collect our coats first. At least Kevin and I did; unfortunately, Adrian had forgotten his which became a recurring theme throughout the week. The thought of a whole afternoon of shopping was taking its toll and we wondered how on earth we were going to get through it - food. Yes, we needed to take on enough fuel to get us through the next few hours so we headed to the little café on the corner of the square where they serve massive slices of pizza for 1 lev (which at current exchange rates amounts to the princely sum of 40p) but we hadn't expected a lunch guest. Just as we settled down to eat an 'interesting' looking beetle sauntered across the table looking for a few tasty morsels which we might have dropped. Clearly he didn't know us very well as we would never drop any of our lunch. As we left we checked outside to see how many Michelin stars the establishment had because we thought anything more than three would demand a strongly worded letter from us. However, we couldn't find the plaque which would have told us it's rating and we guessed that it must have been in the post.

Having run out of excuses to delay doing the shopping we made a start and were very pleased that it all went rather well. Having done this for several years now we are beginning to learn which shops sell what and Alex is better at interpreting our ridiculous mimes in our pathetic attempts to describe what a 'spoke shave' is. So we got back to the orphanage relatively quickly and deposited our purchases in the room allocated to our building materials. This meant we had time to play a few games with the children; one football and a lot of imagination gave rise to great fun and laughter.

However, the games gave rise to a stark reality. Once upon a time Kevin, Adrian and I played football together on the same team and although none of us were particularly brilliant, in our own minds we were of Welsh International standard. Sadly, our minds had failed to take account of the intervening years and fooled us into believing we still had at least some talent. We were smart enough to realise that maybe we weren't quite as good as we once were but it was a crushing blow to discover just how far we had fallen. Our deterioration to utterly useless was completed there in that yard at Krivnya Orphanage. Our heads said 'flick the ball up with my left foot and sublimely stroke it with the heel of my right foot' but by the time the message passed through rusty synapses, cracked nerve endings and clogged arteries the ball was long gone and feet swung aimlessly at thin air. I think we all aged about 30 years in that one moment so we took to throwing the ball around instead as the only advantage we held over the children was height. As we tried to hopelessly hang on to what was left of our dignity the children continued to run, play and laugh as a reminder of what was really important.

If we had had any energy left Kevin and I would have done a rain dance as unfortunately it hadn't rained so we couldn't poke fun at Adrian for forgetting his coat. Not to worry there were still a few days left and rain was still in the forecast.

That evening we decided to visit a different restaurant and sat down to read the menu. In Bulgaria, menus are more like books. Whereas at home we may be used to an A4 sheet of choices in Bulgaria you are presented with a folder with at least 10 pages of options so it takes a long time to choose your food. Eventually, choices made, we attracted the attention of the waiter and I went first. "This one please" I said as I pointed to a tasty looking Kavarma. "No", replied the waiter, "not this" and he drew a long line through a whole section of the menu with an imaginary pen. "How about this one?", "No". "This one?", "No" and so it went on until finally I found something he could actually provide. Kevin had better luck with his first choice of Mixed Grill so when Adrian had his first choice declined he took the easy option and went for the mixed grill as well. While we waited for our meal Adrian pointed out an interesting menu item called 'Sausage Hoof'. We had no idea what it was but thought it was probably the one thing on the menu that they never ran out of.

After our meal we returned to our room where we turned on the TV. Obviously the choice of channels is limited as naturally they are all in Bulgarian but there is the odd 'imported' channel which is in English with Bulgarian subtitles. Our options therefore are Discovery Channel, Animal Planet or CNN. We opted for the Discovery Channel and began to watch a program with the intriguing title 'The Wildmen' about American turtle hunters. What a load of old tosh that turned out to be. We had more chance of understanding the Bulgarian subtitles than understanding the rubbish which poured out of their mouths. Their antics would have been more at home in an episode of Dick & Dom on Cbeebees so we quickly turned over to CNN where they were reporting on the riots in Baltimore, followed by a feature on the Baltimore riots. Then they did the weather forecast from Baltimore district where the riots were. The sports section was all about the games which had been cancelled because of the riots. Then they interviewed the mayor of Baltimore about the riots, followed by a chat with a psychiatrist about the reasons behind the Baltimore riots. After half an hour we realised that there was only one thing happening in the whole world and if we watched any longer there would be an interview with a Baltimore hairdresser about how a decent haircut was the remedy Baltimore was crying out for. So the TV got turned off and we went to sleep.

THURSDAY
The next morning we travelled into Varna for the large superstore called Praktika where we were going to buy the laminate flooring. We needed 120m2 plus underlay, skirting and fixings so it was quite a big order. Thanks to Alex everything went very smoothly again and we were soon in the loading bay spreading the laminate around the minibus to distribute the load.

If the shopping had been boring (is there any other kind?), the journey home certainly wasn't. We were casually driving along the dual carriageway minding our own business when we spotted a man walking up the slip road carrying a pair of crutches. We couldn't think of any possible scenario which made sense of this bizarre sight. But just when we thought we had seen the strangest thing ever on a dual carriageway we all did a double take at the sight of a white haired man in his 60's riding a child's scooter along the hard shoulder. For a moment we were concerned that our clapped out, heavily laden minibus might not be able to overtake him but a hill came to our rescue and we coasted past him with looks of incredulity on our faces as he scooted along oblivious to the absurdity of his actions.

We hardly had time to scratch our heads in wonderment at what we had seen before our exit junction approached; but wait, what is that? No, it can't be. It's the man carrying the crutches. We had travelled about 20 miles since we saw him walk onto the dual carriageway and whilst our old jalopy might be slow it wasn't so slow that a man with crutches could beat us over that sort of distance; even if the crutches were turbo charged.

After unloading all the wood we asked Ivelina if she could help us with something. One of the Orphanages where we work, Barzitsa, had been 'downsized' as part of the government's policy to overhaul the state care system and we were trying to track down the children. We were aware that some had been transferred to Novi Pazar about 25 miles away and wanted to go and see them so we asked Ivelina if she would phone the director there and get us permission to visit. She agreed on the strict understanding that we were not to find work to do there as she needed us in Krivnya. She said it in a joking manner but we were aware that it came from her heart. We promised not to desert her and she made arrangements for us.

There was just time for lunch before we set off for Novi Pazar so it was back to the pizza place and our friend the beetle. It was about 2 o'clock by now and the staff at the pizza place were sat around chatting as the lunchtime rush was over, even the beetle had left. I ordered my pizza and the lady asked me if I would like a bag but I said we would eat in. Afterwards Adrian pointed out to me that I should have read between the lines and what she actually meant by offering me a bag was 'please take it out as we want to close now' but instead we made them stay another ten minutes while we ate our lunch. Fortunately there was some sort of soap on the tiny TV in the corner which looked about as cheerful as Eastenders to keep the ladies entertained.

I've often commented on the state of the roads in Bulgaria but when we got to Novi Pazar we discovered what I thought at the time to be the worst I had ever experienced. I have also commented on the lack of 'Health & Safety' evident in various work practices and this was no exception (I will leave you to judge whether the lack of H&S makes things better or worse). There were massive craters in the road big enough to swallow one of the diggers being used to create the many drainage ditches which snaked their way down the roads. There wasn't a barrier in sight, no road closures, no warning signs, no flashing lights; cars just weaved their way around the gaping holes which looked like hungry mouths just waiting to swallow up any car which misjudged the amount of available road. Eventually we came across a mound of rubble which even the old man on the scooter wouldn't be able to pass round so we parked up and walked the rest of the way to the orphanage.

A wonderful reception awaited us; pre-warned of our arrival a few of the children were waiting outside for us and Radjostina let out a huge cry of joy when she spotted us and ran to greet us. We were escorted into the home where we signed in and sat and chatted with the children for about an hour. It was lovely to see that the orphanage in Novi Pazar was modern, clean and on the face of it, a much nicer environment than Barzitsa. However, despite all her joy in seeing us, Radjostina concealed a heavy heart. When the children were first informed that Barzitsa was downsizing and they would need to be moved, Radjostina and her sister both visited Novi Pazar and 'agreed' to be transferred there but for reasons unknown only Radjostina was transferred, her sister was left behind in Barzitsa and the girls were separated.

We had a quick chat amongst ourselves and agreed we could fit in a trip to bring the girls together for a short while so that at least they could visit one another. The director at Novi Pazar agreed, the director at Barzitsa agreed but Social Services would not authorise it. Whilst very disappointing, it was completely understandable; it is not unknown for 'strange' men to disappear with vulnerable girls in Bulgaria. It was somewhat heartening that Social Services took this stance and evidence of an improving situation - or so we thought!!

When it eventually came time to leave we were once again escorted from the building by the children but as we got further and further away from the orphanage we still had Radjostina in tow and she eventually accompanied us all the way back to the minibus. No one asked her where she was going, no one tried to stop her leaving, no one paid any interest whatsoever in her disappearance. If we had evil intentions it would have been the easiest thing in the world to simply drive off with her never to return.

So whilst it would seem that there are child safety protocols in place they are not practiced. A cynic might say the protocols exist not for the safety of the children but for the appeasement of the EU.

As we returned to Provadia on the dual carriageway we were once again treated to some novel sights such as a car suddenly doing a U-turn in the inside lane to exit the road via the joining slip road. Maybe this is normal in Bulgaria but if I had been coming along that road preparing to join the dual carriageway I would have been very surprised to see a car coming towards me.

Back in Provadia Alex returned to her home so I proudly took on the role of translator. Since my last visit I have learned another new Bulgarian word taking my total to four - I'm practically fluent now. We sat down for an 'al fresco' cup of tea and as the waiter approached I rehearsed my lines and by the time he got to us I was able to order two teas with milk and one with honey; imagine my relief (and surprise) when the waiter returned with exactly what I had ordered, what were the odds of that happening? Flushed with success I was very quick to tell Alex of my amazing linguistic prowess the following morning.

FRIDAY

This morning we were woken by the dulcet tones of a man in the next room trying to clear his throat. From the sounds he was making we could only guess that whatever it was he was trying to clear, it was lodged firmly in his boots. This unpleasant and persistent hacking lasted a full 20 minutes and only ended when he finally coughed up a lung. The silence which followed made us think that perhaps it was his only remaining lung so filled with deep concern we went out to buy breakfast.

If he had known in advance, Adrian might have gone back to the room next door and picked up hacking man's lung off the floor as we were about to discover that Adrian had forgotten to pack his own lungs (he must have left them with his coat). We had about an hour to spare and decided to trek up to the castle ruins on the top of the hill. It's a fairly steep climb with lots of steps to get to the ruins but the views are amazing and for a little extra effort you can cross the meandering footbridge and climb a final small hill to get to the highest point and then soak up the best views from a small, raised viewing platform. Kevin and I reached the platform first and could hardly believe what was happening behind us; Adrian was making the final ascent of six steps on his hands and knees while muttering, "I didn't know I was so unfit" between gulps of air. That extra lung would have been useful now and may have allowed Kevin and I to avoid this pitiful sight. I was reminded of an old favourite song of mine 'More Life In A Tramps Vest' by the Stereophonics. Until this day I had no idea what the song was about but know I know exactly what they meant.

It wasn't easy but eventually Kevin and I stopped laughing long enough to take a look at the steps and wondered how they managed to support Adrian's lifeless body. Those steps which remained were rotten and held in place by 4" nails of which about 3" protruded ready to penetrate the sole of any flimsy trainer which may stray onto them; or in this case any flimsy body which may drag itself over them.

As we couldn't find the defibrillator we paused a while and then started the decent to lower ground where the oxygen was in greater supply and Adrian could get off his knees and start walking normally again.

Back in town we decided to sit down and have a drink. After yesterday's amazing performance the order for two teas with milk and one with honey tripped off my tongue like a local and smugness enveloped me like a warm glove but the waiter said something back to me. Clearly the finesse of my accent and the accuracy of my grammar fooled him into thinking I was a native Bulgarian but I had no idea what he said and smugness made way for panic. I had used up all my words, I had no more (except for 'gypsokarten' which is Bulgarian for plasterboard and that wasn't going to be much use in a café!). I realised that the waiter hadn't understood my order, for a moment there was a glimmer of hope, maybe he simply hadn't heard me so I repeated the order a little more slowly and a little more loudly but to no avail.

I ended up doing the walk of shame to the counter and pointing at the various ingredients of a cup of tea with milk but I couldn't even point in Bulgarian as what arrived only vaguely resembled what I thought I had ordered. I guess I will need to learn yet another word for next year - when will it all end?

Today we really hoped to able to meet up with Zuska. We have known Zuska for many years and a few years ago a friend of the charity (Demi) who came on one of our College trips (students from Okehampton College go to Barzitsa where they run an activities week for the children) arranged for Zuska to receive some important plastic surgery for burns to her face which she suffered as a small child. Demi knew a world class plastic surgeon who, from time to time, would take on charitable cases without charge. He agreed to help Zuska (after the College students collected enough money to cover the anaesthetist's fees) and perform essential surgery.

Since then Zuska reached 18 and therefore had to leave the orphanage and our lines of communication all but broke down. However, thanks to the power of social media (and Google Translator) Zuska contacted Demi and said she needed help. Life after the Orphanage is very tough and she was really struggling. Emails and texts flew around and very quickly I agreed to meet her to see what we could do to help. We had been warned that she would probably ask for money which wouldn't be used wisely and that our efforts may be a waste of time but we were determined to give Zuska every possible chance to improve her life, after all, improving lives is at the core of our charity aims.

As the time drew closer to meet Zuska we really struggled to confirm arrangements. The plan was to meet her with a few of the children from Barzitsa orphanage in a Pizza Café where we would treat them all to lunch but Zuska wouldn't confirm that she would be there and presented us with all manner of half excuses. We couldn't understand why she was being evasive and were unable to get any confirmation that she would be at the café, it all seemed a little odd.

However, when we arrived at the café we were delighted to see her sat at the end of the table with a big smile on her face. We all tucked in to some very nice Pizza and had a good time catching up with some of the children we have known for many years. After we had eaten I took the opportunity to spend some time with Zuska and find out what she wanted and to see if it was something we could help with.

Almost every time I go to Bulgaria I encounter an experience which leaves me humbled and brings home to me the reality of the world in which some of these young people live; I was about to experience one of those moments.

Having been warned that she may simply be looking to 'extract' money out of us for some unsavoury purpose I was on guard. I was not expecting what came next. She simply asked if it were possible for us to pay the bus fare for her to return to her old school (approx 25 miles away) so that she could collect the documentation she needed to enrol in night school. The amount required was 10 lev which is just £4.

As is common with children growing up in orphanages, Zuska did not finish school and so did not have the necessary level of education to find decent work. At best this typically means she will end up doing menial labour for a pittance or at worst it means turning to the gangs and ending up as a prostitute. But Zuska had other plans; her desire was to go to night school, to finish her education and get herself a job which paid a living wage. To kick start this dream she needed £4 to get the documents required to enrol in night school.

We ended up giving fuel money to Didi so that she could take Zuska to pick up her documents in her car (which she subsequently did). During our chat we also discovered that she had had to borrow money for bus fare to get to the café (which was several miles from where she lives), obviously we helped her with that but it also revealed the reason why she wouldn't confirm that she could make the meeting; she simply didn't know if she would be able to find the bus fare.

We know that Zuska faces tough times ahead, we know that she will have moments when she wants to pack it all in, we know that over the next two years (that's how long finishing school will take) she will probably make some bad decisions but we are keen to help her through these tough times and do all we can to help her realise her dream of finishing school and finding meaningful employment. We explained this to her and asked her to talk to us if/when any of these events occur so that we can help her through them.

After our time with the children and Zuska in the café we returned to Provadia where Kevin suggested we go for a walk around the town. I looked quizzically at him but a slight nod of the head towards the sky revealed his dastardly plan. He had spotted a dark cloud in the sky that foretold of possible rain and we were determined to make sure Adrian got at least one soaking so that we could poke fun at him for forgetting his coat. Having checked I had my own coat on me I agreed that a walk seemed like a fine idea. So far rain had been forecast every day but had always failed to deliver and Adrian was getting very smug, action was needed or we'd never hear the last of it. Kevin and I were delighted when half way into our walk the first few spots of rain dabbed our foreheads, we tried not to get too excited as when you have foreheads as large as ours (our hairlines might be receding just a little) a few drops don't mean much. Nevertheless, we reached for our coats and in a display of blatant cockiness put them on and looked expectantly at Adrian. "Aren't you going to put your coat on?", "Where's your coat?" we asked and waited. Within a few minutes it started to rain properly and it was our turn to look smug - and dry! I'm sure Adrian will try to tell you that it was only a small shower and hardly got him damp but in our memories it will always be a monsoon which soaked Adrian to his very core and left him as wrinkled as a prune.

As a point of interest for anyone reading this who has been on one of our trips (or feels like they have after reading the endless reports) and have met Maggie you may like to know that we bumped into her on our walk and discovered that she is pregnant, the baby is due in September. We were very pleased for her. Very few girls leave an orphanage, get married and start a family like Maggie.

Our next stop was Provadia orphanage. In 2010 we had saved Provadia orphanage from closing down and dumping some of the children onto the streets by starting the essential renovations there. Subsequently the EU had provided funding to finish the job and what an amazing transformation had been accomplished. Whilst the building work had been going on the children had been moved to Barzitsa. The work took

many years and at long last children were now resident there. In addition to providing residential care there is also a rehabilitation centre providing day care to children with physical and mental needs. Children from Barzitsa had been relocated there and we knew nearly all of them. It's a fantastic place and the children seemed very happy to be there.
So we had traced some of the displaced children to Novi Pazar, some to Provadia and we were told that more had gone to Balchik (although we were not able to go there). However, this does not account for all the children whose whereabouts remain unknown for now.

Later we began to plan the following day. We needed to get the minibus back to Kichevo which would normally mean driving through Varna but our last Varna trip revealed the extensive road works going on there and the subsequent traffic chaos so we wanted to look for a route which avoided Varna altogether. I knew roughly how to do this but wanted to check it on a map. Strangely Adrian had his Sat Nav on him (instead of his coat I guess) and was keen to show us what a wonderful piece of technology it was; meanwhile I reached for my road map.
"Adrian, why are you hanging out of the window in such a precarious manner?"
"Just trying to get a GPS signal, won't be a moment"
"It's OK, I've found what I need on the map"
"I'll check it on my Sat Nav"
"No need, the map confirmed the route and I know the way"
"Well, it would be useful to have it on the Sat Nav as well. I think I may need to go out onto the staircase to get reception"
And so the saga began. We moved to the staircase, nothing. We moved to the courtyard, nothing, we moved to the street, nothing. We walked to a bigger street, nothing. Eventually, after 40 minutes and a mile further up the road the GPS finally fired up and Adrian announced, "Yes, the map is right". Thanks Ade, that's 40 minutes of life we will never get back.

SATURDAY
With the security of knowing that Adrian's Sat Nav approved our route we headed to the outskirts of Varna as no trip to Bulgaria would be complete without a visit to the Happy restaurant. We walked into the centre of town and found a window seat in the restaurant but when we looked out of the window we thought we had been magically transported back in time to the 1980's as it seemed as though everyone was wearing Adidas shell suits. As we casually people watched we saw some amazing sights

and wondered if we were the only normal people in Varna that day but we weren't, there were in fact no normal people in Varna.

As we walked back towards the minibus we noticed that the Varna streets weren't too bad, nowhere near as chaotic as we had seen them the other day so we decided to risk the much shorter and more direct route to Kichevo through the centre of Varna. Well, that's what we told Adrian; Kevin and I had decided three hours of traffic delays was probably quicker than waiting for Adrian to get a route up on his Fisher Price Sat Nav.

At Kichevo we were pleased to see several of the Barzitsa children (past & present) working on the land. In 2012 a team had gone out to make a start on preparing the land which was earmarked to compliment the work being done at the camps held in the Hope & Future Foundation Centre. Now the youngsters were digging gardens ready for vegetables and building a small stable for a horse. It was great to see the kids getting stuck in to the work.

And so our time in Bulgaria came to an end with a trip to the airport; we were able to reflect on a successful time where our main objective to prepare everything for the builders (who were arriving in a week) was met. In addition we were pleased to have located many of the children who had been displaced when Barzitsa orphanage downsized and made a start on helping Zuska turn her life around.

As always we are extremely grateful to everyone who has helped us. For those who have donated money, thank you. Without you we couldn't buy all the materials the builders will need. And there's a wonderful lesson here, even the 'small' gifts are valuable. £4 may be all it takes to start the process of turning Zuska's life around
For those who prayed, thank you. God answered all your prayers. We know that we can do nothing in our own strength and everything which is achieved is because of God and it is to God we give all the glory.

Andrew

CHAPTER SEVENTEEN
When Earl Grey Just Isn't Good Enough
May 2015

After everyone arrived safely at the airport without any incidents we began to hope that maybe, just maybe, this would be the year when nothing went wrong.

A little early concern crept in when we couldn't find our flight on the board but was soon dismissed when we realised that we were reading the arrivals board not the departures board. Satisfied that we were in the right airport on the right day at the right time we settled down for a cuppa.

The first murmurs of a problem came when Barry announced he had lost the key to his suitcase and was unable to gain access to his passport. While he disappeared to see if he could find some help breaking into his luggage his dilemma set off a chain reaction of people checking their own passport situation. What is it with passports that one feels the need to check them so many times. You spend several days in the lead up to the journey making sure you know where your passport is and that it's in date and the picture still has a faint passing resemblance to you. Family members will have driven you mad with constant reminders 'have you checked your passport'. On the night before you leave you put your passport out where you can't possibly forget it. When you leave you check over and over again that it is in your pocket. Then when you are at the airport you still feel the need to check it again.

One by one people reached into their pockets to check their passport and one by one a sigh of relief filled the air. Relief turned to humour as people joked, "Are you sure that's not your wife's passport?" Then a small quiet voice next to me said. "Oh no, I've brought my wife's passport." I raised a polite giggle as to be honest I thought the joke had worn rather thin by now. But Nigel repeated, "No, really, I have brought my wife's passport" and in order to prove his point showed me the picture. It was surprisingly difficult to get the rest of the team to accept Nigel's error as, like me, they thought he was simply milking the joke which was doing the rounds. Eventually, reality hit and a disturbing silence fell to reveal only the sound of whirring cogs inside our heads as we tried in vain to come up with a solution to Nigel's problem. I don't think we were terribly helpful when the result of our combined intelligence came up with the idea that Nigel could wear a wig and put on a bit of lippy. We visited the Help Desk but the message was crystal clear, Nigel could not travel without his passport. The only option was for him to postpone flying for two days (the next scheduled flight) by which time he could arrange to collect his passport. There was a rare moment of genuine sympathy but normality was quickly restored as suggestions were made as to what jobs we could keep as punishment for his foolishness and some interesting arrangements were discussed for how to greet him when he eventually arrived.

Meanwhile Barry had returned having found someone who could break the lock on his suitcase and release his passport. He phoned home to let Jan know that if she found his key, not to panic as he had got into his suitcase and all was well. There was a moment's silence then Barry sheepishly opened his wallet under Jan's careful direction, to find the key he had placed there so carefully before he left home.

We waved goodbye to Nigel and made our way through security which for most of us was fairly straight forward. However, security is never straightforward for Adam who is a magician and had a bag full of magic tricks which for some reason always means he gets stopped to have his bags thoroughly searched. As we waited for him we imagined the security officer reaching into Adam's bag and pulling out a rabbit, a bunch of flowers and a few doves but unfortunately it wasn't nearly so exciting.

Equally as unexciting was the flight which after many years of recurring drama was a huge relief. We arrived in Provadia on time and as relaxed as being curled up in the foetal position on Hobbit Airlines will allow.

WEDNESDAY
Work started today and the most important job of all was to organise a tea/coffee list. On the face of it, it was a simple task of collating a list of how people like their drinks (e.g. tea, white, no sugar) to post in the kitchen so that when anyone was making drinks there was a list of everyone's preferences to hand. In reality it wasn't quite so straight forward. Neville kicked things off with a request for tea in the morning but coffee in the afternoon, Ross then complained that we could only find Earl Grey tea and that was rubbish but "I suppose I could have it without milk"; he ended up with coffee!!

If only Ross was as fussy and particular about his workmanship we wouldn't have ended up with our roof timbers being several centimetres too short. Never mind we can always stuff the gaps with Earl Grey teabags!!

Despite the minor measuring error good progress was made and half the roof timbers were erected on day one by Ross, Andy & Adam.

Meanwhile Barry, Ken & Neville cracked on with laying the new flooring in another room.

"Hang on" I hear you say, "that's only six people but there were eight on the trip." Well, Nigel was still in London looking for a wig and some lippy and I was shopping of course. No matter how hard I try I can never get out of doing the shopping. Builders are a demanding lot and their need for a 2mm, concave, zinc based, 90 degree, plastic coated, heat resistant sprogget never seems to end and no matter how triumphantly I present them with the very item they requested there is always another shopping list ready and waiting. I am becoming convinced that as soon as I set off for the shops they all retire to the kitchen to make a new shopping list over a cup of tea, not Earl Grey of course as that would be completely unacceptable, unless it's the afternoon in which case it would be coffee..

The children, however, were keen to work and often helped with little jobs. They were like a line of worker ants in the afternoon as they helped us to move hundreds of square metres of wood flooring into the next room to be given a new floor.

It's not easy to see where the children get their eagerness to work from as the two caretakers who arrive at the site everyday clearly have first class honours degrees in work avoidance. Observing them is like watching a master class in skiving and emotions from the team range from petty annoyance to sheer admiration of an art form which has been perfected over many years. Every now and again they are called into action and today's job (as they can only manage one a day) was to remove a door from one of the classrooms which needed replacing. Faced with the enormity of a task which could take up to five minutes, with no tea break, Dick & Dom applied all their years of experience to find a way to do it quicker so that they could return to the more important job of keeping their seats warm. In one swift move the door was jemmied from it's frame and to the sound of splintering wood the door fell to the floor with much of the frame still attached. Phew, time for a break!

To be fair, the men get paid an absolute pittance and it must be difficult staying motivated for such little reward. Occasionally we get a little grumpy about it but most of the time we smile and enjoy the humour in it all.

After work we made our way to Niko's restaurant which is a particular favourite of some of the regulars as the food is great, the service often hilarious and on request, he will open a barrel of his special ale. Everything was going well until Niko committed commercial suicide, the ultimate catering sin. He served a bad bottle of wine! Within the maelstrom of anger and the mayhem of disgusted tutting a mini battle was being played out as men tried to out 'connoisseur' each other using phrases that contained words like 'bouquet' 'nose' and 'palette' while swilling glasses of red round and round and verbally touring Europe quoting every wine region they could think of.
Niko gracefully accepted the criticism and replaced the wine but it was too late, the damage was done. One bad bottle of wine is one bottle too many and our allegiance to Niko's restaurant was irreparably damaged.

THURSDAY
More shopping! When I got back to the site with the latest request for a three quarter, inverted, left handed screwdriver I was looking forward to doing a little real work but that wasn't to be as I was ushered off to meet a local tradesman who would supply and fit a couple of new uPVC doors. I rely on being on site for some relief from the tedium of shopping but things had reached a new low with the introduction of 'on site shopping' as I purchased two new doors and frames. The rest of the team used the time I took with the door man to create another shopping list and I was sent back to town for some striped paint.

Eventually I managed to sneak back onto site without anyone seeing and start preparing one of the exterior walls for painting. I had bought some stabiliser and was applying this to some bad areas of the wall when one of the caretakers came over to see what I was doing. He was very curious about the stabiliser I was applying to the walls, so curious in fact that he deemed it important enough to wake up the other caretaker to show him one of the bottles. Together they read through the information on the bottle and were clearly amazed to discover such a thing existed. It reminded me that they are having to work with such a small budget that a simple thing like a stabilizing solution is not available to them and the majority of work they do is with recycled materials and basic tools. Before we left we gave them a bottle we had left over and they were truly delighted.

The work continued to progress very well and after lunch I was able to leave the site to do something other than shopping. Today was the day that Nigel would join us. He spared himself the misery of cross dressing to look like the picture in his wife's passport by having his own passport delivered to London and was on a flight to Varna. Alex agreed to drive her car so that the minibus could be left for the men on site. We took the chance to do a detour to Kichevo so that we could leave some money for Zuska. Regular readers will know that we have been helping Zuska for several years; firstly with an operation to deal with some severe facial scarring and more recently with help to finish school. A few weeks ago on our previous trip we had been able to help her retrieve the necessary paperwork to apply for night school classes and now we wanted to help her with the costs of obtaining a medical certificate.

Our journey meant a trip through Varna during rush hour. Having experienced the chaos of the roadworks in the centre a few weeks ago Alex decided on a different route around the outskirts. As we approached Varna Alex randomly decided to put on her seat belt, I asked her, "Why have you suddenly decided to put on your seatbelt, you've been driving around without it all week?" She replied, "Well I might not know the police here like I do in Provadia." Unfortunately, our plan to avoid the traffic was unsuccessful and we got caught up in the worst of it. With one eye on the clock (as we had to pick up Nigel from the airport) and one eye on the traffic we painfully picked our way through the traffic and eventually made it to the Hope & Future Foundation (HFF) in Kichevo - mission accomplished. Well, not quite as there was no one there! We took the suspension killing, back wrenching road to the 'eco farm' where HFF are building a new property but there was no one there either. It turned out to be a wasted journey.

Well, wasted except for one moment of triumph for me. The thought of fighting our way back through the traffic of Varna to the airport filled us with dread and it was then that I had my epiphany. "I know a way to the airport which doesn't go through Varna." It was a dangerous shout from me as my navigational skills are famously awful and I was in a foreign country with a Bulgarian National who naturally knew the roads much better than I did. Either my confident cry of "I know another way" fooled Alex or she was just so desperate to avoid Varna she would have done anything but she pointed the car in the direction of my pointing finger and off we went. Not only did I get the route right but we made it to the airport in time to meet Nigel off the plane.

The trip back to Provadia, with Nigel on board, was much simpler and soon the team was re-united and complete once more.

Whilst we were gone the teams had finished the flooring in a further classroom and the ceiling joists were all up. Andy took on the role of bus driver in my absence and was pleased to have got the team home safely but then he spoiled his moment of pride when, returning to his room, he found that the key wasn't working in the door. A few moments of frustrated cursing passed before realising it was the wrong room!

After the trauma of Niko's awful wine last night we tried a different restaurant where the mixed grill attracted a lot of attention. Some of us had experienced this mighty fayre before and were trying to describe it to the others. Adam quickly regretted his question, "Is it all pork?" as a chorus of voices pointed out that the clue was in the title 'mixed grill'. Adam's little error was soon forgotten when the conversation turned to wine again and Ken proudly announced that he knew a man in France who sold the berries for a particular wine. He may have got away with it as I'm not sure anyone noticed until Ross delighted in pointing out, "They're called grapes Ken".

FRIDAY

The purchase of a new jigsaw caused much excitement amongst the flooring team who had now moved to the home to work in the bedrooms. The excitement soon turned to frustration as no one could work out how to fit the blade. It was comical watching experienced builders fight with the tool while the others looked on offering unwanted advice. One by one they gave up as another took hold of the tool to show them how it's done but failed. Screwdrivers, allen keys, hammers and knives all got thrown down as each failed to fit the blade. Finally, in a final act of desperation, Ken handed the manual to Alex and pleaded with her, "Please can you translate these instructions" There was a moment's pause before Alex replied, "But they're in English!" How we laughed and it was only a matter of milliseconds before we sympathetically shared Ken's humiliation with the rest of the team working at the school.

Surprisingly, I found myself shopping again very shortly afterwards but as we left the DIY store disaster struck - the minibus wouldn't start. Alex suggested that it might be the battery but after running a few tests I confidently concluded it was not. Fortunately there was a garage just around the corner and within the blink of an eye 8 men appeared and pushed the bus into the inspection area. While they ran a series of diagnostics Alex repeated her opinion that it was a fault with the battery and whilst I was in full flow explaining why it couldn't possibly be the battery the mechanic came over and announced, "It's the battery." I secretly hoped that it was some kind of practical joke that Alex had arranged to make me look stupid but it wasn't. I had managed to look very stupid all on my own. A few minutes later a new battery had been purchased and fitted and we were on our way again. I consoled myself with the knowledge that the fitting of a new battery had in fact doubled the value of the minibus.

Another productive day on site meant that the new ceiling was now up and new flooring had been laid in one bedroom and half of another (thanks to the new jigsaw and Alex's translation of the English instructions into Devonshire).

SATURDAY
Today was Alex's birthday and we were pleased to be able to give her a card and a small gift.

Because the flooring team were making such good progress we needed to buy more flooring so another trip to Varna was hastily arranged. We managed to speak with Didi at The Hope & Future Foundation and arrange to meet her at the Praktika store to pass over the money for Zuska. When we arrived we were delighted to also meet Maria, Dari & Milen who were with Didi for the day. I have known these children for many years and it was great to see them again. We chatted for a little while and handed over the money before going into the store to buy the flooring.

Back on site Ken and Adam started work on a leaking window. It was a very large window which had recently been renewed but the reveals were in an awful state and letting in water which had damaged the ceiling inside. Access to the window was a precarious climb over a couple of flat rooves around the back of the building but all went well and the job completed without incident.

After work that evening we paid a visit to Provadia Orphanage. Back in 2010 a team had been to Provadia Orphanage and fitted 30 new windows. The fitting of the windows was a critical part of saving the orphanage from closure. We agreed to help if there was some input from the Mayor who agreed to fix the roof and deal with some subsidence. As a consequence the EU then stepped in with some funding and the orphanage received a major overhaul plus the building of an extension. The site now houses a rehabilitation day centre and residential units for the children. It may have taken 5 years and a lot of concern, doubt and worry to turn that crumbling wreck of a building into the modern facility that it now is but it was definitely worth it. I was keen to show the team what was possible and to help them grasp the vision for Krivnya. Also, for Andy who was on the original team from 2010 it was an opportunity for him to see the fruit of all his endeavour. It was an added pleasure that most of the children living there had been transferred from Krivnya so we all already knew each other.
It was truly fantastic to see the children in such a wonderful environment and to know that we had played a part in making it happen.

SUNDAY
Once again I made the mistake of thinking that Sunday would be a shopping free day - it wasn't!! Unfortunately, paint in Bulgaria is not what we are used to back home. In fact, 'paint' is probably not the right word as the insipid, watery solution which passes as paint in Bulgaria is so thin it would be more useful as a milk substitute for Ross' Earl Grey. After what felt like 15 coats of the first batch I purchased earlier I was sent back to the shop for more as you could still see the wall through the paint - I wasn't happy and fuelled by grumpiness I set off on my own without the safety of a translator. It must have been my lucky day as I managed to return with more paint thanks to a lot of pointing and a patient shopkeeper.

Lunchtime revealed a new talent which had been overlooked until now - Adam can cook. He prepared a lunch which could loosely be termed as some sort of stew and despite the mystery of its content it tasted very good and proved very popular.

I spent a pleasant afternoon in the sunshine painting the outside wall with a beautiful soundtrack provided by the nesting house martins who were feeding their young. However, my pleasure was rudely interrupted when one of the house martins came in for a closer look at the person at the top of the ladder but when I took a closer look at it I discovered it wasn't a house martin but the biggest, baddest bee I have ever seen. The ladder rocked violently beneath me as panic swallowed me up as a giant bee would obviously have a giant sting. To my great relief the buzzing monster flew straight past and carried on his merry way without so much as a passing glance in my direction and eventually the ladder stopped shaking enough for me to climb down and learn how to breathe again.

Whilst recovering a monotonous drip, drip, drip took me back to an incident last year when I was fitting a new toilet and despite a cloudless blue sky and 30 degree sunshine, an inexplicable drip was drawn like a magnet to the back of my neck. Once again the haunting sound of , what I believe was the same infernal drip, played like a metronome just behind me. We hadn't had rain since the night and it was about 2 o'clock in the afternoon. The sun was shining, it was hot and bone dry everywhere else, where could the drip be coming from? It didn't make sense. But it continued to drip onto one of the sills which needed painting and there was nothing I could do but wait for the impossible drip to stop. Meanwhile it continued to taunt me by defying all the laws of nature by existing.

The day finished with the 23rd and final coat of paint being applied and a hatch fitted to the new ceiling. Great progress had been made with the flooring as three bedrooms were now finished.

MONDAY
Alex turned up at the hotel with a very bad toe which she had stubbed overnight and was in a lot of pain but if she was expecting sympathy she made a bad mistake. This particular morning she had her mum with her who had just been to the market and bought a big bag of strawberries. In a battle for attention between Alex's bad toe and a big bag of strawberries there could be only one winner - the fruit. One by one we tucked in to the strawberries which were particularly delicious while completely ignoring the grimace of pain which marred Alex's normally smiling face. I watched with a hint of embarrassment as slowly but surely

the big bag of strawberries was reduced to a rather small bag of strawberries by a flock of gannets masquerading as builders.

Strangely we didn't see Alex's mum again as she disappeared back to the market to replace her lunch.

Today the new doors arrived and were fitted which put the finishing touches to two of the rooms we had been working on. One of the rooms will soon become a computer room. Holsworthy College have offered us 15 computers (plus screens, keyboards & mice) which later on this year we will take out and install. The creation of a computer room will mean a huge boost to the children's education and we are very pleased to be able to provide this. As orphaned and abandoned children with special needs the odds are already stacked against them but a good education can help to reduce the odds in their favour.

Since returning to the UK we have collected the computers and are hoping to take them out mid September in time for the start of the new term.

The rest of the day was spent finishing off all the jobs we had started and as each one was completed so the men would come and join the rest of us painting the outside.

We also had a chat with Ivelina (orphanage director) about what jobs she might want us to do next year which was going well until she mentioned the one thing which could possibly strike fear into the hearts of the team - toilets. And not just any toilets but the outside toilet block at the home. I have looked at these toilets before and assumed that the condition was so bad they couldn't possibly be in use but sadly they are and even more sadly for our team we were being asked to repair them. There is no running water to the toilet block which is used throughout the day then sluiced via a long hose before being shut down for the night. I took some of the team to inspect the block and seek advice on the practicalities of renovation and all credit to the team, they offered me the encouragement I needed to confirm we would take the job on.

Whilst on the one hand it is an horrendous prospect on the other hand it will be amazing to provide the children with a clean, hygienic toilet where they can do their business without the risk of picking up some horrible disease and struggle to complete the process within the length of time they can hold their breath.

The other jobs on the wish list are not so scary and include:
- New perimeter fencing
- Create a 'leisure' room at the home
- More classrooms in need of new flooring
- Repair internal walls
- An outdoor shelter

One more treat awaited us before we left for another year; Ivelina had bought us all a parting gift to thank us for the work we had done. Whilst this was completely unnecessary it was none the less very moving and whilst we didn't understand a word of the speech she gave to the assembled staff and children the emotion in her voice and the tears in her eyes said it all. There was a photo call during which we all took pictures, shook hands, embraced and said our goodbyes. It is during these moments that hearts and minds are committed to returning again the following year and carrying on the work.

The children are amazing and so happy despite their circumstances; it really is a joy to be able to do this work and do our bit to improve their future chances of breaking out of the poverty cycle.

TUESDAY

Unusually, we had a late flight meaning we had most of the day free before heading to the airport so Alex arranged a day of sightseeing including a visit to the local museum.

In 2012 the oldest civilisation in Europe was discovered in Provadia and an archaeological dig recovered many artefacts which are now on display in the museum. For a brief moment in time, the discovery propelled Provadia into the world's media as the discovery was of significant archaeological importance.

The museum also tells the story of how the Provadia economy and thus the town was built on 'White Gold' i.e. salt

After an interesting tour of the museum we headed for the town centre and to the array of little café's lining the main square where we sat in the sunshine enjoying a cold drink and reflected on a successful week.

The journey back to the UK was relatively uneventful and we all arrived home safely. Time to start planning for next year!! (Must check my passport).

Once again I thank God for all He has done and is doing through us in Bulgaria.

Andrew

CHAPTER EIGHTEEN
Rex's Mysterious Bag
September 2015

SATURDAY
With every TV channel broadcasting images of chaos at Calais and borders being closed on a daily basis we had no idea what we would face on our journey across Europe. We were travelling through ten countries in all: UK, France, Belgium, Netherlands, Germany, Austria, Slovenia, Croatia, Serbia and Bulgaria. All of these countries were closing their borders in response to the growing refugee crisis.

We were very mindful that the refugee problem was far greater than the issues facing us but we wondered what difficulties we might face as Europe tried to find a way to deal with the humanitarian crisis on its doorstep.

Kevin and Adrian travelled from Cardiff to Okehampton where our journey began. Mum had kindly prepared another food parcel for us which we added to the box of food which would sustain us through the next few days of travelling.

Regular readers might recall that last time the three brothers went to Bulgaria there was an issue with Kevin's bag; well, I say 'bag' but 'purse' might have been a more appropriate description of the ridiculously small piece of luggage he brought having been asked to allow extra room to carry clothes for the children. So we had no concerns this time that we had to fit our luggage into a space in the car which a sparrow would struggle to squeeze in to. But no, this time Kevin decided to bring two bags! What was he thinking? Last time, with a whole plane at our disposal he brought a purse, this time with only a car which was already full of 15 computers, screens, mice, keyboards, cables and the clothes we couldn't take last time because of his diminutive bag, he brought two bags. There was a bag with his clothes and a mysterious rucksack which never left his side. Adrian and I constantly wondered what might be in there but we never found out; it will always remain a mystery.

As we had no idea what troubles might await us at the Eurotunnel we had a quick cuppa at Jo's and left an hour ahead of schedule. For the first time ever we had the luxury of a Sat Nav so with all the necessary information input we left Jo's full of confidence. At the end of Jo's road the SatNav said 'turn left'; not a great start since that was a dead end. But we weren't concerned as Kevin was responsible for navigating and he had a full set of instructions printed out. We asked him to check his notes to which he responded, "I don't know, I can't see anything with these glasses"

So our trip began with a Sat Nav which wanted to send us the wrong way and a blind navigator. What could possibly go wrong?

As you can imagine it's not too long before our thoughts turn to food so we rummaged around in mum's food parcel. I have noticed that mum has realised that if she puts a funny note in with our food that she will get a mention in the report but I have decided not to pamper to her childish whims so if you want to know what she wrote on the box of Welsh cakes you will have to ask her.

SUNDAY
When we arrived at the Eurotunnel we were pleased to find that there were no problems or delays and we were offered an earlier train which we were pleased to accept. We reached Calais without any problems and the Sat Nav helpfully announced, "Continue on road". What a stroke of good fortune that was because without this valuable advice we might have ended up in the sea.

It was a shame that we had chosen to make this trip during International Road Works Week but despite the plethora of red and white cones our journey was not unduly slowed. It seems that the UK have a lot to learn from our European cousins about how to manage road works. Germany seemed to have made a determined bid to collect all the traffic cones in the world and have them displayed like a trophy along their roads but we continued to make good progress and made our first stop in Austria in excellent time.

Due to a previous bad experience it is always a relief to me when the check in goes smoothly and we find we are in the hotel which I actually booked. The hotel is on the border of Germany & Austria and our 'view' is of the motorway, which on this occasion was more reminiscent of a lorry park. The traffic going from Austria to Germany was virtually at a standstill. The lorries were all backed up and stationery while the cars crawled at a snail's pace to the temporary check point which had been put in place. We made a mental note of this for our return journey.

MONDAY

Breakfast was served from 6am so we got up early to be first in the queue at the self service counter. As we sat down to eat we compared each other's choices and Kevin, the culturally challenged one of us, commented, "I don't know what this is, I just picked it up". It was a croissant. Anything which doesn't come in a box with microwave instructions is a mystery to Kevin and so it was he dined on the delights of 'foreign muck' that morning.

Back on the road we encountered the first of the many tolls which we would encounter. As we were in a right hand drive vehicle, responsibility for paying the tolls fell to whoever was in the passenger seat which was always Kevin as Adrian and I were either driving or sleeping in the back. Very few of the tolls are manned as most are now automatic which presented a bit of a problem for Kevin, prompting Adrian to comment, "It's like working with Stan Laurel". I couldn't help but point out, "Well, that makes you Oliver Hardy"

Obviously anyone who knows us will consider us three mature and sensible adults so you will be shocked to learn that we burst out laughing when the toll machine, in its robotic voice bellowed, "Gute Fahrt". OK so it may be incredibly childish but I defy you not to laugh when a machine chooses to compliment you on the passing of wind. We never tired of that joke.

Eventually we reached the border of Slovenia and Croatia so it was time to get out the passports. Adrian and I handed ours to Kevin who handed them over to the border guard. When she opened my passport a piece of paper fell out in what looked like a contrived attempt to bribe her to allow us through. She looked at it scornfully, replaced it and handed the passports back. When we looked to see what the paper was we discovered it was a voucher for 50 eurocents off the entry price to a service station toilet. How embarrassing, it must have been the worst attempt to bribe a border guard ever.

Before we left Croatia we needed to buy a 'vignette' (tax disc) for travel through Serbia so we pulled over at a garage and I got out to make the purchase. As I don't know a single word of Croatian I resorted to the international language of pointing. I put my finger on the chart on the counter to indicate that I wanted a 7 day Vignette and noted that it said E8.70 so I handed over a 10 Euro note. The lady at the counter said something in Croatian and handed the note back to me. In response to the blank look on my face she said, 'more'. With a condescending smile I once again pointed to the chart and tapped the bit which said E8.70 in an effort to draw her attention to the fact that I was right and 10 euros should cover it. With minimal effort to disguise her loathing of the idiot in front her she put her finger next to mine to point out the big black picture and said 'motorcycle'. Then just in case my humiliation was incomplete slid her finger all of 1 cm to the even bigger black picture of a car and as if to clarify what was already abundantly obvious said 'car''. Next to this it quite clearly said E15.70. With nowhere to hide I handed over the money and hoped that the rapid reddening of my face would be mistaken for too much sun while waiting what seemed like an eternity for my change. Naturally, I neglected to mention this to Kevin and Adrian.

By now it was time for lunch so we pulled over at a roadside café and were drawn in by the English menu printed on the window which boasted. Roast Chicken, Lamb on a spit, Hamburgers and much more. As we wandered inside trying to decide between chicken and lamb we got a sense that something was not quite right. Where was all the food? Obviously it was kept out the back and cooked to order. One more look at the menu to finalise our decisions was interrupted by the man behind the counter. "You want sandwich?" "Do you have hot food?" we asked pointing to the menu. "Hot sandwich" came the crushing response. On the counter there were two plastic containers each with about half a dozen sad looking rolls and the full extent of our choice was to have the sandwich hot or cold. We considered for a second and went for the hot version in the hope that the microwave would kill all the bacteria currently partying on the contents which bore some resemblance to meat of some sort (most definitely not roast chicken or lamb!).

You think you know someone then something happens which surprises you. As brothers we have clearly known each other all our lives and thought we knew everything about each other but the regular tolls revealed something which we did not know. Kevin has unusually short arms. This inspired Adrian to invent a new and very entertaining game of placing the car exactly the right distance away from the toll to cause Kevin

maximum discomfort and embarrassment as he forced half his body out through the window in order to reach the machine and on the odd occasion necessitating him getting out of the car simply to press the button which delivered the ticket. Obviously I found this type of behaviour very distressing and when it was my turn to drive, if I happened to pull up a little too far from the machine, it was, of course, an accident.
The revelation of Kevin's unusually short arms earned him the nickname Tyrannosaurus Rex (or Rex for short)

We were making good progress and although the constant road works were a little tiresome, the new roads which are being built are making a big difference to the time it takes to cross Europe and we were taking full advantage arriving at the Bulgarian border well ahead of schedule. It was looking good for an early arrival at our next motel - but the border guards had other ideas. "Open the boot" as soon as I heard those words I knew were going to be here a long time. As soon as they saw all the computers we were directed to the 'search' zone and our passports retained. "Wait here".
Now in a very untypical moment of thinking ahead, I had, a few weeks ago, anticipated this and arranged for the Director of Krivnya Orphanage to send me a letter accepting the donation of the computers on official headed paper with a very official looking stamp. So, while I was waiting for the border guard to return with his colleague I got the letter ready. The guards ordered me to open the boot again and I obliged then handed then the letter and hoped it would do the trick. I was delighted to see their officious demeanour melt into one of compassion upon reading the letter and they immediately said "OK, you can go". We collected our passports and drove straight to our motel where we arrived in time for a good meal before retiring for the night.

TUESDAY
We took breakfast at a much more civilised time today as we only had about 5 hours of travelling before we reached our destination, Provadia. Breakfast looked good but we were all bemused by the little packet which accompanied our toast. It had a picture of a pine cone on it but what possible relevance could that have to its contents? Sure enough, on closer inspection, what we had was Pine Cone Elixir. With some trepidation we carefully sampled the unusual fayre and surprisingly it was ok.

Back on the road Adrian and I were discussing whether to go clockwise or anticlockwise on the ring road around Sofia. I was advocating clockwise from the map I was holding but the Sat Nat was suggesting anti clockwise so we asked Kevin, our navigator, what the route plan said. "Dunno, haven't looked at it!"

By now we were a little road weary so thoughts turned to the Happy Restaurant where we always stop en route. This was our motivation to push on through the tedium of rubber on tarmac and we were almost salivating at the thought of lunch that day. The choice would be far more than a sandwich, hot or cold.

For some strange reason, although we always stop at the Happy Restaurant we can never remember where on our route it is so it adds a little excitement to our eager anticipation. Is it round this bend? Is it over this hill? We must be getting close now. And then like an oasis in the desert the garage which straddled the road came into view and we instantly recognised it as the site of the Happy restaurant. We pulled in to the car park all misty eyed like we were meeting a long lost friend. But as the tears dried and vision restored we could not believe the sight before us - it was closed! What a disaster, we were crestfallen and could hardly summon up the desire to carry on with the journey. What was the point of it all now? We rummaged around in the back of the car for what food might be left and found a soft mint between two of the seats. We brushed off the dirt and cut it into three but its minty flavour was lost in the sadness of the moment.

The next part of the journey was completed in silence as we were in mourning for the loss of the Happy Restaurant. We tried in vain to console ourselves by considering what a good journey we had had and how it was probably the best ever but it was no good and as it turned out, a bit premature. As we reached the dual carriageway which heralded the final stage of our journey we were faced with yet more road works but this time it was a bit more serious as the road was closed and there were diversion signs in place. We only just spotted the Provadia diversion in the nick of time or else who knows where we might have ended up?

Eventually we arrived in Provadia, booked into our guest house and met up with Alex. We wanted to go straight to Krivnya to unload the computers rather than leave them in the car another night. It would also give us chance to inspect them as driving in Bulgaria is a bit like being in a washing machine with a wonky leg on maximum spin cycle. We literally bounced our way through the country trying to pick out the smaller of the potholes to drive through as there is no smooth road available. And as for Bulgarian drivers!! Lesson one for Bulgarian drivers is 'rip up your highway code, it is meaningless' Lesson two is 'overtake, overtake, overtake'. One of the drivers in front of us while Adrian was driving had been on the Advance Motorists Course where they teach you to stop suddenly in the middle of the road without any indication and without brake lights for no apparent reason. The ferocity of Adrian's braking caused me to scream - £1000 excess!! Yes, our hire car insurance carried a £1000 excess and 1000 pound coins flashed before my eyes as the car parking sensors tried to out scream me as we stopped millimetres from the offending vehicle.

Onward to Krivnya where we received a fabulous welcome from the children who were delighted to see us again; they really know how to make us feel very special.
We went to the home first to wait for Ivelina (Director) who would open up the school for us to deposit the computers. The school is only about 400 yards away and so Adrian asked, "are we going to walk to the school?" I gently pointed out that the purpose of us being there was to unload the computers which were in the car so maybe it would be better to drive!!

A couple of the lads helped us to move all the computers from the car into a storage room in the school and a visual inspection suggested they had all survived the journey but we wouldn't know for sure until we set them up and tested them. We stopped and played with the children for a little while before returning to Provadia for some well earned rest.

Once we had settled into our room we decided to search the TV for a news channel broadcasting in English so we could get up to date on the refugee crisis and check the various borders which we would cross on the way home. There are so many channels to flick through that Adrian suggested we look at the menu. Good idea we thought oblivious to the obvious fact which was about to be revealed - the menu was in Bulgarian and we couldn't understand a word of it. However, we did eventually find CNN where we learned of all the troubles unfolding on the Serbia, Croatia border.

Whilst sorting out our bags we discovered why Kevin had found it necessary to bring two bags, he had packed gloves. Given that the temperature was around 30°c we thought it was a strange thing to pack and wondered if the secret contents of his rucksack were a scarf and a balaclava.

The disappointment of the closure of the Happy Restaurant was put to one side as our thoughts turned to dinner and a trip to Fawlty Towers, our favourite comedy restaurant. Actually the restaurant is called 'Classic' and the owner is Nikolay but we call him Basil because of his comedy antics which never fail to amuse us. And as an added bonus, the food is fabulous.
He didn't let us down and was as entertaining as ever. I was a little disappointed that my pork in mushroom sauce was missing one small ingredient - the mushroom sauce. So actually my meal was simply pork.

We wandered up to the shop to buy food for tomorrow's breakfast and as it was getting late I picked up my jacket. Adrian decided to take the mick going on at me about how it was a balmy summer evening and a jacket was a ridiculous item of clothing. My defence fell on deaf ears as he continued his tirade of abuse culminating in "if only I'd brought my snowing gear" clearly he meant skiing gear but I pounced on his mistake and with Kevin's help managed to turn the attention onto him saving me further abuse.

WEDNESDAY
Today was the big day when we would make a start on installing all the computers. My expectations were low as none of us has much skill in this area but once we started we got into a good rhythm and the work progressed very well.

I must pause a moment and give full credit to the team at Holsworthy College who prepared and donated the computers. Every component worked exactly as it should so that every computer was ready to go as soon as we plugged everything in. We didn't experience one single problem and we didn't find one single piece of kit that didn't work exactly as it should do. Thanks to their brilliant work our job was very easy indeed.

We set up computers in the staff room and 8 classrooms. It was such a joy going into the classrooms and seeing the wonderful environment in which the children were working. For three years we have been working at Krivnya and much of the focus has been on improving the classrooms. What were once dark, dingy old rooms were now bright, clean and cheerful. The improvement in the children's learning as a result is very pleasing indeed. Now every classroom has access to a computer and all of them are linked to the internet. Having access to a computer and learning basic computer skills will dramatically improve the lives of the children and something as apparently simple as this will be life changing. Huge thanks to Holsworthy College for making this possible.

We only experienced one small problem during the whole installation and that was with an internet cable on which the plug was broken. It was a very long cable which passed through several walls in order to get to the router and we didn't fancy chasing a new cable through but it was a sealed plug so a new one couldn't be fitted. So we decided to cut another cable with a plug on it and splice it to the existing cable. It was extremely fiddly as there were 8 very fine wires in total and no guarantee that it would work. Armed only with my trusty Swiss Army Knife I set to work with the encouragement of my supportive brothers ringing in my ears - "I don't want to be around when you plug that in", Don't cut the blue one, you'll blow us all up", "wouldn't it be funny if you took down the internet for the whole village" All very encouraging.
I was very relieved when I plugged in the finished wire to find that the internet came on and no one got injured.

We celebrated our success with a trip into town for some lunch. Whilst in town I decided to visit the ATM as I needed some cash to pay the guest house bill so I stood and waited as there was already a lady using it. As she finished and walked away two ladies made a bee line for the machine totally ignoring me stood patiently in the queue. I was happy to let it pass but Alex was not. With a look of thunder on her face she stomped across the path of the oncoming women and gave me a look which said get in there now. As I have always said, Alex is so much more than a translator; now I can add 'bodyguard' to her growing list of talents.

On the subject of Alex I am delight to be able to share her good news that she is pregnant. The baby is due March 6th.

After lunch we returned to the school and put the remaining computers in the car to take them down to the home where we were going to set up a computer room for the children to play in. At the home Adrian took the computers out of the boot and loaded up Kevin with two computers and a box of accessories. As Kevin entered the home with his heavy load Stanislav ran up to him with his hand raised to offer a high five closely followed by Turgut who held his hand out to shake Kevin's hand. How they thought he could possibly oblige I have no idea but it made me laugh.

The computers went in with minimum fuss and we were finished with time to spare. We used the rest of the afternoon to visit next year's building project - the dreaded toilets!
They really are in a dreadful state. Adrian asked if the children really used them and I had to confirm that they did. They are little more than holes in the ground surrounded by crumbling walls. The list of diseases one could contact from a single visit is endless.
Kevin and I entered the retch inducing pit with a laser measurer a note book and a huge amount of trepidation in order to take all the measurements. It's not a place you would wish to linger so we completed our task as quickly as possible.

Having survived that there was one more challenge awaiting us. We needed to get up on the roof to inspect that. The walls don't look like they can even support the roof but would they take the weight of a full grown man too. Unfortunately, as the lightest member of the brotherhood, I had the unenviable task of testing out the load bearing capacity of the near derelict building. For a brief second I thought I detected a note of concern in my brothers as they rushed to hold the tree trunk I had rolled into position to use as a step for getting onto the roof but it quickly passed. I am pleased to report that I survived my ordeal and I think I got everything I needed for the builders.

Despite an extremely successful day there was no thought of self congratulation on the way back to the guest house as all our attention was firmly focussed on getting into the shower and scrubbing off the stench of those awful toilets. Suitably freshened it was time to start thinking about dinner, we decided to give Fawlty Towers a miss tonight and head into the centre to one of the other restaurants.

If there is one thing which Provadia can boast about it is the quality of its restaurants. There are several in the town and each of them serves up fantastic food so why oh why did I order a salad! I have a few athletic challenges coming up and laughably consider myself to be 'in training' so felt that the luxurious, rich food I normally feast on should be set aside in order to maintain my racing snake physique (or to be more accurate in a fit of panic I foolishly thought that one salad may offset years of overeating and magically shed two stone of excess fat and increase my athletic prowess by a factor of 100).

For a brief moment I was pleased with my decision as the salad was very nice but then the other meals were delivered and the smell of meat, hot potatoes, herbs and gravy filled the air. I was gutted. Salad! What was I thinking? I tried desperately to trade a slice of tomato for some chicken and a cucumber for a roast potato but all to no avail. My ever compassionate brothers thought it was hysterical as they tucked into a hearty meal to watch me nibble on my rabbit food. Salad, what an idiot!!

Back at the guest house CNN was reporting an ever worsening situation throughout Europe and we watched helplessly as so many of the borders we had to cross to get home were being closed. We began to consider the possibility of leaving Bulgaria early to allow for delays. Because everything with the computers had gone so well we were ahead of schedule and an early departure was possible. Complicated but possible.

THURSDAY
We spent the morning finishing off all the little jobs we needed to do and discussing future plans with the director before heading back into town for lunch. Whilst we were sat around eating pizza Alex disappeared and returned with a paper bag which she placed on the table. Adrian asked, "What's in the bag?" "Beer nuts" Alex replied and seeing the look on Adrian's face felt obligated to ask, "Would you like to try some?". Adrian didn't need to be asked twice. Just as he was swallowing his mouthful of nuts Alex added, "They're for the orphans" Kevin and I were disgusted that Adrian would steal treats from the orphans and we made our feelings very clear. Adrian tried to use ignorance as his defence be we were having none of it.

The afternoon was free for us to play games with the children which we thoroughly enjoyed. Out came our Euro Hockey set and we played a great

game of hockey despite a dearth of any perceivable talent. The kids enjoyed running around chasing the ball with a stick for what seemed like several hours and it was only the extreme heat which finally defeated us. The temperature that afternoon was somewhere up in the 30's and so we changed our activities to ones we could do in the shade of the one tree in the area.
Incidentally, construction of a shaded area in the yard is on our list of jobs to do in 2016 and we got a good understanding of why it was deemed so necessary this afternoon.

One of the boys, Marin, asked me if I could spin the ball on my finger (like you see basketball players doing) but he might just as well have asked me to play Beethoven's 5th using only my nose. However, whilst I couldn't spin the ball I knew a man who could, step up to the plate Adrian. Marin was delighted and had a great time trying to learn how to do it himself. This was Adrian's moment as the children gathered round to watch and so he showed them his awesome juggling skills with three, yes three, tennis balls. One girl in particular was amazed and wanted to learn so the rest of Adrian's afternoon was taken up at juggling school. She got on pretty well and didn't seem the least bit bothered by failure after failure, she just kept on trying. She loved watching herself back on the video I took of her and laughed and laughed at all the fun she was having. We had a fabulous afternoon with the children who could play for ever if only we could keep up with them. These are the times you remember why you do this work, all of the fundraising, organising, planning, admin etc becomes worthwhile in moments like these.

We decided that we would leave tomorrow morning, a day ahead of schedule, so one more visit to Fawlty Towers was called for. It's almost like a routine now whereby we ask for something from the menu, Nikolay does his best Basil Fawlty glance at his watch, rolls his eyes and goes to fetch his bike in order to ride to the shop to buy the ingredients. Once again it was Adrian's banana split which had him reaching for his cycle clips.

FRIDAY
We left at 8:45am. Adrian set up the Sat Nav and we pulled away from the guest house. Immediately the Sat Nav kicked in with "when it is safe to do so, make a U turn" Why it should want us to go in a completely different

direction I have no idea. The further we drove the more annoyed it got and kept insisting we should turn around but we ignored it.

We made good progress but were aware that we may face a diversion soon as one of the roads we came in on was only allowing one way traffic and sure enough we were diverted but what a pleasant diversion it was. We zig zagged up the mountain through countryside and villages we had never visited before which made a pleasant change. We were soon back on the route and didn't lose much time.

For our next driver change over point we stopped at a petrol station which had toilet facilities so we decided to take advantage. As he approached the entrance to the toilet Kevin walked past three ladies waiting at the door and went straight in. Unfortunately, he discovered that there was only one toilet to be shared between the sexes and so had to do the walk of shame back past the ladies to the rear of the queue.

Our route takes us through many tunnels, the longest being in excess of 10km and on the way Adrian had been marvelling at how the Sat Nav worked in each of the tunnels. On the way home he picked up on this theme again and commented that there is a tunnel in Cardiff Bay of approx 0.5km but it doesn't work in there so somehow, the GPS signal must be piped into the tunnels here. We thought about this for a while before asking the obvious question, "what's the point?" What possible directions could you need in a tunnel? The options are straight on or straight on. Suddenly the marvellous technology didn't seem so marvellous after all.

As it turned out the borders were relatively trouble free and there wasn't a single sign of any refugee problems. The border crossing from Serbia into Croatia was a little slow with a few queues but we were entertained by a French driver in front of us who refused to start/stop his engine each time the queue moved and insisted on pushing his car. Sometimes he would simply stick his leg out and 'scoot' but when this got a bit hard he would get out and push. Clearly someone in the next queue was impressed with his efforts to save a little fuel and tried to copy him but hadn't taken into consideration that the French man was in a medium sized Peugeot whilst he was in a massive 4x4. Getting the car rolling was fine but getting it to stop was something altogether different. We watched with a mixture of amusement and fear as the panic stricken driver tried to bring one ton of rolling metal to a halt before colliding into the car in front. By now the temperature was around 37c and the last place we wanted to be was outside the car away from the air conditioning so we had no desire to follow in the Frenchman's footsteps. We felt that the extra 8.5p we would spend on fuel far outweighed the risk of a heart attack and so continued to start/stop the engine as necessary.

We continued to make good progress and entertained ourselves with trying to pick the best queue at each border and toll. We really didn't do very well. We reached a new low when, faced with only one queue to pick from, we stilled picked the wrong one! How is this even possible? No sooner had we joined the back of the single queue than a man appeared from the booth next door and called all the traffic accumulating behind us to start a new queue. They rushed past us, through the border and onwards while we still sat in the original queue.

Toilet stops were becoming a source of some amusement. At one stop we made for the loo only to be shouted at and chased by a random woman who apparently wanted paying. As we didn't really understand at first we went in anyway. I was first out which alerted the woman to our presence again so by the time Adrian and Kevin emerged she pounced on them and made them pay.

At the next stop Kevin and Adrian went first and once again a woman appeared from nowhere demanding money which they dutifully handed over. Unfortunately, I had left my coins in the car so called after them to let them know I was going back for my money. Luckily for me the woman must have thought I didn't have any money, took pity on me and let me in for free. So in the free wees game I was winning 2-0. (If you are one of the generous people who responded to my appeal for coins for just such an occasion please come and see me for a refund).

Because we did not encounter any of the problems we had seen on CNN we arrived at the Austria, Germany border at 4am, 9 hours before we could get into our motel. We tried to sleep in the car for a couple of hours until dawn broke then headed into the garage for breakfast. There was free wi-fi there so we researched things to do in the local area as we had a whole morning to kill.

We found a nearby town called Shardling which looked interesting and decided to head for that. However, this meant crossing the border into Germany and then crossing back into Austria and so for the first time we encountered a border control set up in response the ongoing refugee crisis. But if you're picturing a scene like one you have seen on the news, forget it. There were three policemen, one of whom was asleep in his van. There was no other traffic just us so we pulled up near the policeman who asked us where we were going. We told him, he looked blank and simply said he wasn't from around these parts before waving us through. The return journey was even simpler as the Austrian policeman waved us through without even requiring us to stop.

We still had a few hours to kill before we could get into our room so Adrian produced a tablet with Monty Python's Quest For The Holy Grail on it so we sat in a car park at a service station in Austria watching Monty Python. I hadn't seen the film for many, many years (I think I saw it when I was 11) and thoroughly enjoyed it. In an effort to play out the final moments before our room was ready we sat down for something to eat - I didn't have salad.

Eventually we got into our room and before too long decided the best plan was to get as much sleep as possible so that we could make an early start the following day as we still had several borders to cross and the Eurotunnel terminal to negotiate.

SUNDAY
We set off at 2am but just like yesterday there was no sign of any problems and once again we made very good progress - except for the toilet stops again. In one place Adrian got annoyed with the hand drier which refused to work before discovering it was a hand sanitizing unit and similarly, in another place Kevin gave up on trying to get the 'sensor operated tap' to work before it was pointed out to him that it was a soap dispenser. Sadly there were no women there to give me free entry, only machines, so I had to pay like the others.

We arrived at the Eurotunnel several hours ahead of schedule so we hoped that we would be offered the chance to take an earlier train which we were but not before paying 8 Euros for the privilege. I drove through the maze of roads and channels until we arrived at what I thought was our queue. After a little while a lady in a hi-viz vest appeared and with a condescending look and wave of her clip board ushered me away from the queue with the big red X to the one with the green tick. A quick glance in my rear view mirror highlighted my error which had caused a bit of a tail back. I wonder if anyone in the tailback behind me is writing a report like this and if so what they are saying about me right now. I think I would rather not know.

Ironically, the early train was delayed and was about 45 minutes late leaving Calais but we were still well ahead of schedule.

Just when we thought that the Sat Nav working in the tunnels while we were driving was about as pointless as it could get we noticed that it even worked in the channel tunnel. The car was on a train, it couldn't go forward or backward, it was just sat there while the train carried us but the Sat Nav kept on working. It even said "continue along channel tunnel" like we had a choice!! Not bad for a gismo which couldn't even get us out of Okehampton

Of all the troubles we could have faced en route the worst traffic was on the M25 and M3 - no surprise there but we still managed to get back to Okehampton early. In fact, early enough to stop at Jo's (where Adrian had left his car) for a cuppa.

The journey was over. Well, it was over for me. Adrian and Kevin still had to get back to Cardiff which they did without any problems.

Just as I was about to pat myself on the back for a job well done, one more moment of panic was still waiting for me. Back in work on Monday I received a text from AVIS, "please ring us about your hire car". I rang and the girl said, "You're car was due back yesterday at 10am, is there a problem?" "No" I said, "I arranged to return it at 6:30pm tonight" and waited for the inevitable argument. I tried to recall the conversation when this was agreed and conjure up an image of the paperwork. Had I made a mistake? How much was the fine? Oh no, what have I done? But the girl on the phone simply said, "Oh ok then, see you later" Phew! What a relief.

With the hire car safely returned I can now formally pronounce the trip as an outstanding success. There was so much scope for things to go wrong not least of which was the danger of working with technology. Computers generally conform to Murphy's law ' if it can go wrong, it will go wrong' but nothing went wrong. Our journey took us through all the pressure points of Europe during the worst migrant crisis since WW2 but we didn't see any problems and experienced virtually no delays as a result. We even got home early.

So a huge thank you to everyone who prayed for us. Your prayers were heard and answered. God blessed us in every conceivable way. And because of your prayers the children of Krivnya Orphanage now have access to computers which will be life changing for them.

Please continue to pray for all our projects as prayer really does work - every time.

Andrew

CHAPTER NINETEEN
Health & Safety Gone Mad
May 2016

With a few years of experience behind us we decided to do things a little differently this year. Previously we had spent a week in Bulgaria sourcing materials and getting them on site before coming back to the UK and returning to Bulgaria a few weeks later with the main team.

However, we now felt that our knowledge of what is and isn't available, our knowledge of where to go to get everything we need and the increase in my Bulgarian vocabulary which now extends to a full seven words (nine if you count pointing and repeating the same word over and over with increasing volume) that we could do it in three days and allow the team to join us in the full and certain knowledge that we will have succeeded in getting everything ready.

Barry and I travelled from Okehampton and met up with Adam at Luton airport at 2am so the three musketeers were ready for what lay ahead. Somehow I managed to get separated from the other two in the check in queue and so had nothing to do other than listen to the various conversations going on around me. Unfortunately, on the same flight, there were a large group of twitchers (bird watchers). Now I'm no stranger to the joy of watching wildlife and birds are perhaps near the top of the list of wildlife worth watching but it was with dismay that I found myself in the queue with the RSPB's 'Boring' branch. In particular the two men nearest to me (and the ones with the loudest voices) were trying to 'out-twitch' each other but doing it in the style of two gentlemanly old friends.

I saw a greater lesser spotted striped finch gull on the Thames last week
How wonderful but if only you had gone to that place only I know about you would have seen the rarer greater lesser spotted striped bullfinch gull.
Oh I know that place and I've seen that bird, you were very lucky to see it. Was it the one with the yellow bill? Oh no, of course not, there's only one of those and I'm the only person ever to have seen it.
Ah yes, I saw you seeing it with my XST2000 multi vision, diamond lens, tungsten, military grade binoculars.

You have those binoculars? Very impressive aren't they. I had a pair when they first came out in 2009 but I've upgraded to the superior XST3000 trinocular. I used them to watch you watching me watching the yellow billed greater lesser spotted striped bullfinch gull.

And so it went on, blah, blah, blah until finally I heard the dulcet tones of the check in clerk calling me forward. "Do you have any items in your luggage you wish to declare?" "Just the dismembered remains of the chairman and director of the Dull branch of the Boring RSPB society" I replied. I was sent to the oversize baggage area to have my bag scanned but it went through without incident although the girl monitoring the x-ray screen did look up at me and mouth "thank you"

During all the many times we have made this journey we have seen some amusing sights but this year we witnessed an all time highlight. Amongst all the chit chat that was going we gradually became aware of a minor altercation at the check in desk which we soon realised was a debate regarding the size of some hand luggage. Wizz Air have a policy that bags up to a given size are free whilst anything larger is charged. The check in clerk was completely impassive as she pointed to the stand with the measuring device for baggage. The animated passenger dragged the bag towards the stand and with the help of her friend lifted its gigantic mass onto the frame. It was obvious to everyone that there was no way it was going to fit and she would have to pay the additional charge. Obvious to everyone, that is, except the girl to whom the bag belonged. She was determined that her bag would fit into the frame and to everyone's amusement she started to push it for all she was worth in an effort to jemmy it into position. This failed so she began trying to manoeuvre it with her foot until she finally dispensed with any sense of dignity, stood on the bag and with her friends help jumped on the bag until it squeezed into the frame.

The impassive check-in clerk almost cracked a smile as she said, "OK, bring it here." The almost imperceptible smile was only hiding her knowledge of what would happen next. The bag was stuck fast, there was no way it was coming out. The women heaved and pulled, puffed and panted, grunted and cussed, levered and twisted but the bag was going nowhere. By now everyone was watching this comedy unfold until it got to be excruciatingly cringe worthy; who would crack first to put them out of their misery? Eventually one gallant knight stepped forward and with the super human strength of someone who couldn't bear to be stuck in the queue any longer heaved the bag from its metal prison like Arthur pulling Excalibur from the stone.

In a strangely British way no one muttered a word, not even a giggle was heard but there was an unspoken collective nod around the departure hall which acknowledged the humour of the situation and the stupidity of the woman. In that one moment of knowing silence everyone was united in their inaudible acknowledgement that we had all shared a special, comical moment together.

Satisfied by this bright moment in an otherwise dull day we completed the journey without further incident and arrived in Varna where we were met by Alex who chauffeured us to the guest house in Provadia in our beloved old minibus.

I took a very early opportunity to show off my mastery of the Bulgarian language and used several of the seven words I know to order four pizzas (the majority of my seven words relate to food) which went down very well after our long journey. Suitably refreshed we headed off to Krivnya to take a look at the jobs we would be doing and assess what materials we would need to buy.

By now we have got used to last minute changes to our work schedule and this year was no different. I'm beginning to have a very sceptical view of the Bulgarian school inspectors who seem to turn up just before we are due and give the director a list of jobs which have to be done in order for the facility to remain open. However, on this occasion, I had to agree with them when they condemned the toilets at the home and demanded instant action. Originally this was going to be our project but the urgency of the job demanded that it was dealt with before we arrived. The inspectors were generous enough to leave us another job instead and just in case we dared to feel relieved that we didn't have to undertake a toilet job they told us that the school had to have indoor toilets and so our job was to build those.

There are no indoor toilets at the school and the existing outside toilets are a bit grim to say the least except for one which we upgraded in 2014 and with 50 children plus staff one good toilet is hardly sufficient.

In the few weeks before our trip we became extremely confused about which room would become the new toilet block so we arrived at Krivnya not really knowing where we would be working or the size of the job but on arrival we were shown the room and all became clear. We did a tour of both the school and the home taking a look at some of the jobs on the list and working out what we thought we could accomplish. With the tour over and a shopping list well underway we left Krivnya and made our way back to Provadia.

As I had earlier paid for our pizza lunch Barry felt guilt tripped into buying us drinks but had hatched a dastardly plan to avoid paying. Once we had selected our liquid refreshment we approached the counter, Barry dug into his wallet and passed the cashier a note; she returned it with a polite smile. So Barry handed her a bigger note just as I walked up behind him to ascertain the nature of the problem which I saw immediately. "Barry, those are Euro notes they only accept Lev here" "Oh no" replied Barry, "I've picked up the wrong bag of money" and that's how he got out of paying for the drinks. Fortunately, Barry had two bags of money and the other one contained Lev so that was the last time he could pull that trick.

We decided on an early evening meal as we had been travelling since 9pm the day before and only managed to snatch a few moments of uncomfortable sleep on the plane and wanted to get to bed early. Now that Alex is a mum she is no longer available to join us for our evening meals and so ordering food has taken on a new and interesting dimension with no one to interpret for us but Adam had a very novel solution. In an extraordinary act of foresight, last year Adam had taken photos of all his favourite meals including ones others had had which he fancied. He had practically the entire menu of all the restaurants in Provadia in picture format on his phone. At first Barry and I scoffed at his idea of showing the waitress a photo of the meal he wanted but we had to defer to his greater intelligence when the waitress smiled in recognition of the food and wrote what he wanted on her pad. As the week went on Adam's phone became the 'Wikipedia' of any info we wanted from years gone by

THURSDAY
Well there was no avoiding it, we had to start the shopping so a trip to Praktiker in Varna was arranged. Despite spending an eternity pushing trolleys up and down endless aisles and gazing at sacks until we were numb trying to work out if they contained cement, plaster, grout,

adhesive or anything else we seemed to have very little to show for our efforts although Adam did have some very nice photos of 90 degree nails which might come in useful next year should we have to hammer round corners.

One shop in a day is more than enough for any man and Barry felt the urge to do some real work and make a start on the ceiling of the new toilet block. Having purchased all the timber we needed we were able to start hanging the first of the joists. Under Barry's direction Adam and I made ourselves useful running back and for to our store room for such oddities as a long weight, striped paint and rubber headed tacks which strangely we could never find but despite this (or maybe because of it) 'we' made good progress. Feeling satisfied with our efforts (once I even held a piece of wood while Barry fixed it in place) we retired for the day and set off for our much anticipated return to Nico's bar and restaurant.

Regular readers will probably feel by now that they have actually been to this restaurant as it always gets a few mentions thanks to Nico's hilarious antics earning him the nickname 'Basil' after the legendary Basil Fawlty. We have come to learn that his larder is about as well stocked as Kojak's shampoo cupboard and take great delight in ordering food which he doesn't have thus sending him off to the shop on his bike to buy the ingredients. This time we had only stopped for a drink and so weren't expecting the Tour De Provadia to start so early but when Barry ordered a beer Nico pulled that face which signals the fetching of his bicycle clips. Quite how a bar can have no beer is beyond me but it's entertaining none the less. In an act of compassion Adam and I took a cursory glance at the soft drinks cabinet and ordered drinks we could see on display.
Later that evening whilst strolling back from the convenience store in the cool night air we were idly chatting about sweets and Barry happened to mention that he liked Jelly babies eliciting my response of "only if they're Bassets!" Clearly Adam hadn't heard me properly when a look of disgust crossed his face and he protested, "battered Jelly babies??!!!"

FRIDAY
One other event which Barry had been looking forward to was the weekly market as, over the years, he had discovered that Bulgarian seeds make for excellent quality vegetables and he is particularly fond of their tomatoes. As a tomato is a food it falls within my extensive Bulgarian vocabulary (the fact that the Bulgarian word is almost the same as the

English is irrelevant, I still count it towards my total of seven words). Anyway, I managed to successfully ask the lady for two packets of tomato seeds. Clearly I impressed the lady with my fluency in her native tongue as she then went on at great length about how to plant them and nurture them but I didn't understand a single word she said. I gambled with a few knowing nods in what I thought might be the right place and I think I got away with it. Either that or I will receive a massive box of courgettes in the post in about a week. It was then I remembered that this has happened before; I offer a few words of Bulgarian only to be hit with a barrage of dialogue in return, of which I understand less than nothing leaving me to resort to the Bulgarian phrase I use more than any other, "I don't understand". Will I never learn?

To add to my humiliation Adam turned to a translator app on his phone but I was secretly pleased to discover it was even more stupid than I am. He took a receipt from his pocket and copied the word CYMA into his phone; his phone clicked, whirred and let out a little steam before responding with the translation of CYMA. Stupid phone even I know that this words translates as TOTAL (or sum).
Andrew 1 - Adam's phone 0.
Time for me to quit as I feel sure I cannot sustain this winning streak of 1.

My momentary triumph was brought back to earth with a bump as we realised we had to go back to Praktiker to get more supplies for the builders who would arrive in a few days. The main things on our shopping list were laminate flooring and toilets. Fortunately, we have gained the wisdom to sit down and work out exactly what we need in the relative calm of the coffee shop the night before rather than our previous efforts to do all sorts of crazy mathematics in store as we try to calculate how much skirting we need, how may couplers, how many corners (internal or external?) while a salesman forces a patient smile. So we were able to hand Alex our list and leave her to get on with all the ordering on our behalf.
Over to the bathroom section where there is a bewildering array of toilets but naturally my eyes were drawn to the cheapest one. Then we discovered that we needed two different types. Two with soil pipes going straight down and one with a soil pipe coming out of the back. One of the men at the orphanage had given Alex these strict instructions but no explanation as to why. We pondered on this and could not come up with a reason but decided to buy what we were asked despite our misgivings.

We returned to the mysterious sacks of powder and with Alex's help picked the right ones for the jobs we needed to do; grout, adhesive, plaster etc.
With chronically overloaded trolleys we left the store and loaded the minibus. Fortunately Kamen, Alex's fiancé, had put a new floor in the bus as the old one had rusted into virtual non-existence. He had also done a lot of work to the engine so that even with its heavy load it was capable of getting us back to Provadia before winter.

As stated previously one shopping trip in a day is more than enough but today we had also been to the market and bought two packets of seeds so you can imagine how exhausted we were. Never the less, as soon as we had deposited the contents of the mini bus at the school we got straight back to work on the ceiling. Now that I was an expert in holding wood we got on really well and managed to complete hanging all the ceiling joists. Unloading the bus was a joy as the children all helped us. Their enthusiasm is infectious, they love to help us. I wish I could apply that much joy to a seemingly mundane task.

After all that work we decided a little entertainment was in order so we decided to eat at Nico's. After studying the menu I asked if I could have a side order of stewed vegetables with my pork. "I don't know" came Nico's odd reply and that was it, nothing more was said. Maybe he was hoping I would forget what I ordered because it took an hour and a half for the meals to come (well there were three of us in the restaurant). When they finally arrived, my side order of stewed vegetables consisted of two slices of raw tomato and one slice of raw pepper, not quite what I had envisaged. I mused on how he could possibly only have one slice of pepper, where was the rest of the pepper from which the slice came and why wasn't it on my plate? Oh well, this was Nico's place after all and this is why we go there.

SATURDAY
Today we made arrangements to go to Kichevo and visit Didi at the Hope & Future Foundation. In 2012 we helped Didi make a start on preparing a site set aside for the provision of an eco unit where children could go for respite and training. Our role in 2012 was to create a driveway and some footpaths, our role today was simply to visit and see what progress has been made.

Over the last few years excellent progress has been made and there is now a beautiful house on the grounds with a small stable and storage shed. We had a tour of the house which is wonderful and we saw some quilts we recognised on the beds. The quilts were donated a few years ago by the Okehampton Quilting Guild and it was great to see them making the bedrooms look so cheerful.

We spent some time catching up on various children we have known and tried to help over the years; there was a mixture of fortunes, some doing well and some not so well.

I was pleased to learn that a previous introduction I had made was proving fruitful. Having introduced The Hope & Future Foundation to FSCI in Bulgaria plans are now well advanced in setting up a safe house in Varna for children who would like to pursue further education. We have previously sponsored youngsters who want to go to college but one of the issues we have faced is the lack of safe accommodation and the associated problems any youngster will face when moving from a small village to a big city (particularly in the absence of parental care and guidance). The provision of a safe house managed by FSCI & HFF will dramatically improve the success rate of those children who have a desire to improve their lives with further education. This is a very exciting development in which we were delighted to have played a small part.

On the return journey (via Praktiker for more supplies) Alex and I were recalling the time that we were driving through Varna and witnessed a motorbike accident when Adam piped up, "I remember that." Alex and I were baffled as Adam wasn't with us on that trip. "Adam, I'm sure that I was with my brothers on that occasion. You weren't with us." I said
"Yes I was, I remember it clearly" Adam replied.
Alex chipped in "No Adam, you definitely weren't with us"
Adams response went something like this;
"Well I've seen a motorbike accident somewhere in Bulgaria on one of my trips.
Or maybe it was in Greece and it wasn't with you but someone else.
Actually I don't think it was a motorbike, it was a horse.
There was no accident but the horse died"
We were just glad that he didn't have any pictures on his phone of the resultant carnage.

One thing which struck me as we travelled back and for between Varna & Provadia was the changes in Health and Safety legislation. Regular readers will know that I have often commented on the total absence of any H&S application in Bulgaria but it would appear that the boys from Brussels have begun taking action and imposing EU law on the highways department. Our regular excursions on the dual carriageway took us past gangs of men strimming the central reservation. Men were standing in the fast lane clearing the over growth for the benefit of the motorists. We were shocked to see that at least one member of each team sported the latest Hi-Vis vest and as if that wasn't enough to satisfy the bureaucrats the gangs were shielded by as many as six traffic cones. Yes SIX traffic cones. I worry that this appalling display of decadence will mean that the rest of Europe will have to go without. What was wrong with the old system when a 16 year old boy stood in the fast lane and waved the cars over with a hanky on a stick (we have actually seen this happen!). Thanks to all this H&S cars now left a gap of at least a foot and a half between them and the strimmers as they flew by at 80mph.

Back at Krivnya we got on with putting up the plasterboard on the ceiling. Having spent the previous two days perfecting the difficult skill of holding wood I was ready and eager to learn a new skill. Barry had clearly been impressed with my wood holding and had the confidence in me to teach me how to hold plasterboard in place with my head while he screwed it in (the plasterboard, not my head). Within minutes I was a master at my new skill and I scoffed at my old secondary school teachers who repeatedly lectured me "use your head boy, you're a waste of space." If they could see me now, using my head, they would eat their words.

Sadly there was bad news today. One of our team Eddie had put us on notice that he might not be able to join us due to an injury to his arm and today he confirmed that he would not be able to make it. Whilst this news was extremely disappointing we all understood that he had made the right decision.

When bad news like this hits us there's only one thing to do, cheer ourselves up with a visit to Nico's restaurant. He didn't disappoint. Ordering from the menu is a little bit like food roulette as you never quite know what will arrive. I ordered a chicken and mushroom meal and Barry ordered pork rolls, when the meals were delivered they were identical in every detail. During the meal a huge electrical storm hit the town which was quite breath taking but we weren't exactly put at ease when Nico ran around the restaurant Basil Fawlty style pulling out all the plugs and plunging the restaurant into darkness and silence. I'm not sure but I suspected it was a ploy to disguise the fact that my chicken and Barry's pork were one and the same unknown meat. My suspicions were heightened further by the strange disappearance of one of the local stray dogs who roam the town.

SUNDAY

At last Sunday had arrived and the rest of the team was due to join us and the work could pick up pace. We were due to collect the men from Varna airport at 11:30 so we had a couple of hours to do a few more jobs at Krivnya. At 10:30 I bid farewell to Barry and Adam and headed towards the minibus with Alex. I put the key in the ignition, turned it and …… nothing. Just a click. I smiled nervously and tried again. Another click followed by a deafening silence. Silence is not something normally associated with the minibus which, despite all the marvellous improvements Kamen has made, is still capable of deafening a man at 100 metres so we knew something was wrong.

I don't know why but I decided to attempt something straight out of my 'when will I ever learn' manual and pronounced a diagnosis. "Sounds like the starter motor to me." Filled with false confidence I was even stupid enough to proffer a remedy. "We just need to hit the starter motor with a hammer." Which is exactly what I proceeded to do. Undeterred by the failure of this action I moved to plan B which was to rock the bus whilst in gear in an effort to dislodge the jammed starter motor. I don't know if you have ever tried to rock a 17 seater high top LDV but there was no way that was going to work. With Adam's help we managed to get the bus rolling and encouraged Alex to knock it into gear when we got over 0.05mph but that didn't work either.

With time ticking on and the men due in to the airport shortly we had to admit defeat and Alex kindly offered to go in her car instead so she phoned Kamen who would come and collect her and take her to her car.

When Kamen arrived he was keen to try and fix the mini bus so I offered him the benefit of my wisdom, "I think you'll find it's the starter motor." He was polite enough to pretend to listen to me and even lifted the bonnet to humour me but as soon as he could see that I wasn't looking he jumped in the driver's seat turned the key and started the engine. Apparently there was a fault with the ignition which was easily remedied by a little jiggle of the key. Another classic misdiagnosis from me; just as well I'm not a brain surgeon!!

By now I had sent messages to the team that there was a problem and Alex would pick them up in the car although she will be a little late. However, with the minibus repaired we decided to take that as it offered more room for their luggage. After spending over three hours curled up in an aircraft baby seat the prospect of driving from Varna to Provadia with their luggage on their laps and balanced on their heads wasn't worth contemplating (although I could have given them a few tips about holding things up with their heads as I now had two gold stars for this activity).

With the men safely collected and delivered to Provadia I enjoyed a rare moment of calm sipping apple juice in the sunshine while waiting for the men to deposit their luggage and freshen up. I actually fancied a mango smoothie but I only know the words for apple juice, I drink a lot of apple juice in Bulgaria!
Being a generous man I allowed the new arrivals to join me for a drink before driving them up to Krivnya to start work. We had a quick tour in order to explain the jobs we hoped to tackle and then got down to some work.

The first job was perhaps the most difficult; levelling the floor in the new toilet block. There was a lot of head scratching, a lot of discussion, a lot of ideas, a lot of nodding but the final solution was to take a bolster chisel and a lump hammer and knock seven bells out of the floor. I must confess I had expected something a little more technical, a little more, well, professional but it wasn't to be. I hung around for a while hoping that someone would teach me how to hold a chisel so that I could add to my rapidly growing skill base but clearly the other men thought this was a step too far. Having already learned to hold wood and to hold plasterboard with my head, it was time to consolidate my skills not expand them. I was a little hurt and went outside to see if I could hold a piece of wood and a piece of plasterboard at the same time but it wasn't to be. I had reached a pinnacle and there was no point trying to stretch myself too far too soon. Maybe I could learn something new tomorrow. I quite fancied removing a lid from a paint pot. I decided to Google it later so that I could impress them with my knowledge.

With Max and Ross fully engaged in knocking lumps out of the floor the rest of the men found other work to do. Some decided to start laying laminate flooring in the counselling room at the end of the corridor. It is a small room and seemed like a good one to start with as there were many rooms which needed doing. We got the key for the room and made our way down the corridor. On opening the door we were a little startled to be greeted by the site of a doll hanging on the wall by means of a rope around its neck. Now I'm no counsellor but I doubt that you would find this idea in any text book on counselling unless it is one written by Stephen King. I tried to sound out the Cyrillic letters on the door and it either said 'Psychiatrist' or 'Psychopath' I'm not quite sure.

The men steeled themselves and entered the room with caution, checking under seats and desks for clowns or Chucky dolls and when they finally decided it was safe, began work.

Adam and Alex busied themselves putting a thermal lining behind some radiators. The heat had damaged the walls which we repaired and the lining was added to cover the repairs and reduce the probability of it happening again.

All in all it turned out to be a very productive afternoon.

After work the team repaired to Nico's for some liquid refreshment. Twenty minutes passed before Nico appeared and said, "Oh, I'm sorry, I don't open til 5:00", it was 5:50!! The men eventually got their drinks and the conversation turned to building anecdotes of which each of the men had plenty. When the debate turned to health & safety in the workplace Ross helpfully noted, "There were only two serious deaths in the construction industry last year." An interesting fact which prompted a further debate about non-serious deaths.

MONDAY
Today the men decided that a ramp was required for the steps outside the toilet block or else there was little point in constructing a disabled toilet if there was no wheelchair access into the building in the first place. For this they needed aggregate, sand and cement. I must admit I wasn't best pleased about this as previous expeditions for sand had been hard work and resulted in us being in a builders yard flummoxed by the prospect of buying it by the bucket load and having to provide our own

bags (which we didn't have). How many buckets in a kilo? How many buckets in a bag? We didn't have a clue.

However, today was Alex's birthday and lady luck was smiling on her as this particular shopping trip went very well indeed. The first builders' yard we pulled into had everything we wanted and it was already bagged. We simply reversed the minibus into the appropriate area and loaded the bags into the back of the bus.

Fantastic, we patted ourselves on the back for a job well done and proudly swung the back doors open back at the school in front of the builders. But wait, where was the applause, where were the cheers and the adulation for our amazing triumph? "That's not enough" said Ross. "We need at least that much again" added Max. Totally deflated we returned to the minibus and drove away, back to Provadia, back to the builders' yard. "Oh no" said Alex. "What?" I queried. "It's closed" she said. "Are you sure?" I said in partial disbelief. "The gate is shut" she said "Look." In a state of denial I kept creeping forward in the minibus in the delusional hope that if I approached the gate it would somehow magically open but it didn't. It stayed firmly shut. It seemed that Lady Luck was now laughing at our misfortune. At Alex's suggestion we tried somewhere else and to my amazement we once again found a yard with everything we needed all neatly bagged and stacked in orderly piles. We purchased what we needed and got back to Krivnya just in time as the previous load was running out and the ramp was half finished. Our second delivery meant that the ramp was completed that day. However, as the skies started to darken and the wind picked up the threat of rain was in the air. If it rained on the newly formed ramp it would be washed away so the men hastily grabbed all manner of metal sheeting and wooden boards and managed to construct a cover to protect the ramp from the elements and it was a good job too as the rain came and it was very heavy. I am delighted to report that the ramp survived.

As we were unloading the minibus I noticed a mark on Max's head which told of a minor accident but his face was split by a grin like a Cheshire cat. Why was he so happy at having banged his head, it didn't make sense. Now despite his name, he is more Mini than Max and is the smallest member of our team (which, by the way, lent itself very well to hours of endless mickey taking) and it transpires that he banged his head on one of the outside toilet door frames - he was delighted. It was the first time in his life that he had banged his head on a door frame and for once he felt quite tall. He was so pleased no one had the heart to point out that these particular door frames were only four foot high. Rumour has it that he went to the hospital and asked if he would have a permanent scar and when they told him 'no' he asked if there was anything they could do to make it permanent as he wanted everyone at home to see this mark of his great stature.

The laminate flooring team finished another room at the school today and were preparing to gather all their tools and head off to the home where the next job was. I commented that there was only one step ladder and it was needed at the school for painting the ceiling so Barry helpfully pointed out that they were doing flooring and therefore wouldn't need a ladder. D'oh!
I decided to hide my embarrassment by helping the men carry their kit to the home and set up there.

When I returned to the school Max was looking a little sheepish clutching a small piece of cardboard. Pointing at the cardboard in his hand I said "What's that?" "Well," he said, "Earlier I needed a wheelbarrow and Alex wasn't around so I approached one of the staff and drew this" he pointed to the cardboard where there was a sketch of a wheelbarrow and continued, "The bloke just looked at me and in perfect English said, "Do you need a wheelbarrow?"" Max had picked the one member of staff who speaks good English with which to play his game of Pictionary. He was rather put out as he kept insisting the quality of his sketch was worthy of a Turner Prize but this was wasted as the bloke (Mladen) understood English and didn't need the picture. I thought perhaps the knock on his head was having an effect as the sketch bore an uncanny resemblance to some pictures I have seen hanging on my daughter's fridge courtesy of her 3 year old son but as the week went on and the injury should have healed he was still banging on about the amazing wheelbarrow he had drawn. To be honest, if Mladen didn't speak English and relied solely on the picture I think Max would have ended up with a Teenage Mutant Ninja Turtle for his efforts.

Every year there are sobering moments when we realise why we do this work and today gave us one of those moments. There's one lad in the home called Nedyalko who is clearly disturbed and spends much of his day running around clutching a ripped magazine making unintelligible noises. He is a lovely boy and well known to us all as he is frequently around and about. Today we learned a bit of his back story. He was born a perfectly healthy boy but was beaten so severely by his parents he sustained severe brain damage. I asked if his parents were in prison and couldn't believe the reply. No, they are not in prison and when the school is closed for vacation Nedyalko is returned to his parents until the school and home open again. I know this is almost impossible to believe but sadly it is true, not just for Nedyalko but for many of the children in state care.

The teachers have a hard time with Nedyalko in the classroom as anytime they pick something up, be it a pen, a drinks bottle or a text book Nedyalko cowers in fear and cries, "Don't hit me, don't hit me." Even as I write this I feel tears in my eyes as my heart weeps for this poor boy. My hope is that the work we are doing to improve the school and the home goes someway to improving Nedyalko's life. The provision of a soft play room and a sensory room, the bright cheerful paintings on the classroom and bedroom walls, the new clean, sanitary toilets and everything else we have done; maybe we have made a difference to this lad, maybe we have improved his life. I feel sure that we have.

TUESDAY

I don't know how many Weetabix these men eat for breakfast, or maybe it's the caffeine in their early morning espressos but just a few days in and they have used all the laminate we had bought so it was necessary to take another trip to Praktiker to buy some more.

Before leaving for Varna I visited the team doing the toilet block to check if they needed anything only to find them deep in thought and debate about the position of the basin. The plumbing had points for two taps (hot and cold obviously) but they were offset compared to the position of the waste pipe which sat directly below the right hand tap point. If they positioned the basin directly above the waste pipe the left tap would not be over the sink. If they positioned the basin under the two tap points it would not be over the waste pipe. Out came several pencils and sketches were made on walls, paper, boxes and anything else which came to hand but no one could solve this conundrum. The best we could come up with was that the left tap point was for hot water and would have to go via a heater unit which would be positioned above the sink and the tap would come from that. Satisfied with this solution attention turned to the ongoing toilet problem. There was still no satisfactory explanation for why we were asked to buy two toilets with downward soil pipes and one with a back soil pipe. It seemed each person we asked told us to ask someone else. The men felt sure it was a mistake and suggested I return the 'back' toilet to Praktiker and exchange it for a 'down' toilet but for some reason I resisted as experience has taught me that there is usually a good reason behind these apparently meaningless decisions. Hey, perhaps at long last I am learning something and not continually repeating the mistakes of previous years. Time to retire?

Meanwhile the men were making excellent progress. Ken had made some repairs to the roof. The roof was in a bad way and there were many faults so Ken had to admit that he didn't know if he been successful but would find out next time it rained. As a minimum the water ingress will be dramatically reduced if not staunched completely.
Incidentally, on inspecting the roof prior to the repairs I followed Ken into the attic and watched him precariously pick his way across the void towards the area of the fault. I was extremely careful to trace his footsteps exactly as I was fearful that one misplaced foot could see me crashing through the ceiling and into the room below. Eventually, Ken ran out of safe places to stand but still hadn't reached the point of the damage; what now? He gingerly poked out a foot and deftly swept away a hundred years of dust and debris to reveal ....
a concrete floor. Yes the floor was solid concrete and easily capable of holding two men. All our dainty ballet moves to keep us from disaster had been as unnecessary as they were ungraceful.

The laminating team added another bedroom to their rapidly increasing tally and returned to the school to check on the progress of the toilet block. This was also going well and tiling the floor was well underway. As the floor sloped from all corners into a centre drain it was not a straightforward task and required a considerable amount of planning and tile cutting to get it right. The tiling team were determined to get the job finished so that the adhesive would dry overnight and the floor would be ready for grouting in the morning but it was not possible to fit everyone in the confined space to help. So the tiling team suggested I take the rest of the men back to Provadia and return for them in about an hour but just before I left they were able to reveal the answer to one of the problems we had deliberated over earlier. The problem of where to position the basin. Having spent a lot of time and energy working out how to position the basin given the two tap outlets they had discovered that it wasn't meant to be a hot tap and a cold tap as we imagined it was, in fact, a mistake which no one had bothered to tell us about. There should only be one outlet, the one directly above the waste pipe, the other one was an error. Arrgggghhhhhhhh!!!!!!

That just left the unresolved problem of the toilets. Two down and one out of the back - why? Still no answer.

WEDNESDAY

For some reason this turned out to be my official stupid day. I can only hope that the rest of the team noticed and it didn't blend seamlessly into all my other days. As usual I spent most of the morning running back and for to the shops for various bits and pieces and delivering them to the teams either at the school or the home. Returning from one trip I arrived at the school where Adam announced, "Our dinner has been delivered" (we were being spoiled by the cooks at the home who had prepared lunch for us most days). I immediately sprang into action, "I'll go and get the men from the home." I jumped in the minibus, drove to the home, ran up the stairs and breathlessly shouted, "Dinner's ready, I've got the minibus. Come on." There was a pause and the men looked somewhat dumbfounded until Nigel broke the silence with, "It's only 11:15." In all my haste and excitement I hadn't bothered to look at the time and it was indeed 11:15, far too early for lunch. Time for the drive of shame back to the school hoping that no one would think to ask me where I'd been.

Fortunately, the men at the school had been distracted by some local tradesmen. We had asked for a quote for uPVC walls and doors to be constructed which would make up the toilet cubicles and the men had arrived to measure up. Subsequently they submitted their quote which was accepted and the work commissioned with the agreement that we would phone them when we were ready for them to be fitted.

Whilst all this was going on the staff member who had made the decision on the toilets arrived and was able to explain why he thought we needed two down and one back. The penny dropped and everything made sense to those who understand that sort of thing. I am not one of those but I was simply so pleased that I had not exchanged the potentially erroneous toilet that I didn't bother to find out. For once a decision I made had been vindicated, I felt a momentary flush of success which I thought was appropriate as I was standing in a toilet at the time.

Not unusually, my moment of triumph was short lived and stupidity returned on this my stupid day. Whilst driving in Provadia (yes, I was shopping again) I embarked on a left turn (they drive on the right in Bulgaria so this was across the oncoming traffic) but completely misjudged the turning circle of the minibus which is akin to an aircraft carrier and ended up against the kerb on the opposite side of the road with the bus at right angles to the oncoming traffic. I couldn't mount the kerb as the pavement was steeply inclined and on an angle which would have grounded the bus in an instant. To the sound of blaring horns I had to reverse across the road and try again to point the bus at the road and make the turn correctly. To make matter worse, the only reason I was at that junction was because I sailed past the correct turning minutes before whilst in a world of my own.

In an attempt to salvage some dignity, on my return to the school, I decided to skip the class on washing a paintbrush and endeavour to do something infinitely more challenging. I would attempt some solo tiling. There was a small patch of untiled floor in the kitchen which needed attention and I decided it was safe for me to creep in there undetected and do the work unsupervised. Ken had previously cemented the floor to bring it up to level so the job should be relatively easy. I don't like to boast but I did an amazing job. I tiled an area at least 1m2. I couldn't count them all but I'm sure there were at least six tiles some of which had to be cut to shape. At least three of them were level and I was very proud of my achievement. I had gone from wood holder to tiler of tiny spaces in just a matter of days. Brilliant.

Sadly not everyone was as efficient as me and the laminating team only managed to complete one bedroom and a landing but at least this meant that the girls block was now finished so I suppose it wasn't too bad a day's work.

The toilet team managed to tile all four walls but there were two of them so I don't think it was quite the achievement of my 1m2 of kitchen floor.

As we were about to leave for the day Ross said, "Do you fancy running back to Provadia?" rather stupidly I had once said that I often thought about running back. Now it's a huge step from thinking about it to actually doing it but I was put on the spot and under a bit of pressure. I was running through all the excuses in my head and about to deliver my favourite when Ross played his trump card, "Max is up for it." Oh no, now what could I do? Despite the fact that in my head I clearly said, "No, I can feel my tuberculosis playing up" what actually came out of my mouth was, "Yes, OK, I'm up for it."

Max and I stood there contemplating a 6 mile run in the clothes we had been working in all day and began making various excuses, "I don't know if I can run in this footwear." "These shorts are so heavy and cumbersome they will restrict my stride pattern." "My T-shirt is thick with dust and will weigh me down."

Our excuses were tripping off our tongues thick and fast when suddenly, from nowhere, Ross appeared regaled in full running gear. He had taken the trouble to get up early that morning and pack his Nike running trainers, running shorts and lightweight vest. There he was doing all his warm up exercises while Max and I just stood and stared in disbelief. It looked like Seb Coe and two hobbits as we departed the school and the rest of team waved as they passed us in the minibus driven by Ken. As it happens it was a good run which Max and I survived despite the odds. (Oh and let the record show that the GPS measured the route at 6.2 miles not 6 miles as we previously thought).

But stupid day wasn't done with me yet. That evening we tried a different restaurant and were patiently waiting for our meals when the waitress turned up with a few plates of food. In my defence quite a long time had passed since we ordered and it was difficult to remember exactly what meal I was expecting but the food on the plate triggered something inside me. At the time I thought it was my memory which was triggered, a vague, distant memory that it was my meal being waved under my nose. But on reflection I think it may have been simply hunger which was triggered and my famished state caused me to reach out and grab whatever was put before me.

As I tucked in heartily, one by one the other meals were brought out until there was just one person left, Nigel. When the final meal was delivered Nigel looked bemused, he didn't recognise it as being what he ordered but as a professor of mathematics he did the sums and calculated that as he was the only one waiting for a meal and this was the last meal left it must, by simple deduction, be his and he accepted it.

Nigel still wasn't convinced though and muttered something about not ordering a kebab. A kebab! Now that did trigger something within me. The word kebab appeared in the meal I ordered, I remembered now. What was I to do? I was brought up to believe that honesty is the best policy but wait til I see my mum next and I'll be having a few sharp words with her. I confessed to Nigel believing that my honesty would elicit wholehearted forgiveness but I couldn't have been more wrong. I didn't hear the end of it. For the rest of the evening every topic managed to turn itself around to the fact that I had stolen Nigel's meal. It wasn't just Nigel; the rest of the team needed little encouragement to join in my character assassination. Any attempt to justify my actions had scorn heaped upon it and I was cast as the evil pariah. I would like to say that having slept on it my friends and colleagues softened their views and let it all pass quietly like a gentle brook, water under the bridge but no! With all the cacophony of a raging waterfall the abuse continued at every mealtime and any chance in between for the remainder of the trip. I noticed a distinct sharpening in Nigel's response to the appearance of the waitress at all subsequent meals.

THURSDAY

I was happy to welcome a new day and put yesterday behind me and even happier when Nigel decided to cook toast. Not because I was hungry but because for some strange reason he decided to put bread in the toaster which had already been buttered. Thankfully, forgetting about last night's "mealgate" fiasco, Nigel became the clown for a few moments and I breathed a sigh of relief. Today had got off to a good start, for me anyway.

My good day continued as I spent much of it at the home with the children. With some help from Rosanka and Rosa I built a simple gate for the outside toilet doorway. It was nice to be outside in the sun, working and enjoying the company of the children who enjoyed joining in or simply watching and chatting.
The children found me an apple of dubious origin but were very keen that I should accept their gift and so, with some trepidation, I did. I survived to tell the tale so look back on this act with great affection. A simple gift but with huge significance.

Not quite as wonderful as the apple, Adam came round with gifts of ice creams for the team but I appreciated it none the less as this was a particularly warm day and I was glad to stop for refreshments. I was just a little disappointed that it wasn't Adam who gave me the apple as I feel there's a gag in there somewhere which I could have used.

Spurred on by the usual one and a half hour wait between ordering food and Nico delivering it the team came up with the brilliant idea of ordering 24 hours in advance. So, having given Nico our orders yesterday we turned up at the pre-arranged 8pm with eager anticipation and we were rewarded with a wait of only 45 minutes. It remains a mystery how it could still take 45 minutes but we have left orders for next year in the hope that we might be able to get a new PB next time.

FRIDAY

The plan for today was to get the toilet block ready for the fitting of the walls and doors which would form the cubicles. Having previously confirmed that they work Saturdays I wanted to give the fitters a day's notice and to confirm that they would indeed be able to come and fit them. But the best laid plans of mice and men and all that - the fitters turned up unannounced this morning and were keen to start work. I could sense a little tension in the air as we weren't ready for them and there was no way we could all fit in the room and work side by side. But while we were trying to work this one out the fitters discovered that they had mis-measured one of the doors and as a consequence needed to take it away to re-size it which meant we could amicably resolve to accommodate them in the room later that afternoon.

I have been doing this work for more than 10 years and I think that for 6 of them Alex has been on the team doing our translating. So why has it taken this long for us to discover a shopping technique which actually works. The number of times we have stood in a store playing charades to try and explain a tool which I don't even know the English name for. I have to demonstrate it to Alex so she can translate my woeful description into Bulgarian for the bemused shop keeper who makes repeated trips into his storeroom bringing out a pigeon, followed by a bicycle tyre, two turnips and a chimney before finally realising I need a hammer. Today we had a eureka moment. I went through the shopping list with Alex on site. Explaining each item with the aid of practical demonstrations in the situation where the tool or equipment was required. Alex then wrote her own shopping list which she was able to use in the store. It worked like clockwork even to the point that I was virtually redundant and could easily have sat in the minibus outside and spared myself the embarrassment of my futile attempts to demonstrate a 15mm elbow compression joint using only my left foot. However, my joy was short lived as I contemplated the fact that my only useful role on these trips is to go shopping with Alex and with the stark realisation that Alex could now drive the minibus as well I began to see a dark cloud on the horizon. Maybe the men could use a hairdresser - I'll start training immediately.

With the end of the week in sight attention turned to finishing off all the outstanding jobs and attending to some minor repairs. Nigel began combing the sites for all our tools and equipment and returning them all to our tool store. At one point he presented me with a case saying, "I'm not sure what's in here, do you know what it is?" Was it a drill, an angle grinder, a jig saw? I opened it as I didn't recognise the case only to find it was a typewriter! Thank you Nigel, I'm sure that will come in very useful next time we need to prop up the leg of a wobbly workbench.

SATURDAY
There was a mix of excitement and trepidation in the air as we travelled to Krivnya this morning. Yesterday we left the fitters installing the cubicles, what would we find we got there? First impressions were good and we were very pleased as we stood back and admired what we saw however, there was one slight problem. The entrance door was hung the wrong way round. It wasn't the end of the world but it really interfered with the available space and banged into the cubicle doors if both were open at the same time. Manoeuvrability was severely restricted and access to the basin difficult. It still all functioned as a toilet block and looked very presentable but apart from not meeting the high standards of the team it simply didn't deliver on one of the objectives of creating a wheelchair friendly facility and so the decision was taken to remove the door, turn it round and re-hang it. This also gave us the opportunity to finish off the reveals and leave the door looking perfect.

Meanwhile, Barry was realising a dream of four years. Every time he has visited Krivnya he has wanted to build a chest for storing the kit we keep there but time never seemed to be on his side. This year however, the opportunity was available and he took it so we now have a lockable chest, with trays in which a lot of our kit can now be kept neat, tidy and easy to find. Whilst doing this he and Nigel also took an inventory for future reference.

It was a busy day of shopping too but with our new system in place Alex and I made short work of resolving the problems with the cistern hose which firstly was too short then had the wrong fitting. We accommodated the last minute changes to the soil pipe which was the wrong angle and managed to keep the builders working by supplying all their needs.

We thought we were going to be called on again as Max began to fret about a lost waste pipe seal. He was wandering around clutching a waste pipe wailing about the lost seal. Alex and I sprang into action and prepared to launch another shopping trip just as Max realised the seal was on the end of the waste pipe in his hand, where it belonged.

Slowly but surely all the jobs got finished and the men gathered around the toilet door which was the last job being worked on until we could finally say all our work was complete.

We thanked the cooks who had prepared our meals and the cleaner who had quietly and efficiently kept the place looking spic and span whilst also ensuring that the school was open for us by 8am and never complaining if we stayed late. We gave out small gifts of chocolates as we really did appreciate what they did for us.

Ivelina (Director) gathered us together to thank us for all we had done and gave a moving speech about how she was concerned that we had all worked so hard but she couldn't guarantee that the children, because of the nature of their disabilities, would be able to keep everything looking so good. We assured her that we completely understood but pointed to all the other work we have done over the years which had been maintained in pristine condition and congratulated her on the amazing work she and all the staff are doing there.

Ultimately, if we have improved the lives of the children it matters not one jot if a tile gets chipped, a wall gets scratched, a gate hinge gets broken or a floor gets drawn on with felt pens. If there is even the smallest improvement we will have achieved our aim and be very happy indeed.

We left Krivnya for the last time and headed back to Provadia where we decided to sit in the park opposite our guest house and enjoy a drink or two in the sunshine. Whilst there three lads from the home in Krivnya turned up and as they recognised us made a bee line for our table. The men were trying their best to come up with three 1 lev coins in order to give the boys a ride on the little cars nearby. We could only manage two between us but they had a great time doubling up where necessary. Just away in our peripheral vision we became aware of a lady stood at the edge of the park. It soon became apparent that she was looking for the boys as one of them ran over to her. We were shocked when she gave him quite a beating, hitting him hard around the head several times. The boys' story began to unfold, they had been taken into the care of Krivnya orphanage because of the risk of physical abuse at home but as this was now a public holiday they had been returned to the temporary care of their mother.

The oldest of the three boys took hold of his mum and became very agitated; he was pulling her towards our table but she was clearly unwilling to come and a scuffle broke out between them. Fearing the worst we were at a loss to know what to do but then all became clear. The boy wanted his mum to share in the popcorn we had given him and his brothers, it was a heart warming moment. Mum drifted back into the distance with a handful of popcorn while the boys came and tried to grab our drinks. As the majority of the team had bottles of beer we had to have our wits about us to stop the boys from swigging on these. Surprisingly, I had an apple juice but was not overly keen on sharing my glass with the boys who's personal hygiene left a little to be desired so poured the contents of my glass back into the bottle and let them have it. However only two of them managed to get a drink so one boy sneaked around the back of us and in a flash grabbed Nigel's beer bottle and took a hefty swig. Naturally we reacted quickly and animatedly snatched the bottle from his hand. Sadly, this attracted the attention of his mum who raced over and dispensed another beating on the poor boy. With this, the boys disappeared and we didn't see them again. It was a strange meeting with very mixed emotions; we had given them a few moments of pleasure, a little food and a little drink but at what cost?

Whatever the outcome of our actions I know that the next time we see the boys we will receive the usual greeting of a snotty nose and a filthy face rubbed deep in to our bellies on the end of a massive hug. These gorgeous children have so much love to give; what a delight they are.

And so another successful trip came to an end. We were delighted to have completed all the tasks we set out to achieve, we worked hard and had a few laughs along the way, we rekindled old friendships and made some new ones but above all we have achieved our aim of improving the lives of these precious children who bless us in so many ways.

The team were amazing and I want to thank each and every one of them for their dedication to the children. I also want to thank all our supporters, those who give financially, those who pray and those who offer words of encouragement. Above all I thank God for being the ultimate provider of everything I need to be able to pull off these trips. I can do nothing in my own strength; I am fully reliant on God. I consider it a privilege to be God's worker in this small corner of His creation.

Andrew

Printed in Great Britain
by Amazon